CHANGE-PROMOTING RESEARCH FOR HEALTH SERVICES

CHANGE-PROMOTING RESEARCH FOR HEALTH SERVICES

A guide for resource managers, research and development commissioners and researchers

A. S. St Leger and **J. P. Walsworth-Bell**

Open University Press
Buckingham · Philadelphia

Open University Press
Celtic Court
22 Ballmoor
Buckingham
MK18 1XW

e-mail: enquiries@openup.co.uk
world wide web: http://www.openup.co.uk

and

325 Chestnut Street
Philadelphia, PA 19106, USA

First Published 1999

A catalogue record of this book is available from the British Library

ISBN 0 335 20221 7 (hb)   0 335 20220 9 (pb)

Library of Congress Cataloging-in-Publication Data
St. Leger. A. S. (Anthony Selwyn), 1948–
    Change-promoting research for health services: a guide for
rasearch managers. R & D commissioners, and researchers/A. S. St. Leger
and J. P. Walsworth-Bell.
        p.   cm.
    Includes bibliographical references and index.
    ISBN 0-335-20221-7 (hb: alk. paper). – ISBN 0-335-20220-9 (pb: alk. paper)
    1. Health services administration–Research–Great Britain.   2. National
Health Services (Great Britain)   3. Medical policy–Great Britain.
I. Walsworth-Bell, J. P. (Joanna Pierce), 1947–   II. Title.
    [DNLM: 1. National Health Service (Great Britain)   2. Evidence-Based
Medicine–organization & administration–Great Britain.   3. Health Care
Reform–Great Britain.   4. Health Services Research-methods–Great Britain.
5. Health Services Research–organization & administration–Great Britain.
W 84.3 S145c 1999]
RA854.G7S8 1999
362.1′0941–dc21
DNLM/DLC   for Library of Congress   99-22321   CIP

Typeset by Graphicraft Limited, Hong Kong
Printed in Great Britain by Biddles Ltd, Guildford and King's Lynn

This work is dedicated to the memory of our friend and erstwhile collaborator the late Professor Harold Schnieden

CONTENTS

PREFACE

This book is about research and development (R&D) in health services being part of all managers' repertory. Managers are people who make decisions and bring about change, at all sorts of levels and in a wide range of disciplines. They include clinicians in many specialities, as well as administrative staff, general managers, directors of finance and human resources and so forth. Their decisions and the change they all manage include the trivial and the momentous, and all can take hard work. Our belief is that at a time when health services globally are continually changing, strategically, structurally and clinically, R&D plays a key role.

Only good research can elucidate and challenge the status quo or future possibilities for effective healthcare. Only R&D as integral to what all managers do can develop a culture which can cope with change and measure and manage that change in ways which make sense to all concerned, and result in beneficial use of scarce resources. This does not mean that all managers have to be researchers. But it does mean that researchers and managers have a duty to collaborate, to understand and make the most of each other's skills. The responsibility is mutual. To illustrate this and explain it we have developed a paradigm of health services research which is not about simple purity in either the research or the management world, but necessitates the complexities of collaboration, engagement with all sorts of issues and opportunities for continued learning, as part of a change management culture and change enhancement which are now inextricably what health service organization is all about.

So who is this book for? Part I is by way of background. We briefly sketch out the introduction of research and development into the National Health Service (NHS) in Britain, and discuss the development of the general management function and attempts to implement effective healthcare. Then we set out our new paradigm, a means of addressing some of the issues raised. Much of the story will be familiar to managers, although not, perhaps, from the point of view that they have experienced, whatever their interests. Unfortunately, many researchers may not be as aware of what has been happening in the NHS. This is one of the reasons for this book and our new paradigm. So, while we hope that Part I will be of interest to many readers, we particularly commend it to people interested in health services research as an essential context for the contribution which we know they can make.

Parts II and III of the book look at the practicalities. There are two substantial contributions on commissioning research. This process may be known, to some extent, to experienced researchers. However, hitherto, many managers may have felt ill-equipped and diffident about becoming engaged in what can be seen and felt as a largely intellectual and dissociated from reality type of activity. So we feel that managers will need to read this section to see that the ideas we have can be taken forward, albeit with hard work – but that is nothing new to any manager in any part of the health service. We also urge researchers to understand the details of what we are putting forward. The results will be an R&D process very different from that they currently experience. Different, but, in the long run, more satisfying and undoubtedly more useful.

Chapter 5 is a commentary on various aspects of research. It introduces basic concepts to the novice and also, for the more experienced, it shows how some of those concepts need to be reinterpreted within our paradigm. Much of this will be elementary for researchers who have spent any length of time on health services work. But inexperienced researchers, would-be researchers and managers should all find it helpful. Much of this is about demystifying apparently impenetrable and irrelevant jargon. Dip into this chapter as you need it. It is about comfort with the language and ideas of research, not about ethereal and distant activities. This is the bread and butter of good research. Everyone who is involved ought to have some idea of what can or should be done. In our new paradigm, sharing and sharpening accessible ideas and practicalities will work best the more informed all the collaborators are.

Finally, we look at using research. This last chapter is for everyone: R&D in health services is everyone's responsibility if it is to work. Again, the process may be challenging and may make some people uneasy, but, at the end of the day, the final project should be really useful health services research: that is what this book is all about.

The ideas presented in this book have been gestating slowly over many years. They take forward the concepts developed in our previous book *Evaluating Health Services' Effectiveness* (Open University Press). This work, though in some respects a sequel, stands alone and may be read without reference to its predecessor.

ACKNOWLEDGEMENTS

In developing our ideas we have been supported by many friends and colleagues too numerous to mention individually here. However, some to whom we are particularly indebted must be thanked personally. Dr Kathleen Rowsell has been a stalwart supporter of our new paradigm as it developed. She has given us tremendous aid, through her viewpoint as both an academic and a health authority chairman, in developing and expanding the implications of our ideas. Professor Colin Roberts, recently retired from the University of Wales, immediately grasped the importance of what we were trying to do, and without his support and encouragement this work may not have been completed. We are also indebted to Dr Roger Johnson who, in his capacity as Medical Director of the Manchester Health Authority and role as Chairman of the Manchester, Stockport and North West Pennine R&D Liaison Group, gave encouragement to the development of our ideas and enabled us to test the practical realization of some. To Gina Evans, R&D Facilitator for the aforementioned R&D Liaison Group, gratitude for her support and enthusiasm in applying the ideas to some of the projects mentioned by way of example in this book and the insights she has shared with us. Our work has also been greatly enhanced by the encouragement given by Professor Maggie Pearson (NHS North West Director of R&D), her willingness to explore new ways of doing things and her aptitude at circumventing some of the more frustrating NHS restrictions. Chris Handley at South Staffordshire Health Authority was endlessly patient in providing typing and other support. We are also grateful to Jacinta Evans of Open University Press for her continuing support of this project.

Part I

BACKGROUND AND RATIONALE

RESEARCH AND DEVELOPMENT IN A CHANGING HEALTH SERVICE

KEY POINTS

Health services all over the world are making hard decisions. In Britain, recognition of the important contribution of research and development occurred in the late 1980s, eventually resulting in explicit arrangements for research and development in the National Health Service from 1992 onwards.

The history of British health services encompasses concepts of equity and universality. Since the 1980s, general management has attempted to control activity and expenditure by shifting power from doctors, a change still developing.

Change requires effective management. Simple dissemination of appropriate information is not enough. Measurement and monitoring of practice is essential.

1.1 The general relevance of the theme

This book is about making health services research work – that is, be a successful part of a concerted effort to achieve evidence-based healthcare. Necessarily, the views are grounded in the authors' own experiences, which are largely confined to the National Health Service (NHS) in England and Wales. This does not mean that the approach is not generalizable. In fact, the opposite is likely. But it does mean that we owe our readers some explanation of the background experience of the NHS, as the field with which we are most familiar, in order to illustrate why certain ideas have developed and appear especially pertinent at this time. The NHS plays a major part in public expenditure. To illustrate, of £260.2 billion planned for public expenditure in 1996/7 the NHS in England was the second largest spend, at £33,800 million, 16 per cent of the total.

What may be felt by some to be undue tardiness in emphasizing the necessity of good research and development (R&D) in an enterprise requiring this level of expenditure might possibly be because of our being relatively cheap compared with many countries, especially because some health workers' pay is considerably lower. This means that for every pound spent on the NHS in the UK, we are able to buy more than the equivalent spending in other countries, such as the USA or Germany. In addition, we rely heavily on 'informal care' (the care provided by friends, relatives and neighbours); this has been estimated as worth £30–40 billion per year in the NHS. This all suggests that, even on a crude basis, the NHS is good value for money.[1]

Health is increasingly regarded as a fundamental value in society, and one which governments should play an important role in promoting and protecting, even in the face of increasing economic pressures. These increasing economic pressures are leading to most countries engaging in healthcare reform, and a simultaneous concern with rationing. Globally systems as diverse as those in the United States (Oregon), the Netherlands and New Zealand are increasingly adopting similar themes: community-oriented approaches, curbing the professional autonomy of providers, attempting to develop consensus on levels of service and developing agreements on access to care. Increasingly, concepts of effective healthcare play a role in these difficult debates.[2]

In the NHS in England and Wales the reality of demand for healthcare outstripping supply has always been present, but the NHS was thrust into more explicit priority setting as a result of reforms in 1991. In common with other healthcare systems around the world, the British NHS is under growing pressure to contain costs, cope with an ageing population, limit the deployment of expensive medical technologies and generally do more with less. Within this there is a belief that the scope for redeploying resources from ineffective procedures and practices is probably considerable, and that there may be far more effective means of reducing rationing pressures and prioritizing than existing imperfect samples of public opinion.

Thus, appropriate criteria for rationing, which are certainly not, yet, adopted as public policy, have been suggested as including effectiveness, cost-effectiveness, need (rather than demand), equity and public preference (such as life-saving rather than life-sustaining interventions). There is a sense that clinicians should now be obliged to demonstrate health gains in the competition for funds. The onus of proof should be on the medical profession to show which of its activities would yield a positive benefit for society. At the same time, this huge organization needs to be efficiently managed, especially in terms of good information. Increasingly, we become aware of the inadequacy of our existing information systems in terms of health outcomes and what works and what does not. In time, as one author has suggested, rationing may be less a central issue, and where it is unavoidable, it ought at least to be better informed by evidence.[3] But being able to demonstrate that resources allocated to the NHS are being used prudently and effectively is not easy in an environment which lacks an appropriate research culture, and where quick results are sought.

One of the most significant changes has been the developing legitimacy of R&D as an always coupled concept. That is, research is not seen as a stand alone, isolated activity, accessible only to researchers. Development is no longer the prerogative of those incapable of research, somehow ensuring that the fruits of researchers' intellectual endeavours are by mysterious processes plucked and digested, to nourish the whole organization. By putting the two together, indivisibly, the British NHS has insisted on a link which has hitherto been unknown to both researchers and developers – or change managers, as we prefer to call them. It is ensuring the reality of the link which is the major concern of this book.

We continue this introductory section with a brief summary of R&D in the NHS. This is followed by a sketched profile of the NHS, past and present, and a glance at some attempts to put effective healthcare into practice. This then leads logically on to the argument on which this book is premised.

1.2 The legitimization of R&D

At the time of writing the United Kingdom (England, Wales, Scotland and Northern Ireland) is governed centrally from London. The government combines both legislative and executive functions. It is bicameral – that is, there are two chambers of Parliament. One, the House of Commons, is made up of representatives elected to serve during the term of the government (up to five years). The other, the House of Lords, comprises non-elected individuals, who may be there by right because of their occupation (the Church and the law), by inheritance (the aristocracy) or through honoured service (with a peerage bestowed for life). As we write, legislation is being prepared by the Labour government to remove the right of hereditary peers to sit in the House of Lords.

Both houses have a number of standing committees, whose membership is drawn from across the political party spectrum. These committees may examine a wide range of topics, including public expenditure and the performance of the health service. One such committee is the House of Lords Select Committee on Science and Technology. In March 1988 it published the third report of the 1987/8 session: *Priorities in Medical Research.*[4] In reaching its conclusions the committee drew on a wide range of evidence, presented orally and in writing, from eminent researchers and doctors. It was this report that triggered the whole 'industry' of R&D in the NHS.

The committee's inquiry started from the premise that the United Kingdom should maintain the research capacity to sustain first class health services. The inquiry addressed a number of issues, including who should lead the research, who should fund the research, who should do the research and who should apply the research, and what sort of organization should contain all these activities. In tackling these complex issues, the committee felt it could identify four main types of research: basic research, clinical research (involving patients), public health research (involving the health needs of the community as a whole) and operational research (which was applied research concerned particularly with the effectiveness of service provision). The last category is the particular focus of this book, and was clearly the area which the committee felt was the most neglected.

On examining the evidence and the report, it is notable that a strong theme running throughout was that both research priorities and medical research itself had largely to be science-led. Many witnesses wanted to combine a strong tradition of basic research with a targeted approach on 'priorities'. Unfortunately, there was no recognizable mechanism for setting priorities or targets. Not only was there no mechanism, there was no easy way of perceiving whether the balance of priorities was right. One witness is quoted as saying: 'No-one can answer this question sensibly; science being the art of the possible rather than the desirable and each of us having his own justifiable priorities.' Not surprisingly, the committee was led to conclude that the science-led approach should be dominant, but with some setting of priorities. It also felt that greater emphasis on problem-led research was essential.

There were, however, largely negative comments when it came to the NHS setting research priorities. There were comments from the committee on the weakness of the NHS input into the determination of priorities, and how priorities in medical research were often influenced to a considerably extent by funding sources. The committee recognized how the funding of applied research in medicine was known to be troublesome – and how this had been previously demonstrated in the abortive transfer of funds from the Medical Research Council to the (then) Department of Health and Social Security, following the Rosthschild Report, and their subsequent return. We comment on this below. The situation was further complicated by the serious divergence of administrative approaches between medical research (which tends to be concentrated in a few locations) and medical services (which tend to be widely dispersed) in the United Kingdom.

The situation obviously worried the committee. It concluded: 'No research system can function effectively when the principal customer has so small a direct input.' One witness had already commented that, 'Because of the way the NHS is organised there seems to be a genuine communication problem between the basic researcher and those that direct health policy.' Another had strongly made the point that the debate about healthcare in the UK was obsessed about either spending money or doing things to patients, but never really looked at the results of those activities and expenditure, and research was desperately needed to look at both the cost and the outcomes of the health service.

Funding was acknowledged as a difficulty. This was not least because the sources of research funding were relatively complex. They included the Medical Research Council and other research councils; the (then) University Grants Committee; the NHS itself; the Health Department; medical research charities; and the pharmaceutical and medical equipment industries. As one witness commented, it was appalling that at that time a department with an annual expenditure of approximately £20,000 million pounds funded a research programme of its own at a level barely over £20 million pounds. It is interesting that, apart from the pharmaceutical industry, the overall expenditure on medical research was estimated to be approximately 1.5 per cent of the health service budget – a proportion considered to be totally inadequate by most major pharmaceutical companies in terms of guaranteeing their medium- to long-term future. This figure of 1.5 per cent is worth bearing in mind, as is the rejection by at least one witness of the idea of ensuring some sort of simple link between research and the NHS, such as a target expenditure.

Other problems related to research skills. The bias towards 'science-led' research priorities was largely justified by the lack of healthcare researchers and of a long-term strategy for training researchers in the field. Relative to medical research, there was no critical mass of skills, people and funding at that time. The lack of application of research evaluating practice was highlighted as an area of greatest neglect, despite the great need by the NHS of this type of research. Again, it is interesting how the majority of witnesses believed that the dissemination of research results through learned journals was quite satisfactory. This implies that, as researchers, they perceived a straight route through from research to publication to appropriate action, with, understandably from their point of view, the greatest need for expertise being at what was then seen as the start of the process, doing interesting research.

As a result, the committee's central recommendation was that the NHS should be brought into the mainstream of medical research. One of the witnesses who was very supportive of such an approach felt that health service research should be done 'near the action': that is, far from Whitehall, with even regions too distant, and the districts as probably the more appropriate focus. The committee wanted a special health authority set up within the NHS in order to undertake this research. This central proposal was rejected by the government when it published its response 21 months later. It is, however, fair to say that a great deal of other change was in hand in relation to the NHS and that the response clearly indicated that the government had understood some of the main issues to be addressed.

In its response, published in 1989, the Government accepted the principal thrust of the recommendations that a new initiative was required to help the NHS identify and lead its own research needs.[5] The way in which this should happen was designed to be consistent with the general thrust of direct management accountability, which was an increasing part of NHS culture: there would be a 'chief of research and development'. This individual would have responsibility for developing the research programme, by directing arrangements for determining priorities. Responsibilities also included helping the NHS to: identify and meet clinical and health service research needs; advise on national priorities; ensure effective dissemination; participate with the Medical Research Council and other scientific committees and advisory bodies; and direct arrangements for assuring the scientific quality of the research directly commissioned by the Department of Health. The reason given for establishing such a post was to ensure that NHS research stayed within the mainstream of NHS management, so that research issues were properly and directly addressed, and acted on. As regards funding, it was felt appropriate that moneys earmarked for meeting the additional expenses of teaching hospitals should be extended to healthcare research and developing other support mechanisms.

It is interesting that, in the context of the proposed restructuring of the NHS, maintaining a strong research base and service support for research in the NHS was felt to be crucial, not least to help districts to articulate and meet their research needs. Thus, it is clear that not only was the need for good health services research acknowledged, but there was considerable movement from this research being led purely by scientists to its being compatible with the way the health service was managed and funded, and the service queries and need for research that might arise as a result.

By 1991, the first Director of Research and Development had been appointed, and the first Research and Development Strategy for the NHS ('Research for Health') had been published.[6] The strategy looked at important issues, such as the coordination of health research, education and training, resources and a national structure through which priorities should be agreed, and research commissioned and managed. In general terms, the structure comprised a central R&D committee, with support committees in each region.

In order to integrate R&D with management, the Director of Research and Development was appointed a member of the Management Executive within the Department of Health. At that time, the NHS structure included Regional Health Authorities. Although those health authorities no longer exist, the regional role has been continued in the posts of Regional Directors of Research and Development. Central funding was provided to ensure sufficiently eminent appointees, supported by staff capable of managing research programmes and monitoring for quality control. Thus, unlike some other NHS initiatives, which are expected to be 'resource neutral', this was felt to be so important that clearly differentiated funding and management should be rapidly put into place. At the heart of the process, the Central Research and Development

Committee coordinated national priorities. One of the first tasks for the regional teams was the drawing up of plans to address the funding of R&D priorities, processes for replacing the previous purely reactive locally organized research scheme, input from interested parties (including senior NHS management) and provision for dissemination of results.

The impact of this shift from research experts owning everything to do with health research to a process of seeking out priorities and managing the accountability of researchers to the wider NHS community should not be underestimated. The contribution of committed and highly professional research managers to the process has been very significant.

Health research priorities have emerged as of two general types: those falling within specific clinical areas and those picked up by the health technology assessment programme (HTA). The early chronology was:[7]

1992   Regional structures. Regional plans.
1992   Commencement HTA. Clinical area: mental health.
1993   Continuation HTA. Clinical areas: cardiovascular disease and stroke, physical and complex disabilities.
1994   Continuation HTA. Clinical areas: cancer, diabetes, primary/ secondary care interface, dentistry.
1995   Continuation HTA. Clinical areas: mother and child, implementing R&D, asthma management.

Since 1995, Regional Health Authorities as separate entities, serving populations of between about three and five million people, have no longer existed; however, the regional structure supporting and managing the R&D process has been retained. These regional structures provide sources for consultation and advice, as well as management of specific research priorities (for example, the first clinical area for research, mental health, was managed by the Northern and Yorkshire Region). Although all these structures are undoubtedly committed to R&D in the NHS as a means of meeting decision makers' priorities, none has been able to let go of the opportunity to fund completely unsolicited research ideas, and therefore all have retained some element of the previous system for funding research in the NHS, the locally organized research scheme. Education and training has been managed within regions in different ways. In general the themes have been the development of individuals (for example, in various types of scholarships) and support for R&D infrastructure (ranging from statisticians and librarians to computing).

Resources, as ever, remained a major problem. The strategy aspired to R&D consuming 1.5 per cent of the NHS budget. In 1989/90, 1.5 per cent of the NHS budget was estimated to be £317 million. In September 1994, a task force chaired by Professor Anthony Culyer recommended that R&D in the NHS be resourced by a single funding stream, conceived as a levy on all healthcare purchasers' allocations, based on existing spend.[8] Using declarations from healthcare providers, the top sliced NHS R&D budget was set at approximately £400 million, related to more than

39,000 projects. The research funding system established as a result was quite unlike any other in the UK, although the process was informed by 'challenge' funding systems used elsewhere in government to fund such activities as urban regeneration and transport infrastructure in local authorities.

The scene was thus set to facilitate the integration of good management (informed decisions) with research 'products' (supplying that information). Progress in the decade since the House of Lords report illustrates the exciting potential, if not the actuality.

1.3 Background changes in the NHS: towards the universal use of the effective, and the erosion of clinical autonomy?

This section looks at some background changes in the NHS in England and Wales, and some recent attempts to introduce effective healthcare. Our underlying thesis is that the implementation of effective research-based clinical care requires both skilled management and high-quality information supporting that function. We start with a sketched history of the NHS, where the changes could be interpreted variously as, for example, attempts at cost control or improving equity. Alternatively, they could be seen as a gradual lessening of local medical influence in the face of enhanced management power. There has been a desire for a diminution in variations in healthcare (dictated by local clinical autonomy), in parallel with the increasing recognition that some methods of care are universally applicable, and that this message regarding effective healthcare should be readily available for use by both clinical and managerial staff. This is followed by a description of some of the widely promulgated information about effective healthcare used in England and Wales in the 1990s, and an examination of the criticisms of the failure to implement such care. A brief summary pulls together the main lessons and leads into our new paradigm.

The beginnings of the NHS are generally seen as contained within Lloyd George's National Insurance Act of 1911. Two features are especially pertinent here: universality and the influence of the medical profession. 'Universality' may seem a strange concept for an Act whose welfare was limited to employed men (not their dependants) and general practitioner (GP) care (not hospital), but it was a contrast with the selectivity of some other welfare legislation, and the desires of social reformers, notably Beatrice and Sidney Webb, who would have preferred a focus on the deserving poor, to the exclusion of other potential welfare recipients. Without this basis, we should not have had the 1948 universal NHS (the Act having been passed two years previously) which thus laid the following duty on the Minister of Health:[9]

> To promote the establishment of a *comprehensive* health service designed to secure improvement in the physical and mental health

of the people and the prevention, diagnosis and treatment of illness, and for that purpose to provide or secure the *effective* provision of resources (authors' emphases).

As regards doctors' influence, their preference for a state-funded service was clear in the face of the alternative: control by friendly societies and the local government employed medical officers of health. Medical influence in the administration of healthcare had grown during the 1930s, and was secured in the 1948 Act, by representation on executive councils for family practitioner services, on local health authorities for community services and on regional hospital boards, teaching hospital boards of governors and hospital management committees for hospital services. Despite the clear tripartite structure, the professional influence was all pervasive.

There was a major reorganization of the service in 1974, and this brought together hospital and community services, while family practice services still remained separate. Although the 1974 structure failed to secure full unification, it was hoped that it would at least end the syndicalism that had marked the first 26 years of the NHS. The 1948 settlement was perceived as giving the doctors and other producer groups too much influence over the way services were provided. The aim of the revised structure was to give greater attention to consumer needs by strengthening central control, as expressed in the slogan 'Maximum delegation downwards, maximum accountability upwards'.

In addition, the notion of 'equity' (resources distribution pro-rata with need) became as much emphasized as 'universality'. National formulae incorporating attempts to assess morbidity as a basis for financial allocation were introduced in England and Wales and Scotland. In 1976, the Department of Health and Social Security created a planning system designed to have health authorities proceed in accordance with national guidelines and priorities. However, this system failed with the cash crisis precipitated by the mid-1970s 'stagflation' (the unusual combination of inflation and recession). The optimism of a nationally available service, incorporating government priorities and funded by a 'fair shares' formula, could not last, and a solution was sought by changing the administrative structures of the time.

It was thought that relief would come by transferring power downwards: in England, 90 area health authorities were replaced by 200 district health authorities, with greater freedom to plan. However, the prevailing management style was retained: consensus, i.e. the hope that multidisciplinary (finance, clinical, administrative) agreements would ensure effective action.

Increasingly, there also came the clear realization that simply distributing money in the general belief of benefit, with no proof of the value of that spending in terms of health improvement, or demonstrable implementation of stated national priorities, was no longer tenable. Thus, a number of important shifts in attitude were signalled in the 1980s:[10]

- standardized information systems (the Körner Initiative) in February 1980 (so that *ad hoc* local arrangements were no longer acceptable);
- efficiency savings, from 1981 onwards (challenging the previous assumptions that all health spending was well used);
- an annual review system, launched in 1982, linking the Secretary of State, regional health authority chairmen and district health authority chairmen (to ensure that national priorities were implemented);
- Rayner scrutinies (quick reviews of efficiency in the public sector) extended from the Civil Service to the NHS in 1982 (no service was so well organized that it could not be improved);
- central control of manpower from January 1983 (in a labour-intensive industry a most significant aspect of resource control);
- performance indicators (covering 70 areas of clinical work, finance, manpower, support services and estate management) from September 1983 (thereby indicating that comparisons were a reasonable basis for judgement, that nowhere was unique or unchallenged);
- compulsory competitive tendering from September 1983 (part of the push towards efficiency of resource use, not security of tenure, as the basis for employment);
- forced disposal of surplus property (again, a far harder line on efficiency).

These initiatives by central government culminated in October 1983 with the publication of The Griffiths Report, a 24-page typed letter which proved to be one of the most important and influential contributions to the health debate in the 1980s.[11] The most quotable observations include:

> In short if Florence Nightingale were carrying her lamp through the corridors of the NHS today, she would almost certainly be searching for the people in charge [a reflection of the inertia and non-accountability of consensus management].

> To the outsider, it appears when change of any kind is required, the NHS is so structured to resemble a 'mobile': designed to move with any breath of air, but which in fact never changes its position and gives no clear indication of direction [a reflection of the lack of clear monitoring].

Despite mention of the importance of the continuing involvement of doctors in administrative and management structures, especially in hospitals, it was the letter's recommendations regarding general management that were the most influential. It was not enough to set targets; managers had to be given power to achieve them.

A general management structure was created from the top to the bottom of the NHS. Medical and nursing representatives on management teams lost their power of veto, and managerial pay, as well as job tenure itself, became dependent on how well managers performed. This was accompanied by a detailed circular directing health authorities to put out to competitive tender their catering, cleaning and laundry services. The era of automatic dependence on in-house staff was over.

The NHS used to be an essentially collegiate institution run, to carica-ture only slightly, by doctors. The general management reforms of 1984 generated a paradigm shift in NHS internal operations. Out went con-sensus management by professionals, in came business-like managerial hierarchies. This was underpinned by the notion that professionals should be subject to the same kinds of accountability and control as are found in contemporary business hierarchies. Thus, what could be construed as an attack on professional autonomy, evident in isolated initiatives from the early 1980s, was conducted in earnest after 1984.

However, none of this gave managers much influence over spending, or the clinical decisions made by hospital doctors. If costs had to be cut, then the main way to do it was by closing wards or hospitals as a whole, and those decisions could be delayed or rejected by the opposition of community health councils, who had to be consulted before such changes were made. Doctors, whether consultants or GPs, really had to make very little concession as regards professional self-government. This is because the NHS in the mid- and late 1980s continued to provide them with defence mechanisms. In the absence of developed sources of in-formation (particularly relating to prices and costings) it was difficult to impose the new disciplines. In many cases doctors simply worked as in the days before the introduction of general management, aware that few possibilities to discipline them existed. The problems were not only that information systems remained crude, but also that no real sanction could be brought to bear on consultants' work patterns and behaviour. Clinical autonomy was protected by this lack of a disciplining agent. There were no clear means by which clinical autonomy could be challenged, and genuine efficiency (and effectiveness) be secured in the NHS.[12]

The 1991 reforms which separated 'purchasing' and 'providing' roles can be viewed as, in part, reinforcing the new managerialism, substan-tially increasing the pressure to replace consensus management with business-like hierarchies. The actual legislation was the 1990 NHS and Community Care Act. But, using the managerial chain of command, many changes preceded the legislation. The structural change was im-mense, not least in terms of medical influence. There was still a bipartite (primary care versus community/hospital care) structure, but instead of representing traditional medical power hierarchies (hospital consultants at the top, GPs at the bottom), it appeared to invert that. The separation was now between purchasers (health authorities and general practitioner fundholders) and providers (community and hospital healthcare ser-vices). Developing alliances between district health authorities and GPs put pressure on providers to improve their performance. GP fundholders required accountability, and were empowered to open up a debate about the standards of care that should be delivered. The old system of planning by decibels, in which providers of acute care won the biggest share of resources, shifted in favour of primary care. With the purchasing power to back their decisions, fundholders were in a strong position to negotiate improvement in services on behalf of their patients, including additional services in their practices, cutting waiting times for outpatient appointments and elective surgery, and improving communication.[13]

The shift in power is nicely illustrated by medical influence over the changes. Managers of hospital and community care services could put forward their services for designation as NHS trusts (the new label for healthcare providers), regardless of the views of the clinical consultants. In contrast, GPs were left far freer to make their own decisions about fundholding; there was no management structure in primary care that could bring about such major changes despite clinical opposition.

The new health authorities were less powerful. The gradual establishment of NHS trusts, 'emerging like butterflies from the shell of a chrysalis', effectively slowed the development of district health authorities in their new role as purchasers, reinforced by the relative neglect of the purchaser role by ministers and the management executive. This is worth bearing in mind as we examine the extent to which effective healthcare patterns have been implemented.

Because GP fundholders were responsible for their practice lists, and health authorities for their local populations, there was potential tension in priorities and responsibilities, and it is not surprising that the principle of equity appeared undermined. The impact on the quality of healthcare by health authorities was limited. Evidence from the use of contracts indicated that a wide range of quality standards tended to cover waiting times, patient satisfaction and a requirement to undertake medical audit, with far less attention paid to standards of clinical quality. This reflected largely the absence of data on clinical quality and the difficulty of comparing providers on a consistent basis.

At the same time, community care, especially for frail and elderly people, was subject to similar 'purchaser–provider' legislation. The NHS and Community Care Act of 1990 gave local authorities the lead responsibility for community care, as enablers rather than direct service providers. There was undoubtedly a risk of cost shifting and buck passing. The emphasis was again more likely to be on cheapness and markers of performance than on clinical effectiveness.[14]

It might be thought that a further requirement of the 1990 Act, the involvement of the Audit Commission, would exacerbate this. The Audit Commission had been established as an independent body in 1982 by the Local Government Finance Act.[15] However, it is notable that among the topics on which it reports are not only probity in the NHS, but rational prescribing, hospital services for children and adolescents and the use of day surgery, all of which have significant implications for the universal implementation of good clinical care, as well as efficient use of cash limited resources. This point is worth emphasizing. Universality interpreted as equity was severely jeopardized by some of the reforms of the 1990 Act. But universality, in terms of a care model being generally applicable throughout the NHS, was reinforced by the Audit Commission approach. Local idiosyncrasies and variations in clinical care were steadily becoming less acceptable. Clinical autonomy was being further eroded.

The speed with which these major reforms were successfully implemented undoubtedly owed much to a combination of factors, including:

- the widely promulgated messages, speedily reaching all levels of the NHS;
- the presence of managers whose jobs depended on getting the change in place;
- management information systems, even relatively crude measures such as the progress of the establishment of trusts, and the recruitment of general practitioners to fundholding.

The pace of change was lubricated by obedient, biddable, links in the chain of command. It is therefore ironic that the final phase of the reforms was 'anti-bureaucracy', culminating in the Health Authorities Act of 1995, which abolished regional health authorities. At last, however, there was a unified structure: family health service authorities and district health authorities were merged.

And what of 'the new NHS'[16] from 1997 onwards? Clearly, some features of the early 1990s are to be retained:

- the bipartite structure (now relabelled as planning (not purchasing) and providing);
- the enhanced power for general practitioners (together with other clinical staff in primary care groups).

Other features are to be discarded, notably inequity ('unfairness for patients'). Although, as ever, there is repeated emphasis on getting rid of bureaucracy, there is a greater emphasis on what could be perceived as 'universal truths' regarding good, effective healthcare:

Nationally there will be:
- new evidence based national service frameworks to help ensure consistent access to services and quality of care right across the country
- a new national institute for clinical excellence to give a strong lead on clinical and cost effectiveness.

In the one NHS, the government is determined that the services and treatment that patients receive should be based on the best evidence of what does and does not work, and what provides best value for money. Variations in the application of evidence on clinical and cost effectiveness are regarded as unjustifiable. Clinical effectiveness will be subject to national monitoring, while 'clinical governance' will be a statutory requirement for all trusts, with chief executives carrying ultimate responsibility. That is, managers are no longer restricted to administrative roles in non-clinical areas. Consistent with the recognition of the importance of implementing research proven standards available everywhere (universally), they now will have the formal power to require those standards to be demonstrably practised. The requirements of clinical governance include:

- evidence-based practice in day-to-day use;
- clinical risk reduction programmes of a high standard;
- adverse events detected and openly investigated;
- problems of poor clinical performance are recognized and dealt with;
- the quality of data collected to monitor clinical care is itself of a high standard.

The focus of work will be health improvement programmes, 'The framework within which all NHS bodies will operate'. These programmes are the responsibility of health authorities to develop and monitor. There is thus an interesting change of emphasis, in the words at least, from production line metaphors to ensuring a 'comprehensive health service designed to secure improvement in the physical and mental health of the people and the prevention, diagnosis and treatment of illness, and for that purpose to provide or secure the effective provision of resources.'

The underlying philosophy has not changed. The means of managing it have. There will still be medical input to local management decisions (GPs through the local medical committee, other doctors in 'aligning NHS trust financial priorities with clinical priorities'), but the key to the whole process is seen as performance monitoring in six dimensions (population health improvement, fair access, effective healthcare, efficiency, patient/carer experience, health outcomes). Universality, not clinical autonomy, is here to stay.

Of even more interest is the strong drive from management, now attempting to shift away from incremental forms of decision making towards the more explicit management of change,[17] an issue explored by a number of researchers interested in social change within our healthcare system. Some of these researchers have highlighted how the rise of the so-called 'new public management' is emphatically not a parochial NHS, or even British, development, but a striking trend in public administration observable internationally from the mid-1970s onward. While researchers may disagree on the extent to which the move towards the new public management occurs similarly in all countries, there seems little doubt that there are many marked similarities between the UK and the USA, and that the broad thrust of change is similar between Britain and Europe, even if the details differ. Hence the changing roles in relationships, with the rise of management and the challenge to clinical domination, while varying in extent, are occurring internationally. Understanding the process of change in healthcare organizations has become a crucial part of the theory and research of investigators of policy making. Thus our changes in the NHS are part of the global shift, and, as such, the balance between power interests and the emphasis on change management rather than day-to-day administration are international phenomena to which change-promoting R&D is key.

1.4 Implementing effective healthcare

Prior to the NHS reforms of the early 1990s, the main means by which change was effected were, first, general management and, second, substantial investment (as in hospital building or medical staffing). The reforms interposed a new decision-making structure between the government's allocation of funds for the NHS and the pattern of expenditure by healthcare providers. Health authorities and GP fundholders, as recipients of funds, were supposed to control the activities of providers through non-legally binding contracts: the purchaser–provider split.

Alongside the devolvement of this responsibility for control came the eventual recognition that means of control included knowledge about, for example, likely healthcare needs in a given population, and research-based knowledge of effective intervention. The climate of opinion which nurtured the growth of research and development in the NHS from the late 1980s also gave rise to central support for widely promulgated advice, based as far as possible on published research.

The process is interesting because it acknowledges, first, that access to research findings relevant to health service decisions may not be easy and, second, that interpretation of those research findings, by judging the quality of the research, requires specialist skills. It is notable that simple promulgation of advice none the less seemed to be sufficient in itself for change to occur, an echo of the evidence given to the House of Lords Select Committee. No one saw that publication was disassociated from and independent of management power and responsibilities, because there was still a belief that clinicians had no difficulty in using this advice and amending their practice accordingly.

The same culture also legitimized the importance of clinical audit, as not only a justifiable but in fact an essential use of clinical time. Again, however, the process was regarded as strictly educational, minimally threatening to clinical practitioners and with little explicit requirement to involve managers in changing clinical care for the better, despite the substantial financial investment in the process.[18]

Methods of promulgating sound advice based on research included the following: NHS Executive funded processes; professional body (such as Royal Colleges) organized processes; nationally (internationally) published journals; and some activities undertaken by the erstwhile regional health authorities as they evolved into regional offices of the NHS Executive. Examples, together with brief descriptions, are given in Box 1.1. The

Box 1.1   Examples of sources of research-based advice

Effective Healthcare Bulletins	These are based on a series of systematic reviews and syntheses of research on clinical and cost-effectiveness. Funded by the NHS Executive, they are produced by the NHS Centre for Reviews and Dissemination at the University of York. They have been available since 1992.
Effectiveness Matters	A new series of publications which began in 1995. It is also funded by the NHS Executive, and produced by the NHS Centre for Reviews and Dissemination at the University of York.
Epidemiologically based Needs Assessments	These were initiated as part of the NHS Executive's programme of work for supporting the developing role of purchasers in the NHS. The first series was published in 1994, the second in 1997.
CRD Reports	These are detailed reports of the systematic review of research evidence examined by the NHS Centre for Reviews and Dissemination, as funded by the NHS Executive.
Professional bodies: Clinical Guidelines	These are systematically developed statements designed to assist clinicians and patients to make decisions about appropriate treatment for specific conditions. They are generated by a number of learned bodies, including the Standing Medical Advisory Committee, Royal Colleges, university departments, and professional associations.
Health Technology Assessments	These are part of the research and development programme in the NHS.
Journals	Examples include *Evidence Based Medicine*, *Quality in Healthcare* and *Evidence Based Healthcare Management*. In addition, the NHS Confederation (formerly the National Association of Health Authorities and Trusts) publishes occasional papers.
Regional Publications	Development and Evaluation Committee (DEC) reports from the South and West region, Aggressive Research Intelligence Facility (ARIF) for the West Midlands and 'Bandolier', from the NHSE Anglia and Oxford.

topics covered are wide ranging. They include the *Health of the Nation*[19] key areas (cancer, coronary heart disease and stroke, accidents, sexual health and mental health) but also influenza vaccination, hernia repair, hip and knee replacement, leg ulcers, diabetes, asthma and cochlear implantation, to name but a few. There should therefore, in theory be no shortage of sound advice for the NHS on an extremely wide range of healthcare topics. There are, in addition, exhortatory documents, as typified by conference proceedings, or a user guide for assessing one's own local clinical guidelines distributed in 1997.[20]

Unfortunately, of itself, dissemination is not sufficient to ensure good, research-based effective clinical care. The previously mentioned brief summary of the development of R&D in the NHS identified one research topic as being devoted to looking at successful ways of ensuring the implementation of research-based care. Others have already attempted to look into this difficult area, and generally take what might be regarded as one of two approaches: managerial or clinical.

The first, managerial, approach tends to be based on surveys of health authorities. Their findings are generally not dissimilar. Thus, despite some good examples, one paper concluded that there were eight main concerns regarding quality management in the NHS, of which four assisted and four impeded the process:[21]

Assisting the process	*Impeding the process*
Senior management involvement.	Uncertain commitment.
Organization-wide values.	Little user involvement (i.e. patients).
Skills.	Little influence on service standards
Integration with everyday activity.	or quality.
	Poor data.

The National Audit Office, in looking at the value for money of the £218 million spent on clinical audit between 1989 and 1994, and a further £61 million in 1994/5, believed that there was evidence that progress had been made towards establishing clinical audit as a routine part of clinical practice. However, there was still a need for monitoring data to ensure that effective clinical audit was being carried out, that it contributed to improved patient care and that there were demonstrable benefits for patients.[22] In other words, the advantages were possible, but the case was far from proven.

Another study, based on a survey and subsequent visits to health authorities and healthcare providers,[23] felt that although some useful steps had been taken regarding clinical effectiveness, there was little evidence of senior management involvement, understanding and support. The authors felt there was a particular need for good information resources, skills development and systems for monitoring the progress of work on clinical effectiveness.

Further work on the quality register (organized by a voluntary consortium of national agencies such as the British Medical Association and

Box 1.2   Adequacy of routinely available data to support various procedures

Effectiveness Bulletins: will we know if we are taking their advice?
Y = yes N = no.

Topic	Do not do	Measure readily available?	Do do	Measure readily available?
Osteoporosis	Population screening	Y[1]	• Extensive research	N[2]
Subfertility	Operate on damaged fallopian tubes	Y	• Use 'adjusted' maternity rates as outcome measures;	Y[3]
			• agree referral guidelines;	Y
			• research	N[2]
Glue ear	Myringotomy/ tonsillectomy for glue ear	Y	• Watchful waiting with protocols;	N[4]
			• research	N[2]
Depression in primary care			• Recognize major depression in primary care;	N
			• encourage compliance with antidepressants in major depression;	N
			• cognitive therapy;	N
			• research	N[2]
Cholesterol screening	Population cholesterol screening	Y[1]	• Give cholesterol lowering treatment to patients with high overall CHD risk;	N[5]
Alcohol (brief interventions)	Only invest in specialist centres	Y	• Use simple screening instruments;	N
			• undertake brief interventions;	N
			• 'seamless' detection;	N
			• research;	N[2]
			• health promotion	Y[6]
Menorrhagia	Diagnostic D & C in women under 40	Y	• Prescribe drugs;	Y[5]
			• endometrial resection/laser ablation;	Y

Topic	Do not do	Measure readily available?	Do do	Measure readily available?
			• hysterectomy;	Y
			• provide information;	N[4]
			• research	N[2]
Pressure Sores	Use prevalence as measure	N	• Use risk adjusted incidence;	N[5]
			• provide mattresses for at-risk patients;	N[5]
			• research	N[2]
Benign prostatic hyperplasia	Overtreat mild symptoms	N	• Watchful waiting;	N[4]
			• more incision of prostate;	Y
			• involve patients in decisions	N[2]
Cataract			• Increase day case rate	Y

Notes: 1 Assume purchaser is charged.   2 May be identified in national R&D programme (e.g. health technology assessment).   3 Published by HFEA but some disputes about interpretation.   4 Requires providers to establish.   5 Problem defining risk group. 6 But primary care health promotion data will no longer be specified nationally.

the then National Association of Health Authorities and Trusts) high-lighted similar concerns: there was little evidence of activity focusing on implementation; the NHS Executive (as the centre of command) itself appeared to be fragmented; and the diverse information sources made keeping up-to-date very difficult.[24] A brief analysis of some of the effectiveness bulletins already mentioned, in order to identify the recommendations for which routinely available data might be available, demonstrated clearly that for most of them routinely available data were inadequate and unavailable (see Box 1.2).

As regards research looking at the impact on clinicians themselves, two recent papers show clearly that simply disseminating information is not enough.[25] Management action is required or we risk wasting considerable expenditure; increasingly, the received view is that clinicians and managers need each other to implement evidence-based practice.[26] The importance of building on constructive relationships with patients and users, of having better links between health professionals and managers, of clinicians practising demonstrably effective and efficient healthcare, is the burden of a recent paper encouraging a new paradigm as regards effective clinical care.[27] The idea is of a 'broader, socialised definition of science', and of shared decisions using all relevant evidence. This could include encouraging clinicians not only to collect their own data (which many do already) but also to adopt a disciplined approach to this so that shared understanding and rapid opportunities for analysis of such data and interpretation of what they mean can evolve.[28]

International work on healthcare accreditation[29] identifies some of the principles of continuous quality improvement, as applied to healthcare systems. These principles include:

- leaders' support;
- involvement of users (customers);
- involvement of everyone, and all processes;
- based on sound statistical analysis.

From a psychologist's point of view, the following are considered crucial: available good evidence; communications throughout the organization; and monitoring the applications.[30]

The message is strikingly clear. Readily available information about good practice is not enough. We need to know how to find that good evidence. We also need senior management involvement in using that evidence, and good quality information to monitor its implementation. Users, as well as professionals, should be closely involved.

The conclusions so far

There is a marked contrast between the extent to which massive change in the structure and function of the NHS has been implemented, and the failure to ensure widespread practice of effective clinical care. We suggest that for change to be successfully implemented the basic requirements are:

1 Widespread knowledge of what is required.
2 Senior management commitment.
3 Management information for monitoring implementation.
4 Clinical information for monitoring the impact on service users.

The implementation of the NHS reforms had much in its favour, as regards change management. The implementation of effective healthcare is, by comparison, lacking.

The best way in which effective healthcare can be implemented is by close involvement of managers from the beginning: in drafting the research questions, in commissioning the research and in using the results. This is the basis of our new paradigm, as discussed in the next chapter.

2

THE NEW PARADIGM

KEY POINTS

There are various types of health-related research. Useful health services research is about change, and so is legitimately a collaborative function, best undertaken by managers, statisticians, social scientists, epidemiologists, health economists, clinicians and, importantly, patients and service users, all working together. This is a participative, not isolationist, model, and the only way, we believe, to make R&D really useful to health services.

So far we have looked briefly at the emerging legitimacy of R&D in the NHS, the thrust of change in NHS organization and limits on the extent to which effective healthcare has been implemented. We have suggested that one of the more salient inadequacies is the lack of monitoring information, while, more positively, the potential levers for change include the recognition that clinical practice can be governed by patterns of effectiveness which are generally (universally) applicable, in the context of clear management structures where managers are committed to making effective use of resources. Hitherto our approach may have appeared somewhat negative as regards clinicians, especially doctors, and their apparent lack of interest in ensuring that only evidence-based medicine is practised, while protecting their professional autonomy.

Although this is undoubtedly an important part of the overall picture, the role of the other main contributors must also be remembered. They are the managers and the researchers. In this chapter we explain their involvement, together with clinical practitioners, in taking research into everyday clinical practice, and hence engaging in what we label the *new* paradigm.

2.1 Nothing new under the sun

For those with long memories, the NHS R&D programme is seeking to pick up from an almost forgotten initiative in the 1970s by Lord Rothschild[1] (then UK government Chief Scientist) which failed. Rothschild sought to make the government-funded research councils more responsive to the needs of government departments through the kind of research they funded. The idea was that there should be a 'customer–contractor' relationship between those who would apply research findings and those awarded grants to do research. The implication was that a substantial proportion of research funds would be directed towards priority issues identified by the customers, i.e. government agencies. After a while, Rothschild's initiative was quietly forgotten, though we are not aware of any formal announcement that it was abandoned. We suggest that it failed partly because the scientific community ('contractors') wanted nothing to do with it and mainly because the 'customers' had little idea of how to commission research and did not work in an ethos which called for evidence-based practice. Peckham's[2] extended trial protocol and an elaborate R&D infrastructure, including the dissemination centres previously discussed, will not succeed where Rothschild failed, as we have outlined. For the heart of the problem is to do with culture – not resources. The R&D establishment was perforce created from the extant medical scientific establishment. It has traditionally owned research and had little regard for wider issues of NHS management and resource use. Moreover, it is optimistic to assume that setting up dissemination centres and the related Cochrane Collaboration[3] (which hand down digested wisdom) will itself be sufficient to influence practice. Indeed, such centres are at risk of becoming insular and preoccupied with academic rigour, such as the finer points of systematic appraisal and overemphasis of the importance of randomized controlled trials.

Nevertheless, this R&D infrastructure has the potential to become immensely valuable once there has been a simple switch of mind-set by researchers, healthcare managers and practitioners. We assert that adoption of a *new paradigm* is the essential prerequisite for R&D to deliver, but this is not of itself the entire solution to the problem. Moreover, the current paradigm will change only if there is a power to force that change. We contend that when those who manage resources understand that it is not in their interests to remain detached from research policy and management they will drive the change. For they have a central role in the *new paradigm* and much to benefit from it.

2.2 Research and paradigms

In this section we define what we mean by 'research' and 'paradigm', and the basis of our argument: that the NHS needs change-promoting research, not just theory-enhancing research. Ideas relating to responsible participants (clinicians, researchers and managers) are examined in turn, and future requirements for us all are summarized in terms of relationships and the detailed implications of our ideas.

Some people use the word 'research' loosely to mean 'scientific research'. In a discussion such as this the various nuances of the term will cause confusion. Indeed, instances of confusion have been seen in the sterile debate over whether or not clinical audit is research. We use 'research' solely to denote some systematic means of gathering information to answer questions; for example, historians do research but do not claim to be scientists. We will explicitly write *scientific research* (we use *theory-enhancing research* as a synonym) or *change-promoting research* (or sometimes *evaluative research*) if that is what we mean – note that a distinction is being maintained.

Our underlying concept of *paradigm* was developed by Thomas Kuhn.[4] It denotes a belief system shared by scientists working within an established discipline. The 'beliefs' include a consensus on the theoretical underpinning of the discipline, the sorts of question worthy of pursuit, appropriate research methods and common standards by which to judge the quality of any piece of research. Thus the paradigm serves to determine what is valued and what is not, and hence the criteria by which individuals are esteemed. It maintains the cohesion of the group, and their 'standards', and guides individuals into supposedly productive (or valued) work. Kuhn's writing shows how the historical development of sciences can be understood through the coming and going of paradigms. When a hitherto successful paradigm begins to fail a period of turmoil ensues, and eventually a more useful paradigm emerges and gains consensus support. Here we shall show a particular paradigm to be redundant and sketch a replacement.

2.3 Theory-enhancing research

Some other definitions are necessary. *Fundamental biomedical research* explores basic biological mechanisms; it elaborates theoretical constructs encapsulating that knowledge which serve as stimuli for further research questions. It is not justified by any immediately tangible practical application. Sometimes it is referred to as 'blue sky' research. Although researchers depend upon the patronage of diverse funding agencies, and hence are accountable, the priorities for research and the disbursement of funds are mainly determined by their peer group. The peer group are the commissioners of research and, as in the Kuhnian notion of the paradigm, its principal consumer. Although many problems have been identified with the way fundamental research is organized, no better method has yet been found.[5] We term activities following this paradigm as *theory-enhancing* research (to make explicit an essential aim of *scientific*

Box 2.1   Features of the theory-enhancing paradigm

Applicable to: fundamental biomedical research and aetiological epidemiology.

Purpose of work within paradigm: to develop the theoretical framework and knowledge base of the particular sub-discipline.

Motivation for work: curiosity, personal satisfaction and, perhaps, a *long-term* desire in some not immediately specifiable way to alleviate human suffering.

Practical application of work to wider world: not usually a major consideration, 'cultural' considerations predominate.

Philosophical base: Popperian principles seem to be applied widely to the diverse theoretical frameworks employed. Uncomfortable with uncertainty unless it is statistically quantifiable.

Typical methods: laboratory and clinical measurement, epidemiological techniques; preference for quantitative methods and narrow range of study end-points pertaining to developing and testing theories; descriptive and uncontrolled studies generally seen as lacking rigour and not able to contribute to answering the questions of interest.

Patrons: mainly research councils but also industry and charities.

Research providers: academics and researchers in diverse institutions.

Judges of who gets funded: senior (and therefore previously successful, according to the paradigm) peers of the research providers.

Research consumers: primarily the research providers.

Judges of valued work areas: senior peers.

Mark of successful work: publication in journal refereed by peers; bibliometric indices such as citations, implying impact on development of discipline.

Judges of successful work: peers; thus it is self-referential.

---

research). Features of this paradigm are detailed in Box 2.1. Of particular note is that it is widely accepted that the logic underlying theory enhancement is the hypothetico-deductive system promulgated by Popper[6] (see Box 2.2). Many might agree with Popper that use of the hypothetico-deductive system is a distinguishing feature of 'science'. We assert that health services R&D (most R and all D) has a different logic and that disentangling R&D from the common conception of 'science' is advantageous.

2.4 Change-promoting research: the new paradigm

Applied research has an end application in view, but those applying the findings are likely to lie beyond the peer group of researchers. They have to decide whether and how to apply the findings. In health services the

Box 2.2 The hypothetico-deductive system

Theories encapsulate knowledge and understanding about the aspects of the cosmos within their domains (examples of domains are the macro-universe, the micro-universe, biological entities, human behaviour). A theory, to be useful to the development of science, has to be more than an explanation (or myth). It should be capable of making predictions about the behaviour of the entities within its domain. These predictions should be testable through observation and experiment. Confirmed predictions (going beyond the observations that led to the theory's formulation) help to build confidence in its utility.

However, science develops conceptually as a result of failed predictions. Once experimental technique and error have been excluded as the reason for the failure it has to be concluded that the theory is flawed. Karl Popper described this *hypothetico-deductive* reasoning as being the underlying logic of science. Hypothetico-deductive means: set up a hypothesis (e.g. theory), deduce its consequences and then test whether the deduction accords with reality. If there is no such accord then the hypothesis (assuming the deductions were logical) must be wrong. Scientists should strive through observation and experiment to test their theories to the limit and ultimately falsify them. Falsification is a spur for correcting and improving a theory. Theory formulation and modification is an imaginative process but testing is a strictly logical one.

There may come a point when *ad hoc* corrections are so insufficient (or inelegant) that someone is driven to reformulate the theory in an entirely different way, such that it encompasses (most or all of) the confirmed predictions of the old theory, opens out a range of new confirmed predictions beyond the power of the old theory and yields the possibility of yet further predictions by which it too could be falsified. These dramatic changes in theory coincide with the paradigm shifts described by Thomas Kuhn. Examples are the move from classical mechanics to quantum physics and the abandonment of the blending theory of inheritance in favour of Mendelian ('bean bag') genetics.

Thomas Kuhn and Paul Feyerabend have each written interestingly about how an abandoned theory and its successor may be strictly incommensurable in the sense that they view their domain in such a different way that concepts and constructs from one do not translate to those in the other in a one-to-one fashion, e.g. the shift from classical mechanics to quantum mechanics at the microphysical level. Discredited theories may still have utility for applied work. For example, Newtonian mechanics, rather than general relativity, is used by engineers for designing and navigating space craft.

It follows from this description that every theory (unless someone succeeds with a theory of everything) is strictly false. Nevertheless, theories are useful. This brings us nicely to William James's pragmatism, which does not require one to bother with the niceties of truth and falsehood but rather with utility: 'What is the cash value of this idea?' James, rather than Popper, is the philosophical patron of the new paradigm.

decision takers require a range of information concerning potential benefits, disbenefits, costs and broader social acceptability.

For them there is no single research question with one answer, but a range of points of view which need to be integrated if healthcare is to be provided as effectively as possible. Making decisions about the 'best possible' is part of the change management process. Successful change management requires some conditions to be met. These include a wish to change, a vision of where the changes will lead and some feasible and palatable first steps to bringing about the change. These conditions apply not only to the leaders of an organization but also to those being led.

We call the contribution of applied research to this process *change-promoting*. The stereotype of this research paradigm is multidisciplinary, a complex web of clinical, sociological, economic and epidemiological perspectives, firmly placed in the context of decision making. In addition, it is itself paradigm challenging, in terms of continually reassessing common belief systems about models of healthcare provision. That is, we become so comfortable about ways of doing things that we do not realize how restrictive our mind-set has become. A quick glance at the recent list of health technology assessment priorities[7] confirms this. For example, who should provide rehabilitation for elderly people with osteoarthritis? This involves challenging the notion that physiotherapists are effective and, as such, the only appropriate care givers. Value is placed on changes in anatomical and biological impairment, so that 'scientific' evaluative criteria may include, for example, changes in the range of joint movement, and this is regarded as proof of productive work. An alternative approach might be to explore sufferers' self-esteem and body image, their psychological and not just physical suffering. It is a major paradigm shift to value how people feel about themselves more than exercises which extend the range of joint movement. Another example is 'the extended nursing role'. Here any research would have to confront ideological opposites: the medical notion of ultimate responsibility, hence superiority, coupled with a task-driven approach, compared with a nursing profession seeking to establish its own and valued identity, quite distinct from the doctor's handmaiden, and a 'holistic', not piecemeal, contribution to care.

We argue that most of the 'research' in healthcare R&D should be seen as *applied* research and that in consequence R&D should be seen as primarily *change-promoting* (see Box 2.3). Moreover, it will follow that *research* and *development* cease to be confusingly different in kind; they differ in degree but can only usefully be understood as inextricably linked. From this stance it becomes possible to elaborate important elements of the new paradigm.

It can be seen from Box 2.3 that there are major differences, apart from one aspect: who does the research, the research providers. Academics and researchers have opportunities to engage with both models. They are central to the process of successful research, and, as can be seen from

Box 2.3 Features of the change-promoting paradigm

Applicable to: NHS R&D (and, perhaps, R&D in other contexts).

Purpose of work within paradigm: to develop preventive, diagnostic treatment and caring procedures and services for the benefit of the population, and to provide those charged with the disbursement of NHS resources with the necessary information to make informed decisions so that change can be successfully managed.

Motivation for work: the realization of relatively short-term goals (months or years rather than decades) for the improvement of health services through the application of fairly secure existing knowledge which might help to bring them about.

Practical application of work to a wider world: the predominant consideration.

Philosophical base: the theory of evaluation against goals, decision theory plus a good helping of William James's pragmatism embedded in sound management practice; willingness to accept uncertainty and use diverse evidence of varying rigour to define the current best state of the art. Prepared to 'paradigm shift' in terms of healthcare models.

Typical methods: quantitative and qualitative within clinical research, epidemiological, economic and social science perspectives aimed at specific evaluation against goals and understanding the broader context within which the work is applied; descriptive studies and those not using explicit comparison groups acceptable as part of overall programme of work from 'R' through 'D' to implementation.

Patrons: primarily the NHS but similar work within closely defined boundaries also funded by the pharmaceutical and medical equipment industries. Some input from charities but not necessarily in a form consistent with NHS priorities.

Research providers: academics, researchers and practitioners in close consultation, and often collaboration, with NHS decision-takers.

Judges of who gets funded from NHS sources: representatives of the interests of NHS decision-takers. These taking advice from research providers about methodological issues.

Research consumers: NHS decision-takers, e.g. health authority management, provider management and clinical professionals using the resources at their disposal. These consumers are ultimately holding a responsibility in trust for the population at large, which if appropriate mechanisms could be devised should be directly involved in these decisions.

Judges of valued work areas: the research consumers based on their own priorities but taking into account advice from research providers (e.g. concerning fundamental work which looks promising for application).

Judges of appropriate methods and standards: the research providers will advise but the consumers will not accept that advice uncritically, as they will have among their number people with research experience, who know which questions research should address.

Mark of successful work: the impact on the health of the nation; research providers can still have their own brownie point systems if this keeps them happy.

Judges of successful work: the consumers; thus it is externally referential.

our summaries, and as will be illustrated below, contribute most successfully in our new paradigm when they acknowledge and are acknowledged by their essential collaborators: clinicians and managers.

2.5 Three key players: clinicians, researchers, managers

Clinical practitioners are of singular importance in the whole chain of events leading to the practice of evidence-based healthcare. Here we outline contributions from others to understanding some of the complexities they face, but also some ways of working through them. A recent interesting study identified some reasons why links in the chain might be weak.[8] It used published evidence relating to obstetric care, which was the first clinical area for which the government funded the widespread dissemination of summaries of research evidence, with commentary on the research quality, by hunting out the ideal form of research (randomized control trials, or RCTs), and which led directly to the establishment of the Cochrane Collaboration, which is now a global research activity including obstetrics in a large number of clinical areas.[9] This was therefore a well established, professionally approved, widely available source of guidance on good, effective, research-based clinical care. The study we are quoting compared this guidance with local policies in maternity units in relation to four types of clinical intervention. The researchers identified discrepancies between the Cochrane Collaboration output and the printed policies, and used questionnaires, interviews and discussions to explore possible explanations. They identified three main explanations for discrepancies:

1 'Don't believe the research': because follow-up was too short or the processes involved in an intervention were oversimplified.
2 'It's no use here': usually because research was done in other countries where women or clinicians were regarded as significantly different.
3 'We don't know how to implement this': usually a matter of acquiring suitable skills.

The research is interesting for a number of reasons. First, it was necessary to undertake the research in order to find out where the good practice had actually occurred. There were no routinely available data which could be used for that purpose, and one of the outcomes of the research was that, locally, the maternity unit set about obtaining more systematic information about actual practice. Second, because implementation of good practice was so variable, it highlights the complexity of the knowledge–attitude–behaviour model which (despite evidence within health promotion circles that it does not work) underpins so much of our current approach to ensuring the practice of evidence-based care, and which is, in reality, far from simple. The relevance of change-promoting research is strikingly clear. Third, in itself the research could be seen as *theory-enhancing*. This is because the conclusions derive from theoretical models of management, based on either persuasion or command, but with no evidence that local managers had a direct input into how good practice should be put in place. The findings will come as no surprise to experienced clinical and management staff. The value of the investment in the research (which will have been complex and time consuming) could be questioned, except that it certainly does highlight the difficulties of effective change management.

A related editorial[10] explores the cognitive and cultural processes involved, the way in which meaning is given to evidence regardless of source, the importance of contested information and the organizational context of clinical practice. An explanatory metaphor is put forward: the four 'different worlds' of researchers, of reviewers, of guideline writers and of clinicians. Each world is ignorant of the others and defensive about itself. We suggest that our new paradigm acknowledges and builds on the complexities of this system, and so is desperately needed if we really are to achieve effective change.

This is not to assume that a simple model is applicable, but to ensure, for example, that possible barriers to change are recognized in research design. As regards clinicians, there are high expectations of their ability to cope with the flood of evidence-based advice – expectations felt by individuals of themselves[11] as well as by outside observers of clinicians en masse[12] in the face of complex clinical situations which turn on the doctor–patient relationship and how the doctor feels about coping with uncertainty and the clinical decision being made.[13] This is a dynamic, complex and potentially stressful situation. The importance of the 'personal significance' of research findings has been eloquently argued[14] as a dialectic. That in turn comprises the doctor's evaluation of that research evidence, the patient's desires and priorities, and then a synthesis of the two. The final result is predicated on the assumption that 'we see things not as they are, but as we are'.[15] This makes sense in that, presumably, most doctors and other clinical staff practise their vocation motivated at least in part by a desire to provide good care for individual patients. The dialectical model illustrates the need to acknowledge the contribution of assessment of 'good' care and 'individual patients' to what is eventually provided; there is a yearning for wisdom, not just knowledge.[16]

Optimists suggest that there are ways of overcoming these difficulties and barriers by, for example, using information technology in the form of computerized clinical decision support systems, informing patients on a personal basis why they should do as recommended, using reminder systems and developing interactive continuing education opportunities.[17]

Another illustration of a way through comes from the vexed area of measuring the outcomes of healthcare intervention. Rather than simply feeling it is all too difficult and so abandoning our responsibilities, we can clarify our thoughts and identify the objectives of care, and hence what appropriate outcome measurements might be,[18] as illustrated in Box 2.4.

Box 2.4   Examples of outcome measurements

Objective of care   *Possible outcome measure*
Improve survival   Mortality rate
Improve symptoms   Symptoms severity
Reduce risk   Risk factors

Objective of care	Possible outcome measure
Improve survival	Mortality rate
Improve symptoms	Symptoms severity
Reduce risk	Risk factors
Reduce complications	Complication rate
Improve recovery time	Resumption of normal activities
Improve functioning	Activities of daily living scale
Reduce pain	Pain scale
Improve emotional state	Psychological assessment
Improve acceptability	Patient satisfaction
Reduce costs	Quantify costs and their impact

Clinicians do change, or, at least, what is recognized as the 'truth' of research findings changes over time, and there may be some relationship with practice. An elegant study[19] of the half-life of truth in surgical literature (based on whether conclusions of earlier studies were acceptable present day dogma) suggests that clinical statements have a half-life of truth of about 45 years. This will exceed the working lives of many doctors. This in turn suggests that during those working lifetimes science successfully challenges what are held to be existing 'facts' (the role of science, according to the Popperian model[20]), so that cultural acceptance of 'proof' is modified. It also suggests that until we learn to challenge current dogma, and implement change in one coherent R&D approach, patients will be severely disadvantaged by outmoded and potentially dangerous practice.

So clinicians are key, and we have some sympathy with their problems. However, recognition of the issues should open up the possibility of addressing them, especially in a model like our change-promoting paradigm. What are the responsibilities of *researchers*? Are they really as locked into their self-referential world as has been suggested? The earlier illustration (Box 2.1) summarizes what we see as the key features of those engaged in theory-advancing research; unfortunately, these characteristics act as barriers to communication with others, as much as functioning to preserve the purity of science.

This population largely comprises university academics, a label which has pejorative overtones for those engaged in what people see as the real world. The obsession with quantification and methodological perfection may be highly important and very relevant, but is often discussed in a language that is entirely inaccessible and impenetrable for the non-expert. The researchers remain unchallenged in this elite society, because they are their own judges and their own customers, and can exist in a culture which is intellectually challenging and stimulating, thereby reinforcing a sense of superiority and advantage. Some of their internal debates have been cogently criticized for focusing on the wrong issues. They are perceived as emphasizing the perfection of a preferred research strategy at the expense of whether a given research design can actually answer the research question,[21] so that, for example, all time and effort is spent justifying quantitative or qualitative techniques, rather than the researchers being absolutely clear about the research question, and how the answers might most usefully be expressed.

An interesting paper, whose authors notably include a health economist, roundly criticizes the waste of research which fails to answer the question on which clinicians and policy makers are desperate for help.[22] A study of RCT trials of treatment for depression criticizes the research for concentrating on efficacy and side-effects, and providing no useful input to the wider prescribing debate, which hinges on both cost-effectiveness *and* clinical effectiveness and is eager to understand what drugs should be used as a first line treatment of depression. As many health service managers, policy makers and clinicians will know only too well, 'it is remarkable how uninformative many RCTs have been in determining the direction of future prescribing'. Of course, research into efficacy and side-effects is needed, and high-quality research is laudable. But this is familiar and comfortable territory for researchers, perfecting their RCTs within given resource constraints (and hence, because of resource constraints, often undertaking research with no power) and ignoring the interests of the wider world, which may extend to conceptually difficult areas such as values and priorities. All research has costs, not least, in this instance, the opportunity cost of the research which is not then done, and which may have been made of more relevance to a cash-limited health service had our paradigm been part of the researcher's culture.

It is not surprising that researchers are fighting back against the idea of public accountability for their work. 'Under-managed' scientists, free from obligation to document (in detailed protocols), to declare (interests, to mitigate misconduct) or even to publish ('slaves to impact factors'), can be portrayed as the brilliant heroes of a past age, visionaries who, left alone, were apparently remarkably successful, if we are to believe one author (although no examples are given!).[23] Quality research is seen as that which is truly innovative, and even the process of peer review should be stopped because it stifles this innovation.[24] It is possible to quote innovative ideas all characterized by expert opposition (such as accepting the possibility of the viral transmission of some cancers, or the development of radio-immunoassay, or opposition to organ transplantation), and this conspiracy of mediocrity can be perceived by researchers as fear by others (their peers) of what is truly innovative, or, even worse, that successful outcomes might threaten the peers' own research base: 'the advent of cures would herald the demise of most research funds in their field.' So researchers are encouraged to be dishonest, either about the truly innovative ideas behind their proposals or about the fact that the research proposal has already been done, and so will inevitably contribute to a good track record of fully reported products. The authors suggest an alternative method of quality control: there should be far more competition for entrance to research or academic units, but these units should then be left free to research as they wished, conditional on certain performance indications, such as decennial publication quantities.

To us, both the criticisms of researchers and their reactions not only polarize the debate unproductively, but suggest that the only way forward is by devaluing, reducing the status and power, of those who are criticized. This is not helpful. Our model is far more about mutual respect, and taking opportunities for joint work between the various participants who play a part in successful health services research and development.

Some researchers clearly see how 'nowadays ... high quality science pre-supposes, in addition to individual skills, team working, networking and co-operation'.[25] An essential determinant of the effectiveness of research teams appears to be effective boundary management: that is, the ability to cooperate both inside and outside the team. We shall illustrate how this can be done through imaginative skill development, variation in work setting and the processes of commissioning and utilizing research. It does mean that health services researchers no longer regard themselves as defined by their qualities as individuals, but have to see that, in addition to skills such as computing, they will be expected to have skills such as team management, leadership and coping with conflict.

They will also have to be able to communicate results effectively, especially given the complexity of much health services research. Here some of the invaluable skills of the experienced researcher may make an essential contribution. For example, in order to be able to interpret aggregate statistics in a way that makes sense to clinicians caring for individual patients, those patients' heterogeneity should be anticipated and sought upfront.[26] The researcher's experience can be used to anticipate the likely complexity of answers, and to check those out with whoever is posing the question. All parties need to be able to cope with the grey areas of life, in addition to our desires to have unequivocal, black and white, results.

This ability to manage multiple ideas, values, questions and answers is not new to health research, although it may be unfamiliar to many workers in the basic sciences or clinical areas. Because the basic sciences may deal in biological concepts and the clinical sciences in physiological ideas, they are not necessarily grounded in the underlying source of all the information: the individual patient. The patient's lay perspective and lay knowledge of the meanings that health, illness, disability and risk have for people should be an integral part of health research.[27] For example, the wives of the victims of asbestosis are reported as complaining to coroners' courts that the deaths were due to exposure of something at work, long before modern science studied the problem. A notably serious iatrogenic effect identified before professional experts acknowledged it is the example of women who linked the use of Stilboestrol to prevent early miscarriage in their pregnancy with vaginal cancer in their teenage daughters.

Interventions related to lifestyle can only be effective if they are cognizant of those lives we may wish to restyle – hence the high value of work exploring sensitive sexual information, which elucidated the differences between male and female prostitutes, and those using, or not using, drugs. These sociological insights mean that public health policy regarding HIV and AIDS can be more realistically (and less punitively) directed to ways more likely to be effective. Good epidemiology and rigorous science are still required, but the openness of researchers to ideas where there may be opportunities for effective action and change are obviously crucial.

Similarly enhanced layers of understanding can be achieved by combining different disciplines in the research team. Recent work in the North Midlands in England illustrates nicely how combining classic epidemiology (quantifying self-reported limiting long-term illness in the national census; undertaking a sample survey using a self-administered well-being instrument, the SF36) with ecological variables (the distribution of census indicators of material deprivation) and records of health services utilization (family doctor consultation) led to the pursuit of a greater understanding of coping with physical impairments by supplementing those data with interviews with people identified as reporting the worst health.[28] 'Normality' as a concept integral to people's attitude to ill-health was clearly shown to be part of how people defined themselves, of their behaviour in public and of strategies for maintaining independence, so that despite fear and uncertainty they develop their own ways of assessing their individual risks (in terms of, for example, the significance of symptoms of angina or asthma) and hence often minimized service utilization. The potential for working with patients to empower them is clearly highly significant, and research can be used to ensure that any health service interventions really are of practical help, but also, in a cash limited service, to restrict demands on the service to times when 'normality' is most severely jeopardized by uncontrolled symptoms. We feel that the researcher has an invaluable contribution to make to our model, especially if working alongside clinicians in a way that recognizes the complex day-to-day decisions which are made.

The imaginative health services *manager* could clearly take advantage of this, for mutual benefit. This apparently complex research approach may, in fact, be more fitting for the milieu of health services management, which, it has been argued, differs from conventional industrial or retail sector management in the extent to which four features predominate:

the lack of clear objectives, political salience, network complexity and processing people.[29]

The lack of clear national objectives has its sharpest manifestation in the debate around the process of rationing, where until very recently it has been unrealistic to expect governments and politicians to come to the aid of health service managers, given the exposed and competitive nature of party politics. In England and Wales this situation has begun to change, with a statement from the Department of Health strongly advising that doctors should not prescribe sildenafil (Viagra) because it 'raises issues about the priority which should be given to the treatment of erectile dysfunction under the NHS'.[30] None the less, there is still an emphasis on investing resources (money, human resources, skills, capital) in services of demonstrable effectiveness as a way of trying to focus the objectives of the service, although there will always be counter-claims and covert vested interests. The deliberate engagement of knowledgeable managers in the process of research and development, as illustrated in Box 2.3, can only help the difficult local debates about objectives for a service, partly by investigating those areas where managers can use results for relevant decisions, and partly to look into areas of greatest uncertainty, which so often attract the greatest political overtones.

Health services are almost inevitably politically salient, even in countries whose third party systems (that is, payers for care who are neither the recipients nor the providers of that care) rely on private health insurance. This means that governments are not generally allowed to leave well alone, that healthcare is an ideal forum of opposition politics and that the resulting rhetoric can be perceived as being more important than the substantial matters which the rhetoric addresses. It can also mean that the wise manager leaves well alone unless there is specific advantage to be gained. While much of his or her sensitivity to the political salience of the moment would depend on experience and local knowledge, there is no doubt that sound research can also be invaluable. One interesting example of this is the repeated research surrounding the controversial (in England) debate about water fluoridation, where the nature of the research has been to address two main areas of concerned decision makers, even though they may not be directly involved in healthcare management. These decision makers are now repeatedly confronted with sound evidence demonstrating beyond reasonable doubt that fluoridation is safe *and* that the majority of the general public support it. The repeated research, building up a sound body of evidence which directly answers decision makers' concerns, has been a major contribution to the evolution of the perception of fluoride addition as an acceptable public health policy.[31] Similarly, research in the 1980s showed clearly that car seat belts, already known to be effective in terms of reducing morbidity and mortality from road accidents, would only be used widely if there were legislation. So not only healthcare interventions but the wider area of public health interventions, arguably even more sensitive politically, require good research which addresses the issues faced by decision makers.

The network complexity of health services comprises partly the various interest groups (trades unions, other statutory and non-statutory agencies) and partly the clinical–managerial relationship, already covered in our sketched history of the NHS, where professional autonomy might conflict with managerial accountability. There is a danger that each group will claim sole interest in benefiting the patient when often there may be little evidence that such benefit is feasible, let alone that it occurs. Well conducted multidisciplinary research can help to bring people together to examine the potential benefits from various interventions, and clarify the contribution from all the players. Many people will have experience of, for example, a hospital stay rendered unnecessarily distressing by appalling catering, and repeatedly research among cancer patients identifies their desperate search for good information,[32] before we come anywhere near exactly what drugs are given or operations undertaken. The whole patient experience is a compound of contributions from many disciplines, and this should be reflected in the way we set about researching how to improve health and healthcare.

This is the 'business' of healthcare: 'processing people'. This can be used to argue against standardizing healthcare, or, in other words, as a barrier to implementing some forms of universal standards of effective healthcare. If all cases of, for example, schizophrenia or hysterectomy are different, there will have to be unique pathways of care for each individual patient. None the less, it is possible to carry too far the arguments of the uniqueness of each individual patient. There are conventional approaches to care which do command widespread professional support, as in managed healthcare. The skill and the art lie in making each person feel as though the treatment has been unique, not in using this as an excuse never to be accountable in terms of costs or outcomes. For at least one author these features of healthcare management require a management style based less on a chain of command and more on a corporate belief.[33] This may well be right, although of course the trick is to combine various management approaches as required; a more contingent, pragmatic approach.

One managerial approach could be based on 'quality'. There is a traditional, intuitively simple model of quality control or accreditation. However, quality control could be quite inappropriate in the context of healthcare; the principles of continuous quality management may be far more relevant.[34] This is because it relies on organization-wide beliefs and shared values, demonstrable in terms of teamwork (through the complex networks already described). It is also patient centred, or clinical staff would not be interested, and would not participate. The result is that good accreditation systems should have 'realigned themselves to promote the idea that continually questioning what has happened will lead to better processes and therefore better outcomes.' Good clear questions, and robust results, are the bread and butter of good researchers, and are clearly integral to this. In the United States, the Joint Commission on Accreditation of Healthcare Organizations has now acknowledged that interpersonal skills, as well as technical competence, are a valid component of accreditation. This means that it has to look at continuous quality management within the organization, supported by data collection, which could bear a remarkable similarity to health services research. This is viewed as an 'organizational consultant' role.

In the UK, the process of R&D in the NHS could be seen as predominantly having an organizational consultant role, if all participants in the process – clinicians, researchers and managers – are sufficiently engaged. Grounds for optimism regarding R&D in the NHS could include: the extent to which the programme is already redressing the balance between basic, clinical and health services research in terms of funding; the extent to which awareness of and concern for the outcome of healthcare among clinicians and managers has been raised; the introduction of greater coherence and logic to research funding decisions; the raised profile and respectability of dissemination and implementation of research evidence; the mobilization of scientists and clinicians to become involved in healthcare R&D; and increased funding for training and research opportunities.[35] We contend that, laudable though all these achievements are, we do not believe that it is enough actively to manage and direct a complex activity (that is, R&D in the NHS) with greater effectiveness and efficiency. The accumulation of interesting and usable data will never suffice unless those data are used. One key opportunity for such use is in the management of change – because change in the health services can be seen as a seismic societal paradigm shift,[36] occurring throughout the world.

There are forces driving change from which healthcare is not immune. These forces include a more collegiate, innovative style of management, by which organizations not only survive but flourish. Characteristics of such innovative organizations are summarized in Box 2.5.

The recurrent theme of effective management and effective R&D in the NHS is that the organizational environment should be 'a truly evaluative culture'.[37] Using lessons from various disciplines (organizational and health psychology, health promotion and marketing), we can be reminded of the salience of recognizing the subtleties of the organizational context (including who may find it easy or difficult to change and why), ensuring that knowledge is disseminated, identifying the key players in the process, then analysing for preparedness of the change and developing a marketing strategy for the desired change. It is possible to perceive various forces as either driving or hindering change, including various types of reward; it is clear that education and feedback on their own are quite inadequate. Pressures from within an organization, including a 'total quality system which uses evidence . . . is an important force for change so that teams can themselves be highly influential in encouraging

---

Box 2.5   Characteristics of innovative organizations

From	*To*
Industrial society	Information society
Forced technology	High-tech/high-touch
National economy	World economy
Short term	Long term
Centralization	Decentralization
Institutional help	Self-help
Representative democracy	Participative democracy
Hierarchies	Networking
North	South
Either/or	Multiple options

---

clinically effective care because of the social rewards they provide to those who are committed members.' This presupposes strong leadership that is itself committed to the evidence-based approach, and the teams being linked into the management structure. We would argue that this clearly requires a multidisciplinary understanding of the nature of the research evidence on which high-quality healthcare is based, and that there is no better way of acquiring this understanding than being involved in some of the research processes we shall describe.

A wider participation in health research in the sense of research being done *with* the active collaboration of potential recipients of the results, rather than *to* passive subjects, has been a proud tradition of community participation in health programmes. We have already commented on the importance of recognizing lay knowledge as a foundation of research approaches.[38] Of more relevance possibly is the need for explicit recognition that sharing research and encouraging participation means sharing power[39] and that, regardless of the topic being researched, or the research design, or even whether the methods are qualitative or quantitative, it is this empowering which results in effective implementation of the results of research. It is, therefore, necessarily an iterative, complex process, not a simple linear progression of events.[40] 'Participation must be seen as inherently political'[41] is a statement from a researcher involved in work in developing countries, but which undoubtedly resonates and echoes with our analysis of the complexities of healthcare management.[42] It is clearly impossible any longer to exclude management, and management information, from the process of research, continuous quality and improvement, or the implementation of effective healthcare, regardless of the sophistication, wealth or state of development of the healthcare system being examined.

We address below the implications of the combination of disciplines and interests in the field of research. In terms of the NHS generally, three main methods of bringing clinicians and managers closer together have been advocated,[43] and we feel that these are appropriate for healthcare systems elsewhere: first, joint training, e.g. with clinical problems discussed with managers, budgetary difficulties with clinicians; second, sound information systems, as we have already emphasized; finally, an idea which brings out why we care so deeply about this, a shared recognition that developing clinical services which are effective, efficient and equitable is a central issue for managers and clinicians alike.

2.6 Implications

Doing research – the skills and the setting

Smith[44] has commented on the need for multidisciplinary work in R&D and noted that among those with the skills to support R&D there is mutual ignorance and disdain. For instance, many statisticians are ignorant of economics and disdain qualitative research, many health economists are ignorant of research methods outside their field, some social scientists customarily employing qualitative methods are suspicious of quantitative approaches. Further, many clinician scientists imbued with the traditional paradigm are ignorant or suspicious of the disciplines that can help to provide the broader perspective necessary for change enhancement.

Training programmes for all the relevant professionals need rethinking. For instance, all would-be medical statisticians should be taught the basics of health economics and given an appreciation of qualitative techniques and their underlying philosophies. Managers must be given basic research appreciation skills and trained in project management. Just as managers must understand research, so must clinical and other researchers have an appreciation of the exigencies of NHS decision making. For all these groups an appreciation of the *theory of evaluation* is essential.[45]

To encourage this in the UK the Medical Research Council is emphasizing the multidisciplinary approach in training fellowships relating to health services research. Other drivers for change can be funding (conditional upon multidisciplinarity) and structures. Strategic health planning groups (such as health authorities), as well as universities, as a setting for researchers would nurture multidisciplinarity and would be a continuing reminder of the need for change management. The new paradigm is not about protecting researchers from the distractions of organizational life, but about giving them the skills to thrive in an environment of change, and ensure that their particular contributions are valuable and valued.

Using research – the new success criterion

A key element of the *change-promoting* paradigm is that researchers and decision takers belong to a common peer group which respects individuals' different outlooks and skills. These decision makers include general managers and clinicians, either in direct clinical care or as professionals who manage.

Success is measured through the relevance of completed R&D work to decision making. The extent of collaboration and the degrees of control by investigators and decision takers will vary across the 'R' to 'D' and implementing spectrum. Box 2.6 illustrates some of the issues at each stage from evaluating a screening test for an asymptomatic disease through to the implementation of a service based on the test. The idea that a screening test may be feasible could have arisen from traditional fundamental research; the need to evaluate its implementation might arise through a health need assessment undertaken, for example, by a health authority.

This means a commitment by those managing change to use research results – and that will only happen if they have participated sufficiently in the research process to be confident of the relevance and to understand the meaning of what has been done. Senior managers in the NHS are intelligent and well capable of this. Unfortunately, many perceive research as a purely theory-enhancing activity, irrelevant to change management, and expressed in impenetrable language (sociology) or numbers (statistics). Conversely, managers' interpersonal skills in managing change appear nowhere in researchers' value lists. The new paradigm demands mutual respect between the researchers and those who use research. This could be achieved in several ways. One option is to take advantage of training opportunities for managers. There could be a programme of events centred on 'really useful research', or university networks could infiltrate business school courses for the NHS with sessions on relevant research for executives. Change management always involves balancing risks. High-quality research, according to our paradigm, will inform those risks and support the decision makers.

Commissioning research

Many managers and other decision takers may lack the knowledge and hence the confidence to take an active role in the shaping of R&D. These failings are no reason for maintaining the status quo.

In the traditional paradigm inherent in *theory-enhancing* research, the patrons of research are not in a direct sense its consumers and leave the details of policy and funding to the practitioners of research. Implementation of the new paradigm depends on an entirely new relationship between investigators, their patrons and the consumers of the findings. Those engaged in clinical research, who often are engaged in practice too, are well placed to identify and promote potential service developments. Further, it is they who are most in touch with findings from fundamental biomedical science that might have fruitful application. Nevertheless, the consumers of R&D (see Box 2.3) have a wider perspective,

Box 2.6 The involvement of R&D consumers in work programmes

	Example programme	Some R&D consumer issues
Implementation	Carefully monitored introduction to routine use	Ensuring efficient management and adequate monitoring arrangements in place. Identification of unexpected problems. Monitoring impact on disease in population.
Development	Large-scale trial of screening programme, preferably replicated	Accurate assessment of costs and benefits. Client acceptability. Overall impact on disease control. Public views. Knock-on effects to other services. Consideration of opportunity costs. More accurate modelling of likely effect of routine implementation.
	Piloting the test on a small population	More accurate sensitivity and specificity. Refining simple costs. Client acceptability. Wider public views. Early assessment of likely impact of full-scale screening programme. Modelling and decision analysis.
Research	Small-scale laboratory evaluation of a potential screening test for asymptomatic disease	Magnitude of population problem. Sensitivity and specificity of test. Likely cost of test. Presence of effective, affordable treatment. Ethical considerations.

Degree of consumer involvement increases upward

encompassing issues of service delivery and the identification of unmet needs.[46] They should shape the overall priorities for R&D, taking into account views from many sources of expertise. The consumers are a numerous and heterogeneous group and thus the 'patrons' for R&D must draw upon a range of interests. Clearly represented among these should be resource allocation decision takers among health planners (purchasers), provider management (including clinician managers) and primary care. The core chapter of this book thus focuses on the commissioning process, the high levels of skill required and the potentially rich rewards.

This is especially important in the UK now that the recommendations of the Culyer Report[47] are being implemented, notably that the funding stream of R&D be conceived as a levy on all healthcare purchasers' allocations. For the first time this will make explicit the potential opportunity cost (and benefit) of R&D in the NHS. If 1.5 per cent of revenue is spent on R&D it is not available for, for example, direct clinical care. Of course, direct clinical care may itself be based as much on clinical idiosyncrasy as demonstrable effectiveness. As the report states, carrying out research, commissioning it, managing it and using its findings are all skilled activities. Change managers in trusts and health purchasing groups or authorities will have to learn how to participate in and understand the commissioning process, even if they are not directly responsible themselves.

The commissioning process is time consuming. The work includes the selection of priorities for research funding, the recognition and definition of the precise research question, the assessment of research proposals against transparently appropriate criteria, the documentation and audit of resource commitment and regular feedback on progress. It is essentially a multidisciplinary procedure, requiring high-level management skills and underpinned by collaboration between researchers and the managers of change. Nationally this is exemplified in the regular reports of the NHS Health Technology Assessment Programme,[48] though its interpretation of commissioning is more limited than that we advocate within the new paradigm.

More locally, ways of achieving this could include the previously mentioned NHS-based research teams, an idea we develop further in Part II, as part of our discussion on implementation, with specific reference to the idea of a 'learning organization'. All this and the further implications of our paradigm are expanded upon in the following chapters.

Part II

COMMISSIONING RESEARCH

COMMISSIONING: AN OVERVIEW

KEY POINTS

Commissioning requires the active participation of health service resource managers in defining research questions according to their priorities, in study design, in determining the outcome measures and in thinking ahead about possible routine implementation and its consequences.

3.1 Preamble

Commissioning is the active management of R&D resources to ensure that projects contribute to change-management. Hitherto, a process known as reactive funding has supported most scientific and medical research. This is a method whereby funds are distributed among competing projects, each of which may have different aims, with these aims not relating to any overriding strategy for research. Commissioning is a proactive process. It entails leadership by resource managers.

Below we outline these differing approaches. We show that commissioning is usually the more appropriate for health services R&D. After contrasting these approaches, in the next chapter we go into detail about the process of commissioning.

3.2 Reactive funding

Reactive funding entails seeking bids against a share of a pot of money. The nature of the bids is not specified other than that they fall into a defined area such as neurosciences. The commissioning panel of experts in the field (grant committee), aided by external referees, decides among the bids on the basis of their perceived importance to developing the discipline and their technical merit, i.e. ability to deliver their promises.

Successful bidders are left to conduct their work and are expected to produce publications, and perhaps a report to the committee, at the end of the work. Monitoring of work in progress is minimal and mainly concerned with financial probity. This is a traditional means of financing research in the pure sciences. It is also widely used for applied research, as in R&D in the NHS.

Reactive funding is wholly consistent with the paradigm for pure sciences sketched in Chapter 2. It is based on the assumption that science is the business of scientists, and thus scientists are the best fitted to decide how resources allocated to their discipline should be used. The product of the research 'belongs' to the scientists: it is they who most appreciate its import; its contribution to practical matters or the enlightenment of the populace is a secondary matter. Many criticisms have been made about reactive commissioning. For instance, it is perforce in the hands of an elite of successful scientists (success by the criteria of their paradigm). It could be claimed that by the time one is good and great the sharpness of one's imagination is dulled and opportunities for truly innovative work are missed. Criticisms are raised about the fairness and efficiency of refereeing in the context of both grant applications and journal publication. Extensive efforts to come up with a better way have failed. However, although we are forced to accept that this traditional method is the best we have for the pure sciences, it does not follow that it is best for health services R&D. Indeed, the *new paradigm*, our alternative paradigm for change-promoting research sketched in Chapter 2, shows that there is a better way. In the following, the implications of *commissioning* are developed. There is emphasis on the practical issues of doing it. Moreover, some currently problematic matters are raised and ways forward suggested. We do not entirely abandon reactive funding. We show that it has a valid but smaller place in health services R&D.

3.3 Commissioning

Commissioning starts from the belief that health services R&D is a tool of change-management, as discussed in Chapter 2. The purpose of R&D is threefold.

1 To encourage the exploration and evaluation of innovative solutions to problems.
2 To encourage the critical appraisal of existing, particularly costly, practices which have never been adequately evaluated.
3 To contribute to the evidence base which informs decisions about priorities for the use of health resources and the disposition of resources among options for service delivery.

Therefore, health resource managers should not sit back and allow researchers to determine the R&D agenda. For the researchers' agenda is

---

Box 3.1   Levels of commissioner involvement

- Setting the research question.
- Bringing researchers together.
- Working with the researchers to ensure that the study protocol is capable of meeting the needs of the commissioners.
- Overseeing project management.
- Ensuring the smooth transition of successful development projects into routine service.
- Organizing dissemination of findings and being proactive in seeking cultural changes in the organization to encourage adoption of desired innovations.
- Encouraging an ethos in the organization wherein a questioning spirit is valued, research is seen to be a useful tool for answering practical questions and staff find being associated with research a pleasant experience.

---

likely to be more influenced by their interests than by an appreciation of the strategic context in which their work takes place. Thus, the defining element of commissioning is the involvement in and ultimate control of R&D funding and project management by resource managers. The term resource manager is deliberately being kept very general at present. It is a generic term for those involved in change-management decisions in the health service. As we move from principles to practice we examine personnel and roles in more detail.

The notion of commissioning is not new. In Chapter 2 the Rothschild initiative was mentioned. It failed. It was less ambitious than what we are proposing. So how can our ideas succeed? As argued in Chapter 2, the crux of the matter lies in eschewing the irrelevant, and therefore misleading, notions in the paradigm applicable to pure science. A simple kind of commissioning has been present in both the fundamental bio-medical sciences and applied health research for some time. This is achieved by giving a much more focused research area to bid for than would be the case for reactive funding. At its most focused this is a specific research question. This is an approach adopted by the Health Technology Assessment (HTA) stream of funding of the British NHS R&D initiative.

There are different degrees to which resource managers can be involved in commissioning. These are illustrated in Box 3.1. Below, we look at these in detail. First, however, we present informal case studies that illustrate how our thinking has been influenced by practice. They also highlight some of the advantages of commissioning and raise some problematic issues. We summarize each of the items in Box 3.1 before proceeding to the next chapter.

3.4 Innovations in the north-west of England

In the late 1980s a group of people, including the authors, began to press for an evaluative ethos to be introduced into the NHS of the then North Western Regional Health Authority. This authority spanned the north-west of England from Lancaster in the north to the City of Manchester in the south. It encompassed rural areas and the Greater Manchester conurbation. It was, and remains, an area of higher than national average mortality and morbidity. Moreover, it contains areas of intense social deprivation. We were struck by the piecemeal fashion in which NHS resource decisions were being taken – this mirrored what was going on elsewhere in the United Kingdom. Two things in particular stood out.

First was the tendency to plan in sequence rather than in parallel: that is, to consider proposals for service expansion and development as they arose until resources were committed and no further developments could be funded. Parallel planning entails considering together a range of development options and choosing from among them. Parallel planning gives explicit recognition to the economists' notion of *opportunity cost*: 'money spent on this denies the opportunity to spend money on something else; thus I should go into the decision fully aware of the knock-on consequences.' Parallel planning cries out to be undertaken in the context of clear strategic aims and stated priorities.

Second was the small degree to which resource decisions were influenced by rational factors such as prior knowledge of the likely benefits to accrue: that is, knowledge that would have arisen from a formal evaluation. In the final chapter of *Evaluating Health Services Effectiveness* we discuss at length the factors that influence the rationality of planning decisions. We conclude that health service planning cannot be wholly rational because there is no agreed rationale. Moreover, we suggest that there is unlikely ever to be an agreed rationale because decisions are inevitably embedded within competing ideologies and political agendas. Nevertheless, recognition of the existence of this non-rational domain should not prevent one from seeking to maximize the rational and minimize the irrational. Indeed, even within the non-rational, that area of incompatible rationalities, the clarity of debate is enhanced if such evidential base as is shared is defensible, objective and complete: to deny that such sharing can occur would be nihilistic, as all discourse leading to the possibility of agreement or compromise would become futile. The irrational thrives on ignorance. For if we have not known what questions to ask and how to use the answers, we can only resort to the untested opinion of others.

Thus, our initial concern was finding the right questions. With this in mind, a checklist was published of issues to be considered by those responsible for the deployment of NHS resources to new developments.[1] This checklist is reproduced in Box 3.2. The individual items in the

Box 3.2 Template for a checklist

1 Describe clearly and concisely the proposal, indicating how its development differs from and is likely to enhance current practice. (What does it do, to whom, how, why etc.?)

2 What, in detail, is the proposal intended to achieve?
   (a) Beneficiaries: group number etc.
   (b) Demand
      • Initial – numbers, cost
      • Final – numbers, cost, containment of demand?
   (c) Benefits – projected outcome
      • quantification
      • monitoring
      • assessment
         – change in life expectancy
         – quality of life
         – morbidity
         – etc.
   (d) Problems/hazards

3 What, in detail, are the projected costs of the proposal?
   (a) Any initial capital costs
   (b) Staffing implication
   (c) Anticipated marginal costs invoked on expansion
   (d) If demand exceeds this present proposal, what is the upper limit at which increased capital and manpower costs would occur?
   (e) Will other developments be lost or deferred or altered if this proposal is adopted?
   (f) Will any savings accrue?

4 What is the evidence that the proposal will provide benefit?
   (a) Preliminary formal trial   (Yes/No)
      • Was it randomized?   (Yes/No)
        If not, why not?
      • Were the following aspects adequate?
        Design, size, conduct, analysis, interpretation
      • Was cost-effectiveness or cost–benefit assessed?
      • Were the criteria of *cost, benefit* and *effectiveness* appropriate to the presently envisaged realization of the service?
      • (a) Do the findings of the trial justify the assertions under (2) above, and (b) can they be extrapolated to the kind of populations for whom this service is intended?
      • If there have been several separate trials, are the findings reproducible and consistent?   (Yes/No)
        If not, how do the results affect the answers given under (2) above?

(b) Experience of implementation elsewhere
- Has the proposed innovation been practised elsewhere?
- Is there previously published, or otherwise accessible, work?
- What has been learned from this experience?
- What changes, if any, would be recommended for the present proposal?
- Was the demand for this practice contained?
- What costs were involved?
- Were the benefits consistent with those suggested under (2) above?

(c) If the answers to (a) and (b) are negative or equivocal
- Should a formal study or trial be considered?
- Where should the study be done?
- How would such a study be funded?
- Should a decision on implementation be deferred until other people's findings are known?

5 Are other developments, e.g. alternative methods of treatment or care, likely to overtake the current proposal?
  Should these be considered before any implementation?

6 If the proposal is adopted, how is it to be evaluated for:
(a) Outcome
(b) Cost-effectiveness
(c) Performance – relating to targets for continuation of expenditure?

7 If the service is being introduced on a pilot basis, have criteria been agreed for the circumstances in which ultimately the service might be withdrawn?

checklist were not particularly original. What was original was their concatenation and the insistence that they be employed by resource managers in the context of parallel planning. Hitherto there had been checklists for judging the methodological soundness of individual published studies. However, there had been nothing that asked searching questions about the evidence justifying implementation of an innovative proposal.

Medical Innovation Fund

Checklists of themselves will not change behaviour. Therefore, the North Western Regional Health Authority was persuaded to divert a substantial proportion of its research funds – one million pounds over three years – from its traditional reactive funding scheme into a new Medical Innovation Fund (MIF). The MIF was itself reactive, but it differed from the traditional scheme in three respects.

1 It was to promote the evaluation of the implementation of innovative services for which there was evidence of effectiveness meeting the criteria of the checklist.
2 The proposed developments had to have support from the management of the district health authorities in which they were to take place.
3 The members of the MIF committee were drawn from the regional medical advisory structure, which represented the professional views of diverse disciplines, including public health medicine, and also included management interests. Thus, they were not primarily academics or researchers.

Prospective applicants to the fund were issued with a copy of the checklist and detailed instructions on how to apply.

The scheme was a success in the following respects. It raised awareness of the need for evidence to justify financing service developments. The members of the MIF committee engaged in sophisticated debates about developments in the parallel rather than sequential mode of planning. People in the service and some in academe began to realize that traditional research with narrowly focused end-point measurements is insufficient to answer the questions posed by service planners. A number of developments came on stream in a more disciplined manner than hitherto.

An evaluation of the MIF undertaken by Johnathan Hantman[2] for his master of science dissertation confirmed some of the positive impressions, but also highlighted weaknesses. First, many applicants to the fund could not or chose not to understand the particular requirements placed upon them. Thus, many applicants did not fully heed the criteria and some submitted proposals which were in the realm of basic research rather than evaluation and development. This is understandable because of the cultural shift involved. Perhaps, it highlights inadequacies in the way that the MIF was proselytized. There is no doubt that some people thought that they could play the system as they had in the past.

The second and biggest weakness lay in the quality of project management. The MIF was set up with the intention that management interests in the district health authorities, hospitals and so on would not only be committed to the development and take it on board as routine service if the evaluation was successful, but would also oversee the project. It was clear that in many cases this was not happening. Project milestones had not been met and no one had enquired why. How the project budgets were being spent was not always easy to ascertain. One should have expected that from the point of view of financial probity there would be proper accounting by the institutions in receipt of MIF funds. That the overall project management was weak is, in retrospect, not surprising. We were asking people to do a task for which they were not prepared and we did not appreciate the complexity of the task.

The 1991 NHS restructuring brought about the internal market and a theoretical, and actual, gulf between the providers of healthcare and those purchasing such care. In 1994, further restructuring brought about the amalgamation of the North Western and Mersey Regional Health Authorities into the NHS Executive North West. We and many colleagues could see tremendous opportunities in the purchaser–provider split of the reformed NHS. This separation of strategic from operational management meant that *in theory* district health authorities would no longer be bogged down in the day-to-day affairs of hospitals and could concentrate on commissioning effective services to be delivered in a high-quality way. In this context the R&D initiative which was a consequence of the reforms seemed an opportunity for health service commissioners to drive the R&D agenda according to the needs of the NHS. However, we were fearful of the way R&D was being implemented.

The national and regional directors of NHS R&D were recruited from the universities' professoriate. Many of the influential people on R&D committees were other academics. Few of these had a background that could give one confidence that they had a grasp of how R&D could inform strategic NHS issues. The non-academic and management representatives on the committees for the most part seemed like tokens, for few had previously questioned the right of academics to set the research agenda. Thus, it looked as though up to 1.5 per cent of the NHS budget would be the unquestioned property of the universities. In this context the paper 'Making Peckham work for managers'[3] was seen as dangerous heresy, and an unsuccessful attempt was made to marginalize its author.

Development and Implementation Fund

Fortunately, the north-west of England was spared from the purity of thought that those in most of the rest of the country who believed they were doing science sought to impose. Through the work of the MIF and various other initiatives, a number of health authority chairmen, chief executives, senior managers and public health physicians had begun to grasp the opportunities that influencing R&D would offer. They were vocal in ensuring that the R&D Directorate in the NHS Executive North West would be structured so that it was responsive to the consumers of research. Of particular importance was their insistence that the idea behind the MIF be developed further. Thus the Development and Implementation Fund (DIF) was set up. This ran alongside a traditional reactive R&D fund.

The DIF was essentially a reactive fund modelled on the MIF and seeking to remedy some of the deficiencies of the MIF. The criteria for a project being considered for funding are displayed in Box 3.3. The membership of the DIF consisted of various health professionals and managers drawn mainly from the NHS rather than academe, and supplemented by a statistician, a health economist and officers of the regional R&D Directorate.

Box 3.3   Criteria for patronage by the NHS Executive North West 'Development and Implementation Fund'

NHS Executive North West
Development and Implementation Fund
— a summary of its features —

'The scheme is intended to facilitate the experimental introduction into the service of promising *research based* service, practice or organisational *developments* which could make an important contribution to improving the health of the population of the Region. Priority will be given to proposals which relate to the management of the introduction of health technologies which have proven efficacy and will lead to considerable health gain.'
The guidance to applicants covers the following issues.

Research framework

- 'The project is based on robust research evidence. Each source is credible and reliable.' Also required is evidence that it should contribute to 'health gain'.
- 'An appropriate *option(s)* for models for service delivery has been identified.'
- 'Plans for *rigorous, and where necessary, independent evaluation*' leading to informing decisions about generalizability etc.

Management

- Availability of appropriate skills and expertise – bought in if necessary.
- 'There are plans to assemble sufficient information to *cost* the options and test these costs as the project progresses.'
- An expectation that the development will be suitable for general adoption.
- 'Plans (by the health authority and local providers) to review how to *sustain* the new service if it proves viable.'
- Detailed timetable with feasible milestones.
- 'Plans for *information systems* to support the work . . .'
- Proper consideration of ethical issues.

Relevance to local people and the health service

- 'There is clarity about how the proposed model(s) for service delivery could make a *measurable impact* on local health and health services . . .' Specifies a range of outcome measures.

Commitment from stakeholders

- '*Commitment* from key senior people in the health authority and the main providers (trusts and/or primary care) to see the project through to completion.'

- 'Plans to engage the different local *professional training interests* to explore how changes, if they are successful, can be introduced into professional training.'
- 'Plans to engage appropriate local *community interests* to ensure a patient perspective to the work, for example to guide the choice of outcome measures for the project.'
- 'Agreement to be *part of a region-wide programme* to share the lessons and results of the work, and a *commitment to disseminate* the results of the project.'

Source: Guidelines from the NHS North West R&D Directorate (October 1995).

Although like its predecessor the DIF was reactive, it was, as is clear from Box 3.3, directed towards the needs of the service. Projects would be considered only if they entailed taking forward work for which there was already good evidence that development and service evaluation was justified rather than speculative research. An important consideration was whether the results from the projects would be generalizable and thus applicable elsewhere in the NHS; the DIF was not intended to fund development work in which health authorities and trusts ought to be engaging during the normal course of events. There had to be support for the project from the appropriate health authority or provider unit (e.g. hospital) management. Management had to confirm that it was a potential development consistent with needs and priorities. There had to be commitment to funding the development as a routine service if the evaluation was positive. The intention was that worthwhile developments would eventually roll out elsewhere in the NHS and be aided by lessons from the evaluation.

The DIF was also more proactive than traditional reactive funds. When good ideas came along in a proposal which seemed methodologically or otherwise weak they were not rejected out of hand. Often the problem would be that the proposal had originated from a team that had little experience of research. Such teams were more likely to propose projects meeting tangible service needs than their more esoteric colleagues in academe, and thus they deserved encouragement. There were three ways of assisting them and these were not mutually exclusive. Sometimes a member of the DIF committee with relevant technical skills would offer to discuss the project with the applicants. Sometimes the applicants would be pointed towards the support network (units dealing in statistics, health economics and the social sciences) that the Regional R&D Directorate had created. Sometimes a collaborative link would be brokered with an academic or research unit known to have an interest and expertise in the area of the proposed study.

All potentially acceptable projects were sent to external referees. Adverse comments from the referees did not necessarily kill the project. If the study question seemed to the committee to be of particular importance to the local NHS then further work on the proposal would be encouraged. This could draw upon the support mentioned earlier. Project management was tighter than with the MIF. The Regional R&D Directorate kept a close check on the funding and the project milestones.

R&D Liaison Groups

Shortly after the MIF was formed the Regional R&D Directorate set up another mechanism to make R&D responsive to the needs of the service. This was the creation of R&D Liaison Groups (RDLG). Each group consists of representatives from a number of nearby health authorities, i.e. health services commissioners. For example, one such group is drawn from the Manchester, Stockport and West Pennine Health Authorities, and the experiences of that group are recounted here. The Manchester, Stockport and West Pennine (MSWP) R&D Liaison Group has a membership drawn from the public health and primary care directorates of the health authorities and a representative of the Regional R&D Directorate. In addition, it has its own R&D facilitator, who takes forward the management of the group's activities and liaises closely with project teams.

The groups were allocated a notional budget by the Regional R&D Directorate and authorized to fund R&D projects according to their perceptions of local priorities. The liaison groups approached their remit in different ways and these are subject to an evaluation commissioned by the R&D Directorate. From the outset the MSWP group decided to be proactive rather than reactive. It sought to develop the model of commissioning outlined earlier in this chapter.

Three projects illustrate this. The first undertaken by the group was an implementation project seeking to introduce research-based standards of care for myocardial infarction across three health authorities. This entailed building collaborative ties with diverse health professionals and managers. It was necessary to introduce a standard data collection process across seven hospitals. The work continues but already a closing of the gap between R&D, audit and clinical effectiveness has been achieved.

The second was an implementation project evaluating family support and cognitive behaviour treatment for schizophrenia sufferers who also misused drugs (not just alcohol alone). Some lessons from this Dual Diagnosis Project are picked up below. The third project was nearer to traditional research. It was a multidisciplinary study, in the primary care setting, of musculoskeletal disorders in ethnic minority people. The researchers were university based and keen to take part in the study. However, the impetus for the work arose from local health service priorities. This study was very successful in recruiting primary care practices which had not previously been involved in R&D. It also used community sources (e.g. the Asian Development Project in Ashton) to help to ensure that the research was sensitive to ethnic minority communities.

Further projects under way include the following:

- action to support practices implementing research evidence;
- feasibility and cost of a primary care eczema clinic;
- aspects of air quality and health;
- uncomplicated dyspepsia in primary care;
- strategies for reducing hospitalization in elderly COPD (chronic obstructive pulmonary disease) patients;
- non-pharmacological management of irritable bowel syndrome (see below);
- management of stroke in the community.

A common feature of all these studies is that their overall management lay with the R&D liaison group rather than being wholly devolved to researchers. The group's R&D facilitator had a particularly important and sensitive role. She kept in touch with all key players on a regular basis and was able to smooth out potential difficulties before they became problems. Moreover, being based in a health authority rather than academe, she was in a strong position to effect links among various professions, links with community groups and the mobilization of resources at appropriate times. Even on occasions when she did not have the authority to make certain decisions she could nevertheless expedite them through knowing how the health management system works, who does what and how to express the issues and their possible solutions in language with which resource managers are comfortable.

Our account thus far indicates how the ideas we are developing in this book are rooted not only in a self-evident theoretical basis but also in practical experience of what can be done. In the next three sections we share insights gained from some R&D projects which, at the time of writing, are still in progress. The first arises from the DIF and is an example of how project management involving the commissioners is helpful. The second and third arise from studies commissioned by the MSWP group. The second is similar to the first but exemplifies slightly different issues. The third involves experience in the early stages of commissioning.

Family Therapy for Schizophrenia Project

The DIF funded a project to evaluate the introduction of family therapy for the management of schizophrenia. The purpose of family therapy is to give support to patients and their carers in the community. Sufficient evidence was presented to the DIF Committee to persuade them that research studies in various contexts have shown that family therapy can result in the more effective management of schizophrenia and reduce the need for costly crisis admissions to hospital. However, that evidence was insufficient to justify district health authorities creating such a service, but enough to warrant a formal evaluation.

The research team was based around academic practitioners of psychiatry and clinical psychology in a teaching hospital. The study drew upon a population of people suffering from schizophrenia who lived in the southern part of the City of Manchester. The improvement of services for the mentally ill was one of Manchester Health Authority's priorities. However, the health authority was not sufficiently well funded to promote costly developments in any area. Nevertheless, it gave enthusiastic backing to the family therapy project and undertook to develop it into a routine service if it was shown to improve the quality of care and to be, at worst, cost-neutral. Cost-neutrality, and perhaps saving, would be attained if the promised reduction of inpatient hospital stays was achieved.

The account given thus far illustrates the point made in Chapter 2 that health services R&D is embedded in the delivery of services, impacts upon broader management issues and is itself influenced by those issues. Manchester Health Authority was seeking to improve services for mental illness and formulating an overall strategy. A family support service offers the prospect of better care for schizophrenia, is consistent with the humanitarian NHS philosophy of as far as possible keeping care in the community and offers the prospect of cost-neutrality. But cost-neutrality is only attainable if savings on hospital bed usage are real rather than illusory. That is, the resources used to support those beds have to be diverted to the family therapy programme rather than, as so easily can happen, being used to support some unplanned service development such as is wont to fill NHS vacuums.

The players in the arena are diverse. There are the researchers. There are those providing the service, some of whom are also researchers. The project also involves a voluntary organization, which must plan ahead for the use of its resources. There is the management of the clinical directorate within the hospital responsible for mental illness services. There is the overall management of the hospital, which has to see mental illness services in a broader context of services. The management of the hospital has to contract with a number of district health authorities and must seek financial stability. There is Manchester Health Authority, which is seeking by its use of contracts with a number of hospitals, a community trust and primary care services to influence the overall disposition of mental health services for the resident population of Manchester. There is the regional R&D Directorate, which is anxious to ensure that its resources are used effectively.

It would have been easy to let the project take its course and be written up, with Manchester Health Authority and the hospital then beginning negotiations on introducing the service on a routine basis. If the project is successful, then shifting resources from hospital beds to family therapy would take time. The health authority and/or the hospital would have to find pump-priming resources to fund the transition.

These resource and contracting considerations have to take place within a clearly defined annual cycle. Thus proposals for the financial (and contracting) year beginning in April 1999 have to be formulated by August 1998 so that they can all be brought together for final consideration and detailed contracting in the autumn of 1998. Almost certainly the project workers, including those employed by the voluntary sector, would dissipate and the resource that had gone into their training be wasted. The momentum of the project would be lost.

To ease the way, a project steering group was set up. This was separate from the day-to-day management by the research team. It was chaired by one of us, representing both health authority interests and the DIF. Its membership consisted of the senior researchers and service deliverers, a representative of the voluntary organization and management interests from the mental health clinical directorate of the hospital. There is thus not only multidisciplinary research but also multidisciplinary research management.

Early meetings were concerned with ironing out some technical problems: for example, problems with patient recruitment, a misunderstanding about what some health economists had contracted to do and means of accessing financial data. After the project had been running for nearly a year it was clear that it was no disaster. It was acceptable to patients and their families, therapists perceived that what they were doing was beneficial and morale was good. An interim analysis of the findings was done, of which the principle researcher was kept blind lest it influence his future assessments of patients. We knew that an interim analysis would not give any definitive findings, but it could provide order of magnitude estimates of what any benefits might be – particularly reductions in hospital bed use which must release resources for a routine family therapy service. On the basis of these findings it was concluded that the study might well demonstrate sufficient bed use savings. Thus an interim report was prepared which used these findings to make informed speculations about how resources could be transferred, how much money would be necessary to keep the fledgling service alive from the formal end of the study until a final decision was made and the necessary pump-priming for the transition to a routine service.

If the clinical team were to be effective product champions for a new service then they had to negotiate their way through a complicated resource management structure. For instance, the health authority of necessity is divided into a number of functional divisions. Communications between them are good, but sometimes the divisions are not synchronized on a particular issue; someone has to make it happen. Thus the role of the steering group, particularly its chairman, was to ensure that the right people were informed at the right time, to ensure that the case being made was expressed in an appropriate manner and to bring together the health authority and hospital managements. It was a matter for those managements to argue out how pump priming might be found. For instance, the health authority claimed that the hospital was already in receipt of other funds from the authority to meet this sort of contingency.

At the time of writing these matters are near resolution. Whatever the final outcome of this project, one lesson is clear. Steering towards a seamless integration of the fruits of R&D into routine service is difficult and time consuming. It is, however, greatly helped by knowing one's way around the system and is thus a shared responsibility of the product champions and change-managers.

The Dual Diagnosis Project

The Dual Diagnosis Project was commissioned by the MSWP R&D Liaison Group. It is a pilot research project looking at a way of managing in the community patients with schizophrenia who misuse 'hard' drugs such as heroin. These are a relatively small group among patients with schizophrenia, but are particularly difficult to manage. A number of management strategies have been proposed but none has been evaluated to a degree that justifies incorporating it into routine service. The liaison group was keen to support further research as such patients pose a significant problem locally. The project was funded as a pilot (i.e. small-scale initial study) because there are many problematic issues around researching this type of patient. One issue is the feasibility of recruiting and retaining patients in a study. Thus, there was no expectation that this pilot study would produce definitive findings which could justify the development of a new service. Rather, it would demonstrate the feasibility or otherwise of proceeding to a definitive study to complement work going on elsewhere. The pilot study was expected to give an indication of whether the therapy was practicable, whether there is sufficient indication of patient compliance and favourable outcome to justify further work, and some feel for the costs that might be engendered if this therapy were to be incorporated into routine service.

This study involves a team of practitioners and researchers based at an ordinary district general hospital. However, the hospital has an outpost of academic psychological medicine from the University of Manchester, which forms the nucleus of research expertise for this study.

A steering group was set up, which included the lead researchers, the principle practitioners, a health economist, an external academic advisor researching this field, a representative of a voluntary sector organization involved and a patients' advocate. It was chaired by a member of the liaison group, and two other members of the group attended. It is a local policy wherever possible to involve a representative member of the patient/client group concerned. In this case it was felt that a drug misusing patient with poorly controlled schizophrenia was unlikely to contribute much, so an advocate from an organization that promotes the interests of severely mentally ill people was invited.

This steering group served much the same purposes as the steering group for the Family Therapy Project. It helped to resolve practical difficulties and to ease the link between the exigencies of routine practice and those of research. Although there was no question of planning a transition from the study to the implementation of a service, it was necessary to think of smoothing the way for a definitive study should the pilot study be successful. For this purpose the chairman and a subgroup of the steering group met members of the management of the hospital.

One issue became clear immediately. The pilot study required minimal support from the broader clinical team engaged in mental health services in that district. However, a move to a definitive study would not only involve more people but hold the prospect, if successful, of leading eventually to a different service configuration. Many patients with schizophrenia have some contact with illicit drugs, although few are on hard drugs. Nevertheless, the treatment model being tested may be extensible to a broader group of patients with schizophrenia who misuse drugs. Thus, what could happen would be the introduction of a new treatment philosophy which would cut across the well defined boundaries of the current care in the community and hospital teams.

If a definitive study which has the support of the health authorities is to be undertaken in that locality with, if successful, a view to rolling it out as a routine service, then there must be a commitment in principle to implementation by the health professionals involved. This is a commitment to consider seriously a different philosophy of care, which might lead to the redrawing of the boundaries of teams of professionals, demarcation of responsibility etc.

These issues were discussed with the clinical director of mental health services. He undertook to inform his clinical colleagues and it was arranged for there to be a presentation by the research team to the clinicians. At the time of writing it seems that the study has catalysed some serious thinking about the roles and relationships among various groups caring for the mentally ill. There is also an awareness arising from the experience gained that perhaps it was inappropriate to distinguish between alcohol and other drugs. Further, there is enthusiasm about moving towards a definitive study.

Several insights emerge from this example. Research in the clinical setting requires managing in much the same way as end-stage evaluation and development projects. It is the programme from research, through development to implementation, that should be managed. Clinical research cannot be detached from the organization in which it takes place. Seemingly innocuous research questions may raise a potential for application which is threatening to existing managerial structures, power groupings, 'ownership' of patients and professional relationships. These have to be handled sensitively. The onus for this cannot lie with the research team. Generally, researchers are fully occupied with research and, sometimes, clinical practice. Their position within the organization, outlook, training and commitments usually do not equip them for the task. Thus, there is a need for change-managers to involve themselves in project management.

Commissioning research on irritable bowel syndrome

The final example looks at the earliest stages of commissioning. It shows how a study question can arise from routine service concerns and how by being proactive health authority change-managers can channel R&D to meet their needs. We start with some background about irritable bowel disease (IBS), show why it is an important issue for the NHS, show how IBS arose as a particular issue for Manchester Health Authority and outline the events that followed.

IBS is a collection of symptoms involving persistent lower abdominal pain or discomfort and problems associated with defecation. It is a diagnosis by exclusion of known causes of such symptoms, such as colonic cancer. Estimates of the prevalence of IBS vary, but it may be that more than 20 per cent of the population experience symptoms of IBS in any one year. There is a core of patients suffering from intractable IBS. It can have seriously debilitating effects on work and social life. IBS patients are demanding users of primary care and the severe or intractable cases accrete in hospital gastro-enterology outpatient clinics. IBS patients are often receiving pharmacological therapies but practitioners in the field are sceptical about their worth. A marked proportion of IBS patients suffer psychological disturbance and some have overt mental illness, such as depression. While there is no doubt that in many cases the psychological disturbances are the consequence of a chronic and distressing illness, there is a strong suspicion among practitioners that in many other cases pre-existing psychological disturbance may have predisposed them to IBS. In either case this leads some practitioners to regard psychological therapies, such as hypnotherapy and psychotherapy, as preferred treatments for the more severe or intractable sufferers.

In one of the Manchester hospitals there has been a hypnotherapy service for IBS for some years. The matter came to prominence when nearby health authorities were asked to fund the expansion of this service through contracts. The Manchester Health Authority asked the academic consultant gastro-enterologist who was promoting hypnotherapy to provide evidence of its efficacy. As an aside, note that it has long been the practice of the health authority to demand that those promoting service developments produce a *prima facie* case based on hard evidence before its own officers spend their time seeking or commissioning an independent review of the field. The consultant produced published papers about a number of small clinical trials and follow-up studies of series of patients. One of us was asked to give a 'counsel's opinion', analogous to a common practice in the legal profession. In some respects the evidence was impressive. The consultant seemed to be getting remarkable results with some patients. However, the trials and follow-up studies had limitations which led the officers of the health authority to conclude that the present state of the evidence was insufficient to justify investing in a hypnotherapy service. The officers of nearby health authorities concurred with this view.

That could have been the end of the matter. However, it had become clear that IBS is an important NHS resource issue. Moreover, demand for hypnotherapy was unlikely to disappear, whatever the view of the health authorities. One tactic for procrastination is to hold an enquiry. Her Majesty's Government institutes Royal Commissions; health authorities can commission R&D. Although this might appear to be a cynical ploy, it is a valuable tool in the non-rational arena of NHS micropolitics. The health authorities needed a breathing space to think through the whole issue of the management of IBS, not just hypnotherapy. Moreover, there were research questions which had to be answered before a cost-effective plan for the management of IBS could be formulated. Thus, R&D both legitimizes inaction in resource disposition and aids a more thoughtful approach.

The MSWP R&D Liaison Group wrote a flyer seeking expressions of interest in engaging in research into non-pharmacological treatments for IBS. The flyer specified the broad research questions but made it clear that researchers and the commissioners would work together in producing study protocols. Thus, the prospective researchers were not asked to submit detailed study protocols. They were asked to submit outline bids which justified researching one or more non-pharmacological treatments, indicated their suitability to research this area, indicated their capacity to recruit suitable patients and stated the degree to which they were willing to collaborate with other groups. The flyer was sent out nationally by the regional R&D Directorate in accordance with the regulations covering these matters.

Four outline bids were received – all from the north-west. One was from the National Centre for Primary Care Research and Development (NCPCRD): this proposed evaluating a patient information booklet along lines which had already been successfully used for patients suffering from ulcerative colitis. Another was from academic psychiatrists and gastroenterologists from teaching hospitals: they proposed comparing hypnotherapy and psychotherapy. The final two proposals were independent of each other, but each was seeking to evaluate aromatherapy. One of these came from clinicians in a district general hospital and the other from an academic at a university not involved in medical undergraduate teaching.

The research teams were invited together to a meeting with the RDLG members and representatives of other health authorities interested in the project. The purpose of the project and the manner in which it was to be planned were explained. Each research group gave a brief presentation of their ideas, after which there was open discussion. The RDLG members and health authority representatives retired and decided in principle to fund three linked projects: an evaluation of the information booklet; a trial comparing hypnotherapy and psychotherapy with standard practice for intractable or severe cases of IBS in contact with secondary care services; and a trial of aromatherapy for milder cases in contact with primary care services. The two groups which had proposed trials of aromatherapy were felt to have complementary skills and resources, and they were asked to collaborate in designing their facet of the study. Another meeting with all the researchers was arranged. In the meantime, enquiries were made via the Regional R&D Directorate as to similar work in progress elsewhere in the UK. It transpired that a major trial, funded by the Medical Research Council, of which we were already aware, was sufficiently different in intent that our work would add knowledge rather than needlessly replicate the MRC study.

The RDLG was determined that the three studies to be commissioned would be linked and produce complementary findings which would inform a strategy for the management of IBS. On the assumption that each therapy was cost-effective we envisaged a three-stage strategy.

- *Stage 1*. All patients deemed by their general practitioners to be suffering from IBS to be given a copy of the patient information booklet.
- *Stage 2*. Patients not responding to the booklet and general advice about diet etc. within three months to be referred directly by the GP for aromatherapy. There would be an initial consultation with an aromatherapist leading to a prescription of aromatic oils and instruction on their application. Follow-up consultations would be infrequent.
- *Stage 3*. Patients not responding to aromatherapy to be referred for assessment in a hospital outpatient clinic for psychotherapy or hypnotherapy. It was hoped that the study might throw light on observable patient characteristics which would predict likely success with psychotherapy or hypnotherapy; all other things being equal they would start on the cheaper therapy.

This strategy clarified the research questions and imposed a structure on the study design. It necessitated an evaluation of the patient information booklet in its own right and use of the booklet as an initial therapy in the two other facets of the study, i.e. the evaluations of aromatherapy and psycho/hypnotherapy. Rather than delay the second two stages until the booklet was evaluated, it was decided to commission its production immediately so that it would be available for all three studies. Use of the booklet in the evaluations of aromatherapy and psycho/hypnotherapy would not prejudice the outcome of those studies even if the booklet were shown at its formal evaluation to have no benefit; giving patients written information about their condition, even if that cannot be proven to alter directly the course of the condition, can be construed as good practice.

The next meeting with all the researchers gave an opportunity for everyone to clarify respective roles and to deal with misunderstandings. One of the researchers voiced the opinion that it was not reasonable for us to expect them to put so much time into meeting and planning these studies. We pointed out that if the researchers were to apply for funds by traditional means there would be the same amount of work in producing a protocol, competition with other teams and an unknown chance that funds would be awarded. Under our arrangements funding was guaranteed if a satisfactory protocol was constructed.

Another misconception arose about one of the research questions. Some of the researchers felt that it was important to establish whether aromatherapy has benefit in its own right. Our design does not do this. It tests whether aromatherapy has a cost-effective incremental benefit above that of the cheaper option of the information booklet alone. This illustrates how approaching an issue 'scientifically' differs from pragmatic evaluation: it can lead to different research questions and in consequence to different study designs.

This second meeting led to agreement on case definition. This was to be based on internationally recognized criteria (the Rome Criteria by which IBS can be defined for research purposes), but also allowing a wider definition more consistent with what actually happens in primary care. The reason for this was that the study was intended to reflect practice rather than to apply, as so often happens in clinical trials, to an artificially homogeneous group of patients. This again reflects the pragmatism of the evaluative ethos, as distinct from the striving for purity dictated by the 'scientific' ethos. The remainder of the meeting considered outcome measures common to the three studies and the next steps towards development of the protocols.

At the time of writing, production of the handbook has been financed and the protocol for the aromatherapy study is near completion. Detailed work on the protocol for the hypnotherapy study was deferred until the summer of 1999 when some results from the current MRC IBS study should be available.

It should be clear that our experience and our paradigm necessitate close joint working by those traditionally unimpeded by each other's views and demands: that is, those doing research and those commissioning research, as well as the main disciplines that can contribute insights to the work and its implications. This is a messy world we advocate. But roles and responsibilities can be made very clear. We start with the commissioners' role as the essential underpinning for all else.

3.5 An overview of the commissioners' role

We refer back to Box 3.1. Each of the items mentioned there will be outlined. Detailed discussion follows in the next chapter.

Setting the research question

Setting the research question is the fundamental and principal distinguishing feature of commissioning. The consumers of the planned research, represented by the commissioners, determine what it is they want to know. The issue is theirs and may or may not be of intrinsic interest to the research community. It may never have arisen had researchers been setting the agenda. It is assumed that the commissioners have thought through how the findings will be used. The study may be part of a programme of work initiated by the commissioners, which will lead from research through development into implementation. We discuss programme planning below. For now we note that it is the matter of ownership and control that fundamentally separates change-promoting applied research from theory-enhancing scientific research. However, as the IBS studies illustrate, the fact that commissioners set the agenda does not preclude working in partnership with the researchers. Indeed, this is a central element of the new paradigm. The partnership may lead to the agenda being significantly modified in the light of the expertise the researchers and associated clinicians bring to bear. Moreover, there is no reason why research directed primarily to a practical purpose should not incidentally address questions which the researchers regard as 'scientific'.

Bringing researchers together

With reactive funding a research team puts forward a proposal. The proposal and team are either accepted or rejected. Occasionally, the referees may suggest changes to a protocol and enhancement of the skills represented by a team. The applicants may be encouraged to submit a revised proposal to the next funding round. However, reactive funding is essentially a make or break process. In commissioning it is the particular research question that is of paramount importance – not whether there is a more capable team offering to answer a more interesting question. Thus, the commissioners are free to suggest collaboration between groups that have put in separate bids or expressions of interest. Indeed, they should in principle be free to 'head hunt' particular individuals or teams. This raises issues of probity, but as we discuss below, these are not insurmountable. The need to broker collaborations arises particularly because health services R&D is so often multidisciplinary. There are few extant teams that encompass all the skills necessary to deal with clinical issues, quantitative research, qualitative research and economic matters. Moreover, health service R&D, particularly as it moves towards development, has its setting in the service rather than in centres of academe. Thus, part of the role of commissioners is to encourage the growth of a body of questioning and research active health practitioners. These people may need help in being put in touch with particular areas of expertise, e.g. statistics. The IBS example illustrated how it was possible to bring together two separate and relatively inexperienced teams, and to give them support from the experienced teams working on other components of the project.

Working with researchers to produce the study protocol

In the theory-enhancing paradigm of science it is difficult to find grounds to question the authority of scientists to choose the research topics and determine the appropriate methods of researching those topics. This is not the case in the change-promoting paradigm for applied research. For research, at whatever point in the 'R' to 'D' to implementation spectrum, has practical application as the ultimate intent. The research questions should be consistent with the present and foreseen priorities of those planning and delivering services. The exact form in which the questions are posed and the nature of the answers to be provided are determined by the needs of the service and not those of academe. Thus the 'customers' must work with the 'contractors' in formulating the study protocol, by which we mean the distilled statement of research aims, objectives, background, methods, costs and ethical issues, available so that both the research team and any outsider can see clearly what the research is about, and how it is being done.

The degree of input required from the customers will vary across the 'R' to 'D' to implementation spectrum. We look at this in more detail below. Lest we be misunderstood, let us make it clear that we are not taking the extreme stance of cutting researchers out of the commissioning process. Researchers in a particular field have immense knowledge of the issues and potential offered by their field. Thus it is imperative that they contribute to the debate about R&D priorities. Moreover, people with research skills are essential to the development of protocols that can meet customers' needs. Researchers should be involved at the earliest stages of commissioning. It is their expertise that can tell whether the research questions are answerable and suggest options for answering them. The determination of a study protocol may become an iterative process involving dialogue between the commissioners and the research contractors.

However, researchers are rarely aware of the bigger picture: the issues of service resource distribution, the issues of setting priorities to meet measured health needs and the practical problems of turning research into implemented services. Thus, although they have a role in commissioning, their interests must not be paramount. Inevitably, in the move towards the new paradigm there will be conflict between the culture of researchers who traditionally, but wrongly, see themselves to be scientists and the culture of change management in health services. On the principle that 'he who pays the piper calls the tune' the power to bring about change rests with health service resource decision takers – assuming they have the confidence to assert it.

The points made in the previous paragraph are repeated in different guises throughout this book. The reason is that the matter of control is so central to the new paradigm. However, we must stress that control does not necessitate autocracy or rigidity. The IBS studies illustrate the crucial role of researchers in criticizing, refining and making practicable the aspirations of the commissioners. This will not happen unless researchers are enabled to feel a sense of ownership of the projects in which they are collaborating.

Project management

From the foregoing arguments it becomes natural to expect that the commissioners will take a role in project management. It is their project and they want to be sure that it will deliver. But this is not just a monitoring role. Mostly, it is to work constructively with the researchers to anticipate and to iron out difficulties. Health services R&D differs greatly from fundamental science not only epistemologically but also in many practical ways. Rarely can it take place in the laboratory and be isolated from the exigencies of the external world. It is usually embedded within health service delivery systems. It will often involve interaction with patients and with health professionals who are not themselves the researchers. It is taking place within a managed service. The project itself may have implications for the management of the service in which it is embedded, and vice versa. Issues arise which are most effectively dealt with by people who are actively part of health service management and have the contacts, influence or authority to get things done. The Dual Diagnosis Project, discussed above, is a good example of how research and the environment in which it takes place interact. The move from a pilot to a definitive study could have an undesirable effect on the morale of some of the service providers unless it is managed sensitively. Thus, just as researchers have to share ownership of projects, so do those who host the projects in their working environment.

These considerations become increasingly dominant as studies are located further from the left-hand end of the 'R' to 'D' to implementation spectrum.

Managing the transition from development to implementation

The transition from R&D to implementation must be a managed process. It requires management skills and understanding of the much broader context to which the R&D is contributing. When we discuss this in detail we show that implementation needs to be planned and managed long before the findings of a study, or programme, are known. Part of this is concerned with getting resources in place for a smooth transition into routine service should the project be deemed successful. The family therapy study discussed above is a good example of this issue.

Managing dissemination

Traditionally scientists have been responsible for disseminating their findings to their peers. This is usually done through presentations at conferences and publications in journals. These modes of dissemination apply equally to R&D. However, they do not suffice. Journal publication can take two years or more and it is usually longer before such works begin to be picked up through publication databases and citations. Moreover, databases do not have universal coverage. Conferences are good for spreading information fairly quickly among the cognoscenti of a field, but this can be hit and miss. Further, the format of journal publications and conference presentations is fairly rigid, dominated by irrelevant scientific notions, and can rarely give the detail required by people thinking of implementing findings. However, the main reason why the dissemination of health services R&D findings should differ from that of scientific research is that R&D is part of the change management process. Publications of themselves do not readily change behaviour. Thus, those commissioning work should consider the active management of changes they deem desirable. We pick this up in more detail below.

Encouraging a positive ethos for R&D

We have mentioned how health services R&D differs from more usual notions of research by being embedded in an organization which delivers a service rather than being hidden away in a laboratory. It follows that R&D is more likely to be successfully commissioned and lead to worthwhile service changes if 'research', especially evaluation, is part of the culture of the organization. This can come about if managers (*professional managers*, e.g. chief executives, and *professionals who manage*, e.g. clinical directors) value a questioning ethos and perceive R&D as delivering something useful to them. Moreover, those whose role is primarily the delivery of clinical services and those who provide support services need to feel comfortable in this atmosphere. They may only intermittently become involved in R&D, but when they do so it should be a rewarding experience rather than a nuisance.

The commissioners of R&D have an important role in bringing this about. Partly it will be achieved by commissioning work widely perceived to be of relevance to the immediate and anticipated problems in the service. It will help if commissioned projects are woven into the fabric of the service in a sensitive manner, rather than stamped upon it. This is where the knowledge of the commissioners about the structure and functioning of the service is so important. They can smooth the way for the project and help to get the various management and professional interests aligned to it. Moreover, managing the transition of successful projects from R&D into implementation in a trouble-free manner will surely maintain morale. While the commissioners cannot be expected to achieve this on their own they certainly are key facilitators of the process.

In the next chapter, we draw together a synthesis from both our theoretical perspective and our practical experience which looks in greater detail at the processes of commissioning.

PUTTING COMMISSIONING INTO PRACTICE

KEY POINTS

Commissioning is a collaborative task drawing on diverse skills. Central to these are the skills of the manager in holding a complicated process together and ensuring that it delivers. Resource managers have to be prepared to contribute to the detailed content of commissioning in order to ensure that they and other consumers of R&D will receive a usable product.

The bones of commissioning were presented in Chapter 3. Here we flesh them out. Some of the headings will correspond to the items listed for levels of commissioner involvement presented in Box 3.1.

4.1 Setting the research question

We noted in Chapter 3 that setting research questions is a key distinguishing feature of the proactive process we are calling commissioning. We observed that the new paradigm entails the funders and consumers of R&D setting the agenda for R&D rather than leaving it to the researchers. Specific research questions for specific studies or programmes of work should be posed, so that the answers will directly inform resource management decisions. The formulation of the questions and the design and execution of studies capable of answering those questions are matters calling upon the expertise of both resource managers and researchers.

Translating these ideas into practice is not as obvious as it might seem. The following issues arise.

1 Generating research questions relevant to the needs of the service.
2 Distinguishing between matters appropriate for commissioning and those better left to traditional reactive funding arrangements.

3 The mechanics of refining a question into something workable to study and worthwhile to answer.

These are considered in turn.

Generating relevant questions

Research questions are likely to arise in four ways.

1 Findings emerging from the fundamental biomedical sciences which have seeming potential for application.
2 Clinical professionals seeking to enhance the nature or scope of their practice.
3 Resource managers facing immediate problems or seeking valid strategies for the development of services.
4 Pressures for the introduction of developments, which may be of unproven worth, not affordable or inconsistent with local priorities.

The boundary between the fundamental sciences and the applied R&D which concerns us is not clear-cut. Fundamental science is an important spring from which well up things of potential practical use. Many, however, evaporate in froth. Scientists, being aware that a practical application might enhance funding prospects, are not averse to speculating wildly at the 'more research needs to be done' conclusion of their scientific papers. Moreover, some have no compunction about feeding the popular press with exaggerated accounts of the scientific importance and benefits to humanity of their latest work – seemingly disproportionately often in the cancer field. To keep track of the potential for applications arising from the fundamental sciences is too great a task for R&D commissioners at a sub-national level. Perhaps at national level it is feasible to assemble imaginative experts to try to predict where to bet development money – this is sometimes called horizon scanning. However, on the whole, we do not believe that this is the business of the commissioners of applied R&D.

Most of the applicable things that arise from the fundamental sciences are likely to concern drugs, high-technology therapies and diagnostic procedures. Commercial enterprises undertake most of the intermediate development work straddling the boundary between science and application. Generally, at the level of the commissioners of applied R&D the fruits of fundamental science arrive as packaged products at market or pre-market testing stage.

Clinical professionals are a major source of ideas and pressure for service improvement and development. They are up to date nationally and, often, internationally about developments in their fields. They are subjected to fierce advertising by the purveyors of medical equipment and therapeutics. Their expertise should be acknowledged and their desire to innovate and improve encouraged. However, their quest for innovation arises haphazardly. This does not necessarily fit with wider health service priorities or funding opportunities.

In Chapter 3 we mentioned the problems that arise from pressure to introduce unplanned innovations such as might have arisen from work funded by reactive funding schemes. We outlined how the Development and Implementation Fund (DIF) of the NHS Executive (North West) gave an opportunity for ideas to arise spontaneously from within the service and, if deemed appropriate, to be taken forward in a disciplined fashion. Although the DIF was in spirit a reactive fund it did lead naturally into many of the features that distinguish commissioning. Thus, in order to harness the creativity that arises from clinical practitioners, commissioning arrangements should give practitioners direct access to float proposals.

Resource managers are constantly having to make decisions in the light of incomplete information. They do not share the luxury of academics in being able to take time to dot every 'i' and cross every 't'. A key skill of the manager is to take calculated risks and to be comfortable in doing so – in this respect medical and dental practitioners are in their daily clinical work much more similar to professional managers than many suppose. The calculation sometimes leads to the conclusion that it would be imprudent to proceed without further information. There are two choices: await developments elsewhere or commission research. The former is sensible if there is already work in progress; hence the value of the networks of communication that have been set up within NHS R&D. If the question is not being answered elsewhere then there may be an opportunity to commission research. It is not feasible to commission research for every question that arises. First, national and local resources are constrained. Second, even in the absence of financial constraints, commissioning is labour-intensive and calls upon active input from the commissioners.

The simplest option is to flag the issue up for attention at regional or national level. This is sensible under the following circumstances.

1 The problem is of wide interest and lies within currently designated priority development areas.
2 The scale of the research required is, in terms of its cost, timescale or project management (e.g. a large multicentre study), too great for local commissioning.

Ideally, as R&D at the regional and national levels moves away from reactive funding and more towards commissioning, there should be the opportunity for those proposing R&D issues to contribute to the definition of the precise research questions, even though the commissioning will be handled elsewhere. It is only when strategic and operational resource managers get involved that the research questions, and the anticipated answers, can be sure to be grounded in the reality of the service.

Local commissioning is best employed for issues that are locally press-ing, e.g. the management of irritable bowel syndrome, as mentioned in Chapter 3. Time put into initial commissioning and continuing project management is a justifiable part of the 'routine' work of the officers involved and not the luxury that it would be otherwise. Moreover, if the problem and the associated R&D are seen to be owned by the organiza-tion there is likely to be continuing support and commitment even from those temporarily inconvenienced by any disruptive effects of the project.

The fourth source of research questions is external pressures to intro-duce or expand services. Pressures often arise from clinical professionals and frequently there is an underlying desire to use the latest wares from pharmaceutical and equipment manufacturers. Public expectations and demands might also be fired by the enthusiasts. What is being proposed does not always sit happily with current priorities and expenditure com-mitments. Nevertheless, it cannot be ignored even if it too readily en-compasses the non-rational and the irrational. It becomes particularly irksome when politicians see it as an opportunity to raise their profiles. These are sometimes issues that lend themselves to the procrastination that commissioned R&D legitimizes. In these circumstances it is greatly in the interests of the organization under pressure (e.g. health authority) to be actively involved in commissioning and project management. Other-wise, ill-conceived questions may be answered which give the appear-ance of providing more evidence, and hence increase the pressure, but do not actually address the main issues concerning resource managers. Beware of commissioning R&D in order to divert energy and attention. Such actions will give any future R&D attempts a bad taste, and even low-level R&D consumes resources which should not be wasted.

Commissioning versus reactive funding

As we progress in this chapter it will become clear that commissioning is demanding of time. Although many, perhaps most, health services R&D projects would benefit from the knowledge, perspective, skill and oversight of resource managers, this is not practicable. Resource managers should restrict their input and control to projects that address issues important to them and their sector of the service.

It is arguable under the new paradigm that all health services R&D should be directed to the needs of resource managers and hence be commissioned. We do not think that extreme view is sustainable. It implies a coherence and rationality for health services which we have already denied. It suggests an omniscience by resource managers which in all humility they are unlikely to claim. It denies the innovative entre-preneur the opportunity to explore matters which are not currently the main concern of resource managers. However, a motivating factor lead-ing to the formulation of the new paradigm is a desire that money spent on health services R&D (and thus denied from uses of immediate benefit to the population) be cost-effective in terms of outcomes that are wanted and usable. Another factor is the distorting effect undisciplined R&D has upon service development – resource managers being taken by surprise after something that ostensibly was research creeps unbeknown to them into routine service delivery.

The solution is to maintain a reactive funding stream alongside that for commissioning and to impose a little more discipline on reactive funding than hitherto. Reactive funding may remain closer to the methods used in the fundamental biomedical sciences, in that the academic and research communities are the main arbiters of projects worth funding. However, all projects which impinge on service delivery should have the consent of resource managers. For example, a largely laboratory-based study to develop a new screening test for helicobacter pylori need be of little concern to resource managers. A population-based pilot study of screening, perhaps in primary care, has serious implications. A momentum may build, leading to pressure to introduce the service routinely, even though a detached view of the needs of the population may have identified more important priorities. The problem here is in identifying the appropriate resource managers to express a view. The possibilities include: the clinical director of gastroenterological services; broader hospital managers (do they really wish to 'sell' this screening service?); the health authorities and others purchasing from that hospital; the health authorities' and other service commissioners' broader strategic management.

The key seems to be to ask the question whether or not the issue concerns strategic or operational management of health services. If it is strategic it rests at the level of district health authorities (and the new primary care commissioning groups) or above. If it is operational it lies with the management of service delivery organizations, such as hospital trusts, community services trusts and individual primary care practices. A matter is operational if it only concerns a service delivery organization: particularly, whatever happens will not reduce the quality or the quantity of already contracted services or increase prices charged for them. Strategic matters are those which may impinge on decisions about what types of services to purchase on behalf of populations. The example of piloting population screening for helicobacter pylori falls at the strategic level.

It might usually not be a matter of resource managers vetoing a study. Rather, by being informed they can ensure that the study will not unacceptably distort current service provision and that there are not false expectations held by health professionals or the public as to what will happen when the study is completed.

Developing and refining the research questions

Getting the research questions right is the key to all that follows. It determines whether R&D is capable of meeting expectations and whether it is a worthwhile use of resources. In the quest for action there may be a tendency to undervalue this stage of planning.

We have stressed that the new paradigm entails considerable ownership of research questions by resource managers. Many of the details of research design and study execution are purely technical and may be entrusted to researchers. The determination of what the research is for and how it is to be used must not be delegated. Senior resource managers must be prepared to give their own time to this. Determining and refining research questions can be a lengthy process. This may fall into the following stages.

Stage 1. An issue arises and it is recognized that information is lacking to form a judgement. Initial enquiry will be made using published literature, the grey literature (accessible reports which have not been formally published) and routine health service information systems. The literature search would usually concentrate upon review articles, effectiveness bulletins, reports from the Royal Colleges and other digested commentary, rather than original research papers. Enquiry among peers can be useful. This is facilitated by electronic mail (e-mail) 'mailbases', which serve as a means of circulating e-mail letters from members among all the other members (subscribers) of the mailbase. An example is the Public Health Mailbase, which is maintained by the University of Newcastle in the UK. More often than not enquiry at this level is sufficient. There may be enough evidence to settle the issue or justification to procrastinate until someone else has done so. Sometimes candidate questions for commissioned research will emerge.

Stage 2. At this point it becomes possible to begin defining the boundaries of one's ignorance. It is useful to go back to the issue afresh, with the insights gained from the preliminary studies, and determine what one really wishes to know. This is a suitable time to consult experts in the field: local clinicians, academics etc. Preliminary research questions should be forming. In consultation with experts and other interested parties, one can start to get a feel for how readily answerable the questions might be, whether the scale of research fits local commissioning or should more properly be placed on the national agenda, and to prioritize this area for potential R&D effort.

Stage 3. Once commitment in principle to commissioning R&D has been made it is necessary to do more detailed homework on what has been and is being done in that field. A more thorough traditional review of the literature may be commissioned as the first step towards planning a study. Sometimes it is evident that a formal systematic review of a large and diverse literature is necessary; this will entail searching out unpublished studies and may lead to a meta-analysis. Again this can be commissioned through the R&D process. This is also the stage to consult the national R&D networks about work known to be in progress elsewhere. It might be necessary to request copies of the protocols of similar studies. The international Cochrane Collaboration databases are useful too.

Stage 4. By this stage a set of research questions will have emerged and it will be known in principle that R&D to address those questions is feasible. This is the point at which research teams are invited to tender for the work or to join a collaboration. It is important to recognize that the researchers can make considerable contributions to refining the research questions. This is important for two reasons. First, the researchers must share ownership of the questions. Researchers are not technical automata. They make a considerable intellectual, professional and emotional commitment to their work. They should not be expected merely to operationalize someone else's questions into research. There should be a dialogue that enables the researchers to understand where the commissioners are coming from and how the answers to the questions will be used. The researchers, often being practitioners in or closely associated with the field, may offer a novel perspective on the issue. Moreover, though the research is primarily practical and follows the logic of evaluation rather than that of science, it may still be possible to accommodate research questions that are mainly of interest to the researchers. Second, moving towards the study protocol and the detailed means of answering the questions inevitably raises the need for further clarification, modification of aims and compromises between the ideal and the realizable.

When one is considering any potential research question the following issues arise.

Is the question well posed?
A well posed question predefines its possible answers. That is, when one receives an answer one recognizes it as a proper answer; one has anticipated the kind of response to be got. For example, to the question 'What is the time?', 'noon' is immediately recognizable as a legitimate answer, though whether it is correct or not is a different matter. 'The next street on the left' is not an admissible answer and suggests that the respondent should turn up his hearing aid. An extreme example of an ill-posed question is 'How do square circles reproduce?' The syntax is fine. It appears to have the semantics of a sensible question if one is not familiar with geometry; however, 'half past seven' is as good an answer as any other.

It is not unusual for research questions, when first stated, to be to some degree ill-posed. This is not uncommon because we all bury assumptions about a given situation within what we perceive to be clear language. Even apparently simple descriptive queries ('What is happening ... service?') require explicit definition of what is meant by 'happening' and 'service', *and* the reason for the interest. Hence it is important to spend time refining questions and to involve people who have fresh perspectives on the problem.

How will the answer to the question be used?
Thinking about this helps to identify ill-posed questions and to identify unnecessary questions. It forces one to be clear about how the findings

from the study will inform decisions. Careful consideration of the decisions to be made and the grounds for the various options should have led to the research questions in the first place, but it does not follow that the answers to those questions will in fact be usable and useful.

Many studies will lead to quantitative outcomes, e.g. indices of effectiveness and cost, measures of throughput, measures of quality of life and patient satisfaction. Each of these will be contributing to answering one or more of the research questions. There will be a mass of data which in their raw form will be confusing rather than illuminating. The analysis of these data will be guided by the research questions and should lead to the answers to those questions being expressed in a manner comprehensible to the customers/commissioners of the research. Thus, even before a study design is drafted the customers should have given thought to what usable results will look like.

The overall findings from most quantitative studies can be presented in tabular and graphical form. This should be done even if more sophisticated analytic techniques (e.g. regression analysis) are being used to explore fine detail and consistency among the data. Hence, the customers should at the outset decide what tables or graphs would enable them to take their resource decisions. That is, dummy tables can be constructed. These make clear what kind of numerical values should appear in the tables, and that informs the study questions that must be asked in order to fill in those values. Moreover, knowing what will appear in the tables enables a prior judgement to be made as to what patterns of values will justify which options.

Are the questions answerable?
Ill-posed questions are certainly not answerable in any meaningful sense. Well posed questions may also not be answerable. It may be impracticable in terms of finance and time to conduct a study. It may be unethical to seek a direct answer. Often, there has to be compromise between what is ideal and what is attainable. It is useful to start by considering the ideal study and how that could inform decision taking. Then, in consultation with experienced researchers, it is valuable to explore the effects of the various compromises which would be necessary to achieve a practicable study.

Perhaps some questions turn out to be unanswerable, but it might be possible to creep up on the problem tangentially. Other questions may have to be dropped but the answers to the remaining questions would still usefully but imperfectly inform a decision that has to be made. Even when it is possible to research all the questions it does not follow that the study will be able to deliver unambiguous answers. There will be uncertainties arising from many sources: inevitable data imperfections, problems during the study execution, statistical fluctuation as might arise from sampling and the inherent weakness of the study design. By anticipating these imperfections and by trying to estimate, in an order of magnitude sense, their likely effect on the findings the customers will have an advance feel for how much residual uncertainty will surround their final decision taking. The study is presumably being designed because the present uncertainties are too great to allow a sound decision. Doing research should reduce the uncertainties but it cannot eliminate them.

4.2 Bringing the researchers together

Hitherto, the conventional approach to commissioning research has been to set a broad priority area, and to expect researchers to set out their hypotheses (questions), methods and costs as part of a tender. The process borrows ideas from the private sector in terms of protecting what could be felt to be commercially sensitive information on prices and processes. It assumes that bidders are not part of a price-fixing oligarchy or cartel, but are in relative isolation.

A familiar argument is that researchers should be required to tender for a contract. The commissioners would draw up a detailed specification, i.e. much of the protocol, and ask research groups to offer sealed bids for it. Those offering to deliver at the lowest price would, subject to quality criteria, be awarded the contract. This is an extreme form of commissioning. Its principal aim is to promote financial probity in the award of contracts, though human ingenuity is such that it sometimes fails. The place of tendering in the context of health services R&D is small. It is limited to projects having easily defined aims and merely requiring the 'off the shelf' application of standard methods, e.g. client satisfaction surveys and population health status surveys.

Most R&D issues are not so simple. Above we discussed the difficulty of even the first stage of R&D: determining the questions. This is most efficiently done if it involves people with research experience working with the commissioners. The rest of study design is equally demanding. Even when seemingly standard designs – such as randomized controlled trials of therapeutic agents – are anticipated, particular studies will often throw up challenges for skilled and experienced researchers. Thus, drawing up specifications for tenders for projects of any complexity would usually be beyond the in-house resources of most potential commissioners.

This form of commissioning is not really in the spirit of the new paradigm. Research is not envisioned as an activity readily detachable from the context of either its execution or its ultimate application. Researchers are not merely hired hands working to a preset brief. They are part of a wider collaborative group, which includes those commissioning the work and those who might one day apply it – moreover, researchers are essential contributors to the refinement of the research questions which set the brief.

Having said that, researchers will come from different disciplines or different teams (such as sociology, health economics, understanding technology diffusion), which means that the expertise they bring to developing a good research question is necessarily limited by their own skills in answering the questions. They may contribute excellent ideas on, for example, relative costs and benefits of health service innovation. But they may have little idea about how to explore the acceptability of the innovation. The problem is that health services managers' decisions have to include this wide range of considerations. So we recommend that commissioners manage a collaborative research approach.

Bringing researchers together in this way should be an iterative process rather than a one-off decision. When the research questions have first been tentatively defined, and there has been a determination to pursue them, is the time to start thinking about the kinds of study which might be appropriate. This is the time to consult widely with in-house experts and external advisors. There is a danger that, in rushing too soon towards a particular class of research, design minds will become closed to wider opportunities; picking researchers with expertise in particular designs almost inevitably channels thinking thereafter. This problem persists because at present most research groups and individual researchers are compartmentalized in discrete disciplines. There are few groups and even fewer individuals who can be said to be competent to take a generic approach. Thus, as brainstorming with various advisors proceeds, suggestions will arise as to specific skills that need to be consulted. Whatever the proposed project, no options should be closed off at this early stage. What seemingly might most appropriately be a traditional quantitative study could on deeper reflection be better tackled by qualitative methods, and vice versa. Of importance to the new paradigm is the notion that R&D does not fall within any of the traditional disciplines. Rather, the kinds of answers sought by resource managers need insights and methods from diverse disciplines.

Resource managers planning to commission research should be aware of the various pitfalls that can make bringing researchers together difficult. Some arise from the compartmentalization of disciplines mentioned above and others seem endemic to the mind-set of researchers. Box 4.1 lists some of the issues that can arise. The greatest impediment to fostering a multidisciplinary approach is the, sometimes wilful, mutual ignorance among practitioners of different disciplines. Oddly, it can be an occasion for pride. Not knowing anything about, say, qualitative methods can often be construed as a belief that there is nothing to know. Conversely, the pride with which some sociologists affect ignorance of elementary statistical methods suggests that their outlook on the world is exceedingly narrow. Some health economists live in a fairy land where they believe they can plan health services entirely on economic principles and without recourse to assessing the perceived or objective needs of defined populations. Some medical geographers believe that they have invented epidemiology.

Box 4.1 Impediments to bringing researchers together

- Mutual ignorance
- Pecking order
- Ownership of expertise
- Caution about sharing ideas
- Needs of career researchers
- Authorship

The pecking order is linked to mutual ignorance and disdain. Pure science is more greatly esteemed (in academia) than applied science, quantitative disciplines are deemed more intellectually rigorous than qualitative ones etc. Funnily enough, the researchers being pulled together in the new paradigm are themselves near the bottom of the (current but, it is to be hoped, soon to be changed) academic pecking order because they are working in applied fields. Yet this does not deter some from seeking to differentiate their positions even on the foothills of greater academic grandeur.

Expertise is a consequence of specialization. The skills of the specialist are useful and should be valued. However, expertise can be an impediment to work that transcends the boundaries of traditional disciplines. Experts like to protect their turf. There are two reasons for this, one worthy and one not so worthy. First, complicated tools (e.g. a statistical technique) can produce misleading results in the hands of the unwary. Second, it is threatening to think that someone who did not complete the same arduous apprenticeship as the expert may be just as capable of fulfilling his tasks. It is discomforting, for example, to the health economist, statistician or therapeutic trialist to think that many of the applications of their disciplines are readily accessible to others. Here a distinction may be drawn between scholarship within a field, i.e. developing the theoretical basis and tools, and application of knowledge from the field. The former is the purview of the expert but it is hard to justify ownership of the latter. Just as experts seek to protect their own boundaries so they hesitate to cross boundaries. To trespass and to be found in error by the 'real' experts can lead to merciless public ridicule.

The strait-jacket of expertise is a serious impediment to developing the cross-discipline insights and skills necessary for useful R&D. In the medium term it is likely that multipotent researchers will emerge in the UK from a variety of new undergraduate and postgraduate courses. They will be competent to do most of the tasks currently the preserve of experts and will have sufficient insight into their own limitations to consult with super-specialists when necessary. Researchers work in a very competitive ethos. This militates against openness and the sharing of ideas. People who are reticent with colleagues within their discipline are less likely to work effectively in a cross-disciplinary team. Career researchers face difficulties which should be acknowledged and understood by resource managers commissioning research. Many researchers follow an uncertain career progression. They are vulnerable because they rely on a sequence of fixed-term contracts. Thus, they have little scope for taking risks. On each project they must deliver: for example, through publications in journals. It can be risky to take part in multidisciplinary and multi-agency projects because it can be difficult to identify, in the final work, the nature and magnitude of individual contributions.

For reasons such as those mentioned above and in Chapter 3, researchers often regard publication as the main end-result of their work. Resource managers must recognize this imperative even if it is not of importance to them. When researchers are brought together there should be open discussion about what there is in the project for the researchers' career achievement markers, and how these may be attained. In a later section of this chapter we look at the thorny issue of publication in more detail.

The problems identified above are not always easy to handle. However, awareness of them should enable commissioners to enter their discussions with researchers with due sensitivity. Issues such as training multipotent researchers and introducing a less haphazard career structure for researchers are beyond the level of individual commissioning groups. However, at regional and national level in the UK there has been some progress with the former, though the latter remains to be resolved, and as a matter of urgency.

Having set out the problems, we believe, none the less, that there are grounds for optimism regarding their solution. The most important is the involvement of commissioners who are resource managers in the health service. Even the most junior manager in any health service rapidly acquires experience of the resolution of conflict, be it in the relatively trivial issues around car parking or beverage subscription (and many readers will be familiar with those minefields) or the more serious dispute, say, between a surgeon wanting to undertake major, potentially live saving, procedures and nursing colleagues arguing that resources for such work must include counsellors and not just theatre equipment. The ability to bring people together to debate and resolve differences is the hallmark of the good resource manager.

Second, many researchers themselves are beginning to recognize the value, and the intellectual excitement, of other disciplines. We have seen this in many fields. A nice example is in the area of paediatric oncology, where high-quality researchers pursue information on not only the impact of various drugs on tumour size but also the resultant behavioural implications and challenges for the learning abilities of the children so treated. The researchers share ideas on molecular biology and educational theory. The desire for synergy is often reinforced nowadays by funding organizations requiring multidisciplinary and multi-agency involvement when research bids are put in, and we would wish that this approach be adopted more strongly, and on a more widespread basis, than hitherto.

The third and final reason for us pushing this concept of collaboration so vehemently is that we have seen it work, and work well. But this means that within any group of researchers there has to be absolute honesty and trustworthiness. A willingness to acknowledge that others' thoughts have contributed fruitfully to one's emerging ideas has to be part of the culture of any such grouping – and managers can often set an excellent example in this. If there is this transparency and openness there should be few fears about probity, but it is also useful to make clear that some behaviours are unacceptable and that there will be sanctions: grapevines can be poisonous, failure to recommend researchers will do little for their careers, and ultimately refusing permission to publish (a potentially lethal component of research contracts such as those managed by the Department of Health) is an option.

4.3 Probity in the patronage of commissioning

Probity is an issue that is likely to cause considerable concern in relation to our new paradigm.

We recognize that there are two major issues involved here: first, intellectual property; second, financial reward. For researchers and others whose careers and personal development are dependent upon their being recognized as having something special to offer in terms of ideas and abilities, a general open pooling of research work will be completely unacceptable. A general pool offers no opportunities for being seen as someone worthy of career development and enhanced pay. But, on the other hand, this pooling of disciplines and abilities is also essential to the new paradigm.

How can we resolve the conflict? One obvious solution might be for each organization (the NHS, hospital services, health authorities or whatever) to have its own in-house research team. This would mean research expertise available on tap, which could be performance managed as with any other resource within the organization, and therefore presumed to contribute both intellectual abilities and value for money (in terms of pay) in the same way as other members of the organization. In many ways this could have considerable advantages. Research commissioners would have immediately available to them support and advice regarding the potential and desirability of any research. There would be no difficulty as regards outsiders misinterpreting the desires or requirements of the organization. Politically difficult colleagues, or likely opponents of any research ideas, could be identified almost intuitively and brought on board at an early and appropriate stage.

However, we feel that this solution has two major drawbacks. First, it is unlikely to be cost-effective, in terms of the range of research disciplines we see as making a major contribution to our new paradigm. It is likely that only the larger organizations can afford to have their own team of statisticians, epidemiologists, health economists, sociologists and so forth. Second, and probably more importantly, we fear that such a team might develop the same disadvantages as those we have pointed out in relation to theory-enhancing researchers. That is, it might become too introspective, too self-referential, unaware of the need to obtain ideas from outside. Although the relative security and ability to develop research as a valued part of any organization's structure could have obvious advantages, we need to be aware of the free thinking necessary for good, productive, stimulating research. So this solution, although it has much to commend it, may not be as simple as it appears initially.

We need to explore other options. In doing this we echo the previously described structure required for considering whether or not research really needs to be done: that is, doing the literature research, consulting experts, drafting a protocol and ultimately going to tender, preferably with a collaborative multidisciplinary group of researchers from a number of different sources. Doing each of those steps in a way that respects intellectual property rights and ensures there is not suspicion of undue and unfair financial patronage will now be discussed.

The first area we suggested for any resource managers contemplating commissioning research was a literature search and review. Although there is undoubtedly a level of critical appraisal skill and knowledge of various literature sources required for this to be done competently, there is not necessarily the same level of innovative or creative thinking that academics would jealously guard as 'intellectual property'. In addition, much of the literature that will be reviewed will already be quite explicitly in the public domain, or at least partly so, so that the ownership of the materials used is not open to question. Thus, probity in this initial stage of commissioning research could quite readily be handled by in-house experts, or by, for example, a contract with a local academic institution, in which literature reviews would be delivered according to the resource managers' time scales (and therefore will be of variable length and quality) within affordable costs (and the same applies) and quite explicitly for public use (if the resource managers are accountable to public bodies). It may be useful on a regular basis (for example, every three years or so) to go to tender for some sort of contract with a relevant institution to undertake this work, as it is undoubtedly easier to have this expertise on tap to provide summaries as and when needed, rather than having to find someone on each occasion when a literature search appears to be required. This is, in effect, potentially a self-closing stage. There should be no uncertainties regarding intellectual property or financial probity at the end of the stage. There may still, of course, be issues around the quality of the review, and those issues will be dealt with partly as the resource manager acquires experience in perceiving the value of review and partly as the reviewers acquire experience in answering the resource manager's questions in a way that is perceived as clear and helpful. The advantage of having a contract with a relatively large institution, such as an academic body, is that there is then potential for that body to call on a wide variety of skills in doing the literature review. Sometimes all that is needed is a very basic training in critical appraisal and some brief statistical experience. Sometimes, however, there is a need to tap into either clinical expertise or a deeper knowledge of the social sciences, especially some of the economic concepts which may or may not be contested appropriately in the literature that is reviewed.

The next stage we suggest for resource managers considering whether or not to commission research is to seek the views of experts. These experts may be identified as a result of the literature review. They may also be known in the field – senior academics are readily identifiable, surgeons with a very specialised interest are often very well known. But we can never be sure we know who to ask in terms of obtaining this expert advice. In addition, the input of expert advice may now entail innovative and creative thinking, and hence some relation to intellectual property rights, as well as possibly occasioning considerable time in terms of the expert whose advice is being given, where it would not be unreasonable to pay for that time.

Here we suggest that there are, increasingly, opportunities via various electronic communication systems to seek out experts who are prepared to contribute advice and reviews. Public health departments throughout England and Wales have access to a system known as 'Epinet', which was originally set up in order to ensure rapid communication about communicable disease incidents. The system is increasingly used for seeking out advice on a wide range of other topics. There is also the public health mailbase, which provides another opportunity for public health physicians throughout the country (and internationally) to communicate with each other, and share ideas. E-mail and web sites are other examples of international means of communicating and sharing. We therefore suggest that the means of requesting comments be as open as these electronic systems are, and therefore unlikely to raise questions of probity. Managers seeking expert comments will have requirements regarding those comments in terms of timeliness, relevance, validity (is this really an expert?) and cost (if someone offers to send in written detailed comments for £500 is it worth the candle?). Answers to the first two will be clear in the context of the question that is developing. Answers to the third question will develop partly with the resource managers' acquisition of research expertise and judgement, and in addition be reinforced by views that have been encountered in the literature review. Answers to the last will very much be a matter of judgement, but will also be informed by the literature review (which may, for example, identify considerable areas of uncertainty, not least because there has been insufficient thought as to how the problem should be approached). Advisors may wish to impose conditions of confidentiality on those with whom they share their expertise, for a variety of reasons, which are most likely to be either because they guard jealously their intellectual property rights or because they foresee political implications of an unsavoury nature as a result. It has to be made clear to any experts offering advice that they may be doing so to a publicly accountable body. The comments will always therefore be made attributable, as will the moneys that has been paid or their time in putting together those comments. If experts find this unacceptable then they will lose an opportunity to participate in this stage of the resource managers' thinking.

Protocol development is a very skilled component of research commissioning, and it is here that issues about probity become particularly difficult. Construction of a well reasoned and feasible research protocol takes considerable experience and may draw on research disciplines as disparate as sociology and epidemiology. Creative and practical thinking are essential, and contributors to a protocol might guard their ideas somewhat jealously. This in itself could create difficulties. However, in our paradigm, the situation is even less straightforward because we would envisage, ideally, those researchers who have contributed to a clear and feasible protocol also being involved in the research, so that there is not an obvious separation between protocol development and tendering for research, and therefore opportunities for accusations of inappropriate patronage and lack of transparency about use of public funds or intellectual property. Where many disciplines can usefully come together to inform a good protocol, the interprofessional rivalries might render the sensitivities even more fragile.

Our suggestion here is that, despite our wish for the whole process to be seen as continuous and continually self-enriching, the fairest way to handle it is as a number of discrete steps, which will allow participants to opt in or out as they see fit.

Thus, the first stage will be the development of an outline protocol – early ideas on what is being asked and how the question should be answered, together with the likely resources required. It would seem sensible at this stage to invite people who have already offered comments and advice to participate. Their contributions to the outline protocol would be paid for in relation to the time and seniority of the input, but the result would still have to be a *public document*. This is because the organization for whom the research is being done must be kept informed not only of expenditure, but of the ways in which thinking is developing in relation to answering the research questions. There will be no promise from the commissioning organization that those contributing to the protocol will do the research. They will, however, of course be well placed to bid for any tenders that ultimately emerge, given their advantage in terms of understanding what the issues are.

The next stage is a far more detailed protocol, and this is where we see confidentiality and professional secrecy coming into play. Again, there will be no promise that those contributing to the development of the detailed research protocol will be awarded the tender for the work. However, the detailed protocol will *not* be a public document. It will be made available only to bona fide researchers wishing to tender for the work. Again, contributions to the detailed work of the protocol can be reimbursed. It is at this stage that we anticipate that very skilful research commissioners can start bringing together researchers from a variety of disciplines to stimulate and reinforce each other's ideas, and thus give rise to the potential of a collaborative research team bidding for the tender when in due course the protocol is more finely developed.

The detailed protocol is then the basis for going out to tender for the research to be done. Making the tender available has to be an open process. There is no doubt about that. However, it is open only to those in a position realistically to make some sort of bid for the work. Clear criteria by which 'fitness to bid' can be judged are not well developed. There will be the obvious ones: a well established research department in an academic or other institution, for example. There will also be people who are already known to the commissioner as researchers with expertise. Others will have to be taken on trust. Herein lies the risk with our suggestion. However, careful records of all to whom research protocols are sent will enable subsequent work to be followed up. This may not do much to reassure people in the short term. In the longer term there is no doubt that those who take inappropriate advantage of the openness and transparency we are suggesting will find this very much to their detriment.

The tenders themselves are of course confidential, and subject to the usual procedures. This is the business of a well managed commissioning process. Most healthcare managers understand and are well skilled in these processes. If they involve others in judging the suitability of the bids (as we would advocate given the complexity of good research), then those people too will have to be subject to the same professional requirements as we expect in clinical and similar matters.

4.4 Ensuring that the study protocol meets the needs of the commissioners

The study protocol is a definitive statement of the intentions of the study and how they are to be achieved. It forms the basis of a contract between the commissioners and the researchers. Details about what should be included in a protocol are discussed in the next chapter. Here we shall be concerned with the process of protocol development. We reiterate a theme that keeps recurring under the new paradigm: the protocol must be 'owned' by both the commissioners and the researchers. As with any commercial contract, both sides should be committed to its delivery and should stand to gain from it. Box 4.2 displays the protocol elements of particular importance to commissioners. We have already discussed the

---

Box 4.2   Protocol elements of importance to commissioners

- Statement of aims and objectives
- Study design and how it will impact on the routine service
- Outcome measurements
- Cost
- Overall time scale and major milestones
- Apportionment of responsibilities
- Intellectual property rights and authorship

---

formulation of study questions and in the next chapter we will take this further by looking at how aims and objectives clarify the intent of a study. The point we wish to reinforce here is that even if the commissioners have determined their study questions in-house the researchers contracting for the project should be consulted about the sense of the questions and the practicability of answering them before the aims and objectives are finalized.

The commissioners are likely to have some prior thoughts about the kind of study necessary to answer their questions. They will know how high a priority the issue is, the degree to which an authoritative as distinct from 'a quick and dirty' answer is needed and the kind of resource, including time scale, they are willing to invest. A dialogue, if necessary a lengthy one, with the researchers is time well spent; for rarely is the step from research questions to study design simple, though when approached systematically it is straightforward. There is often more than one way of tackling a question. Even when a particular overall design is obvious from the start, e.g. an RCT for therapeutic options, there will be many choices to make as to how it is implemented. More-over, compromise between the perfect and the attainable is inevitable. This will be informed by the inherent tractability of the research ques-tions, the degree of precision required in the answers, the financial and human resources available and the time scale in which management resource decisions – it is hoped informed by the answers to the questions – have to be made.

Apart from the technical issues of research design, there are practical ones too. We envisage the kind of R&D that is commissioned to be mainly embedded in the service rather than in laboratories, in which case the commissioners must consider how the study is to interdigitate with the routine practice around it. At the very least this entails making sure that key people in the service are informed. It is more likely that their active cooperation will be needed in which case management skills must be employed to put across the benefits accruing from the study yet also deal sensitively with concerns which people may have. Thus, the commissioners will be dealing with senior management in NHS trusts, primary care and other institutions. However, they must ensure that the people in the workplace are also consulted and their concerns heeded. Better than leaving that to the institution's management is to arrange direct contact between the commissioners, researchers and the individuals whose cooperation is needed or who otherwise will be affected.

Strictly speaking, it is impossible to separate the consideration of outcome measures wholly from that of study design. Nevertheless, there are particular matters that should be kept in mind. The commissioners must satisfy themselves that the outcome measures really do pertain to the study questions and really will, after data analysis, enable resource decisions to be taken. This comes back to a point raised earlier in this chapter: the commissioners must ensure that they have a clear idea of what the analysed data will look like (e.g. particular tables) and exactly how they intend to use the findings to inform their resource decisions. Clarity of thought at this stage pays dividends. Related to this, the commissioners must make sure that they are aware of the strengths and weaknesses of the outcomes they seek. Some types of outcomes and their interpretations (e.g. inpatient stays as a measure of resource use) are fairly obvious; others, such as scoring systems for quality of life, are not. The commissioners should ensure that the researchers, or other appropriate experts, have explained how the outcome measures should be interpreted and any pitfalls, errors and biases likely to be associated with them.

The overall cost of the study is a prime consideration for the commissioners. Detailed costing cannot be made until the protocol stage. However, order of magnitude figures must be considered at the stage when it is being decided whether or not the resource issues under consideration warrant commissioned research. The amount considered worth investing (and risking) in research will be proportional to the loss that would accrue from taking a wrong decision uninformed by research. Loss in this sense may be actual or notional. A notional loss might be an opportunity cost. For instance, there is a considerable number of patients suffering from IBS and they use a lot of primary and secondary care resources. Current case management is widely believed not to be very effective – hence the research questions identified in Chapter 3. If nothing is done, considerable resources will continue to be channelled to IBS. If, on the other hand, there is a more effective way of managing IBS using existing, or indeed lesser, resources then not taking the opportunity to implement it (after suitable evaluation) is a substantial loss. Thus, given that the current management of IBS uses resources measured in millions of pounds annually, the investment of a few hundred thousand pounds in well focused research seems prudent.

Decisions on the order of magnitude of investment can, and must, be made before formal commissioning begins. In the UK there will often be sufficient in-house expertise, e.g. public health specialists in health authorities, and, if not, the regional R&D Directorate would surely have a list of suitable contacts. The research budget sets limits to what is attainable. Thus the commissioners must be very clear about what they want and the margins of error acceptable in the answers to their questions. In other countries these may well be staff employed by, say, the hospital or a third party payer (e.g. medical insurance company) who have similar skills or at least an interest in acquiring expertise and experience.

The protocol will contain a detailed breakdown of the research costs (salaries, equipment, consumables etc.) projected by month and annually over the duration of the project. There are many detailed issues to consider, such as appropriate grades and salary levels for hired hands (e.g. research assistants), incremental salary scales, added 'on-costs' to cover pensions, National Insurance and the expenses of the institution (e.g. a university) hosting the researchers, and extra treatments costs for the NHS. These days on-costs are heavily inflated, by as much as 40 per cent. Thus, one consideration must be whether or not to hire staff through the NHS rather than through other institutions. There is no particular need for the commissioners themselves to become experts in these matters, as they ought to be able to draw upon appropriate advice from regional R&D directorates, or similar groups, who will in most cases be administering the funds anyway.

Extra treatments costs are definitely a responsibility of the commissioners rather than the researchers. The current regulations in the NHS require that research projects distinguish between the costs attributable to the research and those attributable to normal practice. Additional expenses for treating patients must not be included in the research costs. Health authorities have an obligation to meet those expenses through their allocations to NHS trusts (e.g. hospitals). However, this obligation is more theoretical than actual. If a research project springs large unanticipated extra treatment costs on to an NHS trust the health authority may decide to be very tardy in meeting them. Thus, the trust managers may be unwilling to bear the costs out of current budgets if they have no clear expectation of recouping them in the following financial year. Hence, a research project that would significantly distort current local funding priorities can in effect be vetoed. Prudent commissioners of R&D will identify extra treatment costs at an early stage of protocol development and begin discussions with appropriate trusts' management and health authorities to ensure that no nasty surprises are sprung on either and that arrangements for funding can proceed smoothly.

Setting and agreeing the project time scale is essential to the proper use of resources and to project management. Within that time scale significant deliverable events – milestones – should be identified. Examples are training fieldworkers, the completion of piloting, the start and end of patient recruitment, the start and end of data analysis and the beginning of the dissemination of findings. The identification of milestones is helpful to predicting how the budget will be disbursed over the life of the

---

Box 4.3   Responsibilities

- Seeking ethical approval
- Seeking necessary permissions, e.g. access to records
- Budget holding
- Day-to-day management of hired research staff
- Detailed division of responsibility among the researchers, e.g. health economist, clinical researchers, statistician
- Liaison with relevant management and health professional interests in the institutions where the research is taking place
- Production of progress reports
- Data preparation prior to analysis, e.g. coding and checking
- Membership of the researchers' project management group
- Membership of the overall project steering group (with the possibility of an external expert advisor)
- Production of final reports in various forms and general dissemination

---

study, for rarely will the costs be evenly spread. It is particularly important to ensure that the milestones are realistic. For example, there is a tendency to believe that the analysis of a study for which data collection takes eighteen months can be completed in one month. Moreover, writing up the results in a way that makes sense to all those involved is a time consuming business. Although research projects must be properly managed there should be recognition that events are not entirely predictable. For instance, patient recruitment may turn out to be more difficult than anticipated and hence have to be done over a longer period, so that the required numbers (for statistical power) may be obtained. Less productive times of year should be borne in mind, e.g. the Christmas (which in universities can involve a two-week shutdown to save on heating) and summer holiday seasons. Hence it is sensible to build in some slack, to overestimate rather than underestimate the time it takes to reach various milestones. When, as is almost inevitable, things go wrong they can be accommodated within the overall time scale and budget of the study, rather than ending in the very unsatisfactory position of seeking an extension of time and funding. In the matter of milestones the commissioners should heed the advice of experienced researchers. At this stage, too, the commissioners should be giving initial thought to milestones for the implementation of the R&D.

A clear and agreed apportionment of responsibilities is essential. Box 4.3 highlights some of the issues to consider. Disputes about intellectual property rights and authorship can be acrimonious and are best avoided. Ideally commissioners should have a policy which the researchers are made aware of before the project is funded. Nevertheless, an open discussion of how this policy applies to the particular study should take place, and its outcome should be documented in the protocol. The commissioners should show some flexibility according to the circumstances. There are two main issues to consider: first, the ownership of any commercially exploitable product that may arise from the project; second, whose names, and in what order, go on the papers and reports that emanate from the study. If it is anticipated that a commercially exploitable product will ensue then it is essential that whatever agreement is reached is compatible with the current standing instructions in the NHS. Universities and other employers of researchers may claim ownership of inventions of their employees. Hence this potential minefield should be fully explored at an early stage and legal advice taken when necessary.

Authorship is a very sensitive issue. Publication in 'reputable' journals is the life blood of academics. The quantity and, to a much lesser degree, the quality of published work determines their career progression and, if they are in British universities, the base funding of their institution. Thus, under the principle of rendering unto Caesar that which is Caesar's, while privately acknowledging that the emperor has no clothes, the commissioners of R&D must try to keep researchers happy.

It should be borne in mind that the dissemination of findings will be through a variety of media, of which the traditional academic paper is not necessarily the most important or effective agent. Appropriate forms of acknowledgement and authorship will vary among the media. Further, not only do the researchers deserve credit for their work but so do the organizations that commissioned it and the members of those organizations who drove the process forward. In academic papers it is customary, and in journals such as the British Medical Journal mandatory, that funding agencies be acknowledged. The position with regard to authorship of those involved in the commissioning process is less clear. This is because the very proactive commissioning we are describing here is not yet common. For reactively funded projects it does not usually seem appropriate for anyone other than the researchers to be authors; though sometimes members of grants committees and external referees make substantial intellectual contributions to research protocols. Commissioning is different because the relationship between the researchers and the funding body is collaborative.

Journal editors have become increasingly wary about inappropriate authorship. It is easy to see why: it can be difficult to understand how, say, ten or more authors each made a substantial contribution to a piece of work. International guidelines, reproduced in the 'instructions to authors' sections of many journals, stipulate that each author should have made a clearly defined intellectual contribution to the conception and conduct of the study and, very importantly, contributed to writing and approving the paper. Clearly, commissioners going through the processes detailed in this chapter fulfil these criteria.

Box 4.4 lists some of the agreements about publication that should be made and documented before a study progresses. A distinction is drawn

---

Box 4.4   Publication issues that need discussion at an early stage

- Anticipated main paper(s) to be submitted for publication in academic journals
- Anticipated subsidiary academic paper(s), e.g. examining some technical matters of purely academic interest or secondary analysis of the data to explore issues which were not the main study questions
- Anticipated academic conference presentations (talks and posters)
- Anticipated publication in general journals (e.g. *The Health Services Journal* or *Health Trends*)
- Anticipated in-house publications(s) for dissemination as grey literature
- Anticipated academic theses if any of the researchers or their assistants are to register for a research degree
- Anticipated special dissemination presentations to health professionals
- The possibility of placing the findings on an Internet web site

---

between the main academic papers in which the commissioners should be partners and subsidiary work which some, or all, of the researchers may publish in their own names and without further contribution from the commissioners. There must also be a clear understanding about what will be published and when. Academic journals do not like publishing material that has appeared in some form elsewhere. However, it can take one or two years for material to appear in these journals, and that is an unacceptable delay of the dissemination and use of the findings. Such old-fashioned restrictive practices have no place in a world of fast communication and the Internet. Thus, it must be clearly understood that the commissioners are free to produce and widely disseminate an in-house publication or report (grey literature). The commissioners must also be free to organize dissemination events for health professionals.

The simplest solution to the authorship issue is to constitute the researchers and key members of the commissioners as the 'XYZ Study Group'. Each member of the group is listed in alphabetical order with his or her designation or role in the project. From within this list can be highlighted, as necessary, a writing subgroup (and, perhaps, lead writer) and a member to whom correspondence should be addressed. It is a matter of negotiation with journal editors as to how this is handled in publication. In this manner everyone gets due credit and, if such venal considerations matter, brownie points too. It is worth noting that readers interested in such things often begin to recognize certain organizations as being particularly productive settings for good research and will be attracted to a given place because it is recurrently associated with such publications, regardless of the specific names of the researchers, managers and authors.

There is one other matter that needs agreement at this stage: ownership and control of the data. Generally the data are best held by the researchers, who will also be delegated responsibility for maintaining necessary confidentiality. During analysis and report writing the data should be available to all members of the study group, with access regulated by a named individual. It should be agreed that after the findings of the study have been published the data will be in the custody of a named individual (or institution). This person will maintain them for a minimum stipulated period and will allow access to the data, in a suitably anonymized form, to bona fide enquirers.

4.5 Project management

Managing research differs little from managing any other project involving diverse people. Project management, in the general sense, is a skill which all resource managers will have acquired through their training and experience. There are publications on the topic, diverse planning tools (e.g. Gantt charts) and software packages to assist in scheduling events. Thus, we do not dwell in detail on project management. We merely sketch the main elements, giving particular emphasis to the issues raised by managing research projects.

The key to managing any project is clarity of thought about what is to be accomplished and the steps necessary to do so. In the context of R&D the starting point is the study protocol; hence, our emphasis above on its importance. The protocol will describe the aims and objectives of the project and the steps by which they are to be achieved. It will detail the human and material resources required and the finance necessary to sustain them. Thus, it is a small step from a well constructed protocol to a project management plan. The elements of a project management plan are listed in Box 4.5.

The project management plan identifies events which must occur, individuals' responsibilities and how the flow of resources will be channelled and monitored. The day-to-day running of the project and management of employed staff is most appropriately handled by an experienced researcher. It is most likely that the funds for the project will be passed to the institution employing the lead researcher, and that institution is likely to be in the public sector (e.g. a university). The finance department of that institution will be responsible for handling the funds according to the strict rules that apply to public sector institutions. Whether the institution is in the public sector or not, part of project planning is to make arrangements for regular reports about the use of financial resources. This is important not just for probity but also to help to identify unexpected cash requirements at an early stage and to take steps to avert the disaster of running out of funds or going into unplanned overspend.

Box 4.5   Elements of a project management plan

- Project aims
- Project objectives
- Detailed steps by which each objective is to be accomplished
- Identify critical events necessary to accomplish each objective
- Identify global markers of progress, i.e. project milestones
- Anticipate the pattern of cash flow over the duration of the project
- Identify individuals responsible for each critical event
- Identify the day-to-day leader of the project (e.g. a senior researcher)
- Identify a steering group (lead researchers, commissioning representatives and other key interests and advisors)
- Identify someone to take overall responsibility (e.g. a commissioning representative chairing the steering group)
- Identify information that should flow among the members of the project team and to the steering group
- List a schedule for regular meetings of the project team, steering group etc.

The project steering group serves two main purposes. First, it monitors the progress of the project. Second, and very importantly, it is a resource supporting the research team. Bear in mind that under the new paradigm the researchers and commissioners are seen as collaborators. The steering group should have representatives of the researchers and the commissioners. It may have representatives of the management of the institutions in which the research is taking place (e.g. a hospital); the presence of such people not only greatly facilitates the resolution of practical difficulties but also helps to promote a feeling of ownership of the project by the host institutions. The chairman of the steering group should ideally be a member of the commissioning group. Since the steering group will meet infrequently (perhaps quarterly), the chairman may liaise with the research team as required. He or she will be in a strong position to deal quickly and authoritatively with urgent matters requiring input from the commissioners.

A steering group can benefit from the presence of an external and independent expert in the field being explored. Such a person can be a useful resource to the researchers and a source of reassurance to the commissioners that all is going well. Ideally, this expert would be someone who had been consulted during the early stages of commissioning and expressed general support for the project.

The role of the steering group extends until the writing-up of the findings, dissemination and implementation. As matters move into implementation the composition of the steering group may need to change to reflect various health professional and management interests.

The researchers, unless they are also health professionals connected to the innovation, will probably withdraw after writing-up and seek fresh avenues of enquiry. This is reasonable: under the new paradigm researchers are required to work within priorities set by the needs of change management but no one is suggesting that they should become change-managers.

4.6 The transition to routine service

In Chapter 3 we discussed the inefficiency of leaving matters of implementation until the project is complete and the answer has been obtained. R&D has been commissioned with the expectation that the findings will be acted upon. Resource managers should have committed themselves in principle to implementing the service changes if the R&D outcomes satisfy preset criteria; otherwise there seems little point in commissioning R&D. Thus, even before the R&D starts there is at least an order of magnitude estimate of what implementing the findings would entail and cost. What it entails is the steps necessary for successful change management. What it costs is the recurring annual costs and, perhaps, one-off pump-priming to facilitate the transition from development to implementation.

There will come a point during the R&D when those actively involved will become aware whether or not the project is likely to justify sustainable service changes. This view may arise from tentative interim analyses and also from the intuition of those close to the work. Although neither form of evidence is sufficient to justify full implementation, they do support placing some time and resources into planning implementation. As in the example given in Chapter 3, there may be good grounds for investing some money to keep service delivery going during the hiatus between the end of data collection and the point when a final decision can be made on full implementation.

Thus, as suggested at the end of the previous section, the composition and role of the project steering group may change. Alternatively, an implementation planning group may be formed, but this will still need input from members of the steering group. Planning possible implementation is a key element of the change management process. For it is at this stage that the commitment of key individuals, managers and health professionals, must be obtained. This will be greatly facilitated if appropriate hearts and minds were won during the setting up of the R&D project.

In moving towards implementation it should be borne in mind that the first time a service change is implemented cannot be distinguished from the development process. This first implementation should be the subject of careful observation and documentation. Indeed, the process itself and the behaviour and feelings of key personnel may fruitfully be subjected to qualitative research. For lessons may be learned during implementation. These lessons should be part of what is disseminated concerning the project. Hence, people implementing the changes elsewhere may find their task more easy.

Non-implementation also has to be managed. We do not envisage that R&D projects will be commissioned purely speculatively. To justify the use of resources in R&D there must be some *a priori* reasons for believing that the project is at least more likely than not to be successful. Many people may have made considerable intellectual and emotional commitment to the project and have high expectations of the outcome. These need to be handled sensitively. Certainly, it should have been made clear to all involved at the very beginning that the implementation decision would be no foregone conclusion. Even so, there may be a considerable sense of disappointment and perhaps of failure too. Managers must make it clear that they value the efforts of all involved. They should try to explain that non-implementation is not 'failure'. It is a worthwhile outcome from a decision informing process which means that resources will not be used inappropriately, and hence will remain available to support other initiatives.

There is further comment on implementation in Chapter 6.

4.7 Dissemination

Dissemination is an active process, akin to marketing a product. Publication in a peer reviewed journal – the end-point for researchers – is an element of dissemination but it is passive. Knowledge diffuses slowly and haphazardly from academic publications. Indeed, in the academic world there is gradual assimilation of new findings into the collective knowledge base. The process progresses through citation of the original paper in other publications, inclusion in databases such as the Cochrane Collaboration, mention in review articles (or journal editorials) seeking to consolidate knowledge and finally to incorporation into textbooks and syllabi, where the findings become 'fact'. This is a cautious process that allows careful criticism before ideas are accepted. It is a sensible element of the theory-enhancing paradigm but insufficient for the change-promoting paradigm.

R&D is a tool of change management. The implementation of good and affordable ideas to improve service provision is a responsibility of all managers. The product champions who conceived the idea and evaluated it have a responsibility to ensure that fellow managers and health professionals elsewhere have the opportunity to implement beneficial changes as soon as possible. They also need to know about changes which should not be implemented.

To this end a number of initiatives have been taken nationally and regionally within the NHS to aid dissemination. Product champions should take advantage of these. However, they should also use their own initiative. Each discipline has its own hierarchy of formality and pathways for sharing ideas. Peer reviewed publication is the most formal and conversation the least. Product champions should seek to ensure that their findings enter the pathways of all relevant disciplines. The researchers will publish their findings and discuss them with peers at conferences. Health professionals can access a range of professional development programmes from local, regional and national meetings at postgraduate education centres to meetings of their professional bodies (e.g. Royal College of Nursing). Professional managers have similar networks and provision for professional updating.

The messages passing along these pathways will differ in emphasis. The researchers may wish to examine methodological issues and implications for further research. Health professionals are likely to concentrate upon the benefits offered by the innovation and to explore technical issues about how those benefits can be delivered and audited. Managers will naturally be interested in the practicability of implementing the changes, resource issues and matters connected to the management of the service when changes have been implemented. These pathways are complementary, particularly the latter two. For the change cannot come about unless backed by health professionals and managers, and this is all part of the learning organization we describe in Chapter 6.

Part III

DOING AND USING RESEARCH

| 5 |

DOING RESEARCH

KEY POINTS

An understanding of research methods is easily within the grasp of those who hitherto have regarded them as esoteric and difficult. Such understanding is essential if research relevant to the needs of health services is to be commissioned and the findings appraised critically by the end-users. Studies sometimes give wrong answers. Commissioners of R&D must take into account the possible knock-on effects to an entire health service (which financially far outweigh those of funding studies) of faulty evidence when deciding how to invest in R&D (study type, outcomes, study power, replicating studies etc.).

Under the new paradigm, commissioned R&D is, perforce, a multidisciplinary collaborative effort. The driving force is the commissioners and the research team. Also involved should be health professionals and managers at the location where the work is taking place. The researchers will be the experts in the technical aspects of the research. However, we have noted in previous chapters that a deep understanding of research methods, as currently perceived, is insufficient to drive change-promoting R&D. We have also noted the tensions that arise when researchers who believe themselves to be theory enhancers are confronted with the exigencies of change promotion. The cultural gap is two-way, for many who might be involved in commissioning and implementation are suspicious of some of the exacting niceties demanded by researchers. The purpose of this chapter is to demystify research. But first let us be clear what we seek to accomplish and what we do *not* attempt.

In this chapter little prior knowledge of research is assumed. We explore some issues attending study design. In particular, we outline the strengths and limitations of commonly employed approaches. We also examine some of the techniques used to analyse and aid the interpretation of study findings. The emphasis is upon the conceptual basis of research: that is, on the deeper 'why' rather than the mechanical 'how'. Thus, this chapter is not a manual of research methods but a commentary on research which we hope may usefully be read before delving into detailed texts or embarking on commissioning the skills of professional researchers. Established researchers will find nothing fundamentally new. However, on reading this chapter they might perceive some subtle differences from the familiar; these arise by viewing research from the perspective of change promotion rather than that of theory enhancement.

5.1 From questions to methods

In Chapter 4 we stressed the importance of spending time, and consulting widely, to develop well posed research questions. We noted that well posed questions inherently presuppose the type of answers that might be expected. One should know before the study is conducted what one would recognize as valid answers. It is as if beforehand nature is in an uncertain state where the whole range of valid answers is possible, and doing the study forces nature to choose and thereby collapse the range to the particular answer that emerges. We noted that when quantitative answers are expected it is helpful to visualize how they may appear expressed in tabular or pictorial form. Moreover, one should at this stage determine the actions that will follow from particular configurations of answer. This last is beneficial in any kind of research; it is vital to change-promoting R&D because the whole exercise is driven by the desire to make choices about the use of resources. These points are illustrated in Box 5.1.

In the theory-enhancing paradigm of science the kinds of questions asked will centre upon 'why?' and 'how?'; arising from these will be concern for delineating pathways of cause and effect. Our change-promoting paradigm inherently demands questions concerning the support for, and the risks and benefits of, pursuing resource use options. These can be expressed in various ways and some are illustrated in Box 5.2. The first three questions are evaluative: they test options against stated goals, and hence our claims in the first chapter that the new paradigm is underpinned by the theory of evaluation. The fourth is exploratory: to document experience and learn from it. The final question concerns risk management. However, none of the questions is particularly usable as it stands. There is a need for explicit criteria by which to evaluate the results of studies driven by these questions. Some markers that such criteria could use are illustrated in Box 5.3.

The outcomes shown in Box 5.3 remain quite general. Each needs to be made yet more explicit so that specific measurables and measurements may be identified. Nevertheless, it is at this level of generality that the decisions about what it is important to study are made. For example, if a therapeutic approach is being evaluated then it is clear that there are

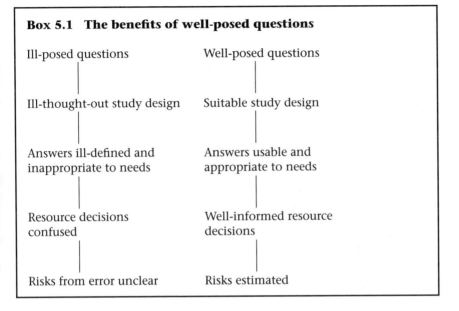

Box 5.1   The benefits of well-posed questions

Ill-posed questions   Well-posed questions

Ill-thought-out study design   Suitable study design

Answers ill-defined and   Answers usable and
inappropriate to needs   appropriate to needs

Resource decisions   Well-informed resource
confused   decisions

Risks from error unclear   Risks estimated

Box 5.2   Broad questions arising in the change-promoting paradigm

1 Does this way of doing things accomplish what it purports?
2 Is this way of doing something preferable to another way?
3 What is the best way of doing this? (There may be ideal methods which are unaffordable, or others less costly but still adequate. Thus the 'best' may be a trade-off among a number of considerations.)
4 What lessons can we learn from implementing this change that we might pass to others?
5 What would be the likely consequences if our (well-designed) study misleads us (politically, financially, clinically)?

---

many more patient-centred measures to consider than just clinical outcome. Indeed, even if the therapy is technically efficacious the benefit actually accruing to the eligible population will be influenced by uptake, which itself is influenced by patients' perceptions and the ease of access to the service. Similarly, resource implications will be important matters for consideration when a decision about the implementation of the therapy as a routine is decided. Thus, thought should be given as to whether to collect cost information concurrently with the clinical evaluation, which is usually better, or to gather it some other way (e.g. retrospectively).

It is only after these matters are decided that it is practicable to begin designing a study or a set of related sub-studies. In given circumstances

---

Box 5.3   Examples of moving towards more explicit outcomes

Patient/client centred
- clinical outcome, e.g. alleviation of symptoms, achievement of immunity
- perceptions of and satisfaction with service
- quality of life (e.g. as measured by QALY)
- function and coping: physical, mental and social
- demand on services (e.g. requests for primary care consultations)
- accessibility and uptake of service (e.g. in screening programmes)
- etc.

Health professional generated
- choices and pathways of care
- patterns of prescribing
- bed usage
- theatre usage
- etc.

Costs relating to resources consumed
- fixed costs
- variable costs
- costs related to outcome, e.g. cost–utility
- etc.

Change management issues for implementation of services
- identifying promoting factors
- identifying blocking factors
- etc.

---

there may be an optimum approach but it should be borne in mind that no design, however well executed, guarantees a risk-free answer. Usually there is a considerable potential flexibility of approach even within such a seemingly well specified class of design as the randomized controlled trial (see below). The final design will always be a trade-off between time, cost and the risk of an equivocal or even a wrong answer. Thus, there is a need for resource managers commissioning R&D to understand the full implications of the chosen study design.

In the next section we discuss the seemingly irreconcilable qualitative and quantitative approaches to research and emerge with a pragmatic view that aids change-promoting research.

5.2 Qualitative/quantitative: the great divide?

The new paradigm does not respect the boundaries of existing disciplines involved in R&D. It demands at least multidisciplinary collaboration and preferably a synthesis from the various disciplinary strands into a coherent new discipline. The former is beginning to happen but the latter is some way off. Elsewhere in this book we examine some of the promoting factors for and impediments to multidisciplinarity. Here we discuss one major obstacle: the apparently irreconcilable divide between qualitative and quantitative research methods. The utility of our paradigm depends crucially upon seeking the broadest understanding of both the humanistic and the mechanistic factors involved in the researching, planning, development and implementation of health service delivery. On the basis of our experience we are confident in asserting that this understanding cannot be achieved without employing both qualitative and quantitative methods. Box 5.4 displays a comparison of these methods.

The divide appears to arise through academic snobbishness on one side and deliberate obfuscation on the other, though debate on the issue is dressed in arcane philosophical argument. People on the quantitative side of health services research see themselves, wrongly, as scientists. They model themselves and their expectations on the hugely successful physical sciences. Theory in physical science is invariably expressed mathematically and measurement is inevitably quantitative. Further, the biological sciences have become quantitative through, on the one hand, their partial reduction to molecular chemistry and, on the other hand, the ability of mathematics to model complicated Mendelian genetics, epidemic spread, prey–predator relations etc. Even domains such as the human mind are not immune to mathematical analysis or mimicry, with artificial intelligence becoming a major branch of computing science. Thus the bandwagon of mathematization is seemingly unstoppable. Disciplines which do not reduce everything to numbers are seen as inferior: qualitative research is obviously trite and worthless. There is some truth in this; from our viewpoint as outsiders we perceive some of what passes as qualitative research to be trivial, incompetent, derivative, pretentious and inconsequential. However, from the firmer ground of our involvement in quantitative research we assert the same to be true of much that emanates from those who consider themselves scientists. The further problem is that those who know or understand little of either way perceive quantitative methods to be the 'big guns' because they appear especially difficult to people who are not numerate, whereas, superficially, qualitative methods appear to be easy and thus readily criticized by anyone.

Those promoting qualitative methods have adopted a defensive stance. They have sought respectability by producing lengthy justifications and pursuing nit-picking scholarly arguments. Theories underlying qualitative research have proliferated and some are inimical to the mainstream beliefs of scientists. These matters are not our concern, for the qualitative disciplines have as much right to their version of theory-enhancing as quantitative ones. What does concern us is pragmatically

Box 5.4 A comparison of the main features of qualitative and quantitative methods

	Qualitative methods	Quantitative methods
Purpose	For gathering and handling data consisting of people's utterances, writing, drawing and body language.	For gathering and handling data that may be expressed using the properties of numbers (classification, ordinality etc.).
Application	To gain insight into people's knowledge, beliefs, attitudes and behaviours without imposing rigid prior constraints as to possible outcomes (as may be the case with quantitative questionnaires). Their use is mainly observational and analytic.	Applicable to all enquiries about people and things where it makes sense to invoke the properties of numbers. Their use may be in observational or experimental studies.
Typical study	An in-depth enquiry of a relatively small number of people (subjects) – at most tens, not hundreds. Usually the interviews are taped, transcribed and then explored for themes common to the subjects and for differences among the subjects. The process of exploration follows a rigorously defined and documented discipline.	A clinical trial of the efficacy of a drug using outcome measures such as length of disease remission, pain relief scales, quality of life scales. Such studies would involve at least tens of subjects, often hundreds. Analysis would follow statistical and economic principles.
Typical presentation of findings	A prose account of the identified themes and the connections between them. This will be supported by selected quotations from the subjects.	Tables, graphs and charts of numerical data together with a commentary on what they show.
Generalizability	The findings may be generalizable in the sense that they provide insights which can be carried over to other people, but not usually in any quantitative manner. The notion of representative sampling is given little emphasis.	Most quantitative studies seek to extrapolate their findings in a numerical fashion to some wider population of which the subjects are a sample. Hence, a strong emphasis on sampling methods and statistical inference from samples.
Weaknesses	Lack of clarity about what may be generalized. Not objective or necessarily striving to be objective. The reader of a qualitative report may have difficulty	Many important aspects of human experience are not readily reduced to quantitative measurables. Moreover, investigators may impose prior

	deciding whether he or she would have come to similar conclusions if duplicating the study or reanalysing the data, or attempting to implement the conclusions in another setting.	expectations on the kinds of responses (e.g. in closed questionnaires) sought, which deny the possibility of the subjects revealing the richness and complexity of their experience, and may therefore be completely irrelevant to the complexities of change management.
Strengths	Put fewer prior constraints than quantitative methods on the experiences to be revealed. An excellent way of capturing the richness and complexity of human experience.	Strive to be objective in the sense that others following the prescribed method should reach similar findings (replicability). Findings generalizable with quantitative estimates of error (e.g. confidence limits).
Examples of contributions within the new paradigm	1 To assist in reaching consensus on research priorities, research questions for particular studies and the selection of appropriate methods. 2 To explore the richness of an area before committing to the necessary rigidity of a quantitative study. This may help in the formulation of really useful research questions. 3 To broaden the picture of patient/client knowledge, expectations, attitudes, demands, satisfaction and quality of life. 4 Useful for in-depth exploratory studies to guide the construction of quantitative instruments such as closed questionnaires. It also helps in constructing questions in language that makes sense to participants. 5 To add the intangible human dimension to what would otherwise be mechanistic, narrow and rigid evaluation. 6 To guide the documentation of experience during the implementation of innovative services.	1 To explore the relationships between recorded processes and events. 2 To study knowledge, attitudes, expectations, demands, satisfaction and quality of life among relatively large numbers of people. 3 To evaluate the quantifiable aspects of service options, such as relating costs to numerically measurable outcomes. 4 To quantify risks involved in resource management decisions.

taking from the qualitative approach what is useful to change-promoting research.

In Box 5.4 we note that one of the weaknesses of quantitative research is its inability to capture the full richness of human thought and expression. Particularly when one is looking at patient/client knowledge, expectations, satisfaction etc., there is a risk that the investigators impose their own ideas of what is important on their subjects. Thus it is possible to produce a very nice closed-question questionnaire that nevertheless misses the issues important to the subjects and in which there is an implicit assumption that the subjects think about those and other issues in the same manner as the investigators. Such questionnaires can be administered to precisely defined random samples of subjects and the responses analysed with the full rigour of statistical methods. Inferences with margins of error (e.g. confidence intervals) may be made about the population from which the subjects were drawn. But if the enquiry is missing the point then the result is precise but spurious. In evaluation of service developments the broad human dimension is of as great importance as clinical outcomes and costs. A service might operate to the satisfaction of health professionals but not be meeting the requirements of its users. Lay perceptions, attitudes, demands, values and so on influence how a service will be used (e.g. uptake) and how well it meets expectations. Thus, any evaluation must take these fully into account. Moreover, resource-managers and investigators should not assume that lay perceptions and behaviours follow the same logic as their own. Similarly, when one is trying to document and learn from the implementation of a service it is not sufficient to note significant events; the feelings, beliefs and behaviour of the participants in the change (e.g. health professionals and managers) are important determinants of how the desired outcome is reached.

Qualitative methods offer a way of exploring these humanistic issues without imposing rigid prior expectations from the investigators. They necessarily involve lengthy discourse between the investigators and individual subjects or groups of subjects. Thus, it is not feasible to investigate large numbers of people – nor is it necessary. Qualitative investigators seek to identify commonalities (themes, or patterns of response widely held) and differences between their subjects. They seek to identify the relationships between the themes and to synthesize an understanding of how the subjects think about the issues at hand. Perhaps the thought processes of qualitative investigators are closer to those of novelists than to those of quantitative scientists. Few would deny that novels can encapsulate a profound understanding of human experience. We do not wish to push the analogy too far, but it is fair to say that qualitative research is potentially every bit as rigorous as quantitative scientific research or writing novels. However, there are serious differences across the divide. Quantitative researchers feel unhappy that some qualitative research is not readily replicable; this occurs in part because the investigator during both fieldwork and analysis cannot attain the degree of detachment from the subjects that is sought in quantitative research. Also of concern is the fact that qualitative research pays scant attention to sampling issues, and does not often seek generalizability other than in a nebulous manner (insights).

In arrogating what is useful in qualitative research to the change-promoting paradigm we make some demands on qualitative researchers. We definitely need some generalizability and this in part depends on how subjects are selected. The purpose of using qualitative methods within our paradigm is wholly practical. We want usable knowledge and insights that help to guide decisions. Thus, if we are to use qualitative methods to understand, say, patient perceptions of the important issues in quality of care, we need to sample patients who represent a diverse range of characteristics. To do otherwise is to risk missing important perceptions shared by sub-groups of patients and perhaps related to age, education or ethnicity. Thus, some kind of formal sampling is required; it is not sufficient to gather a 'sample of convenience', i.e. people who happen to be readily available. Random sampling is in some respects ideal, but with small samples it does not guarantee representation across the range of characteristics of the study population: chance alone can lead to very non-representative choices. An alternative might be strati-fied random sampling: that is, randomly drawing samples from within each separate identifiable sub-group of the study population. There is also purposive sampling, which does not claim randomness but delib-erately seeks individuals with particular characteristics; closely related is quota sampling. Randomness is not important in this context, for we are not seeking to use sampling theory to extrapolate in a quantitative man-ner to the whole study population. Representation is important and, as we have shown, is a concept distinct from randomness.

The demand for representation implies that commissioned qualit-ative studies are likely to need more subjects than sometimes are ap-proached by qualitative researchers. It is hard to see how a sample of ten, even one very carefully purposively chosen, could encompass key features of a heterogeneous patient/client population. Thus, when one is employing qualitative methods within the paradigm it may, for re-source reasons, be necessary to sacrifice depth of interviews for breadth of coverage.

5.3 An overview of qualitative techniques well suited to R&D

Box 5.5 summarizes the features of some qualitative methods that have particular relevance to R&D under the new paradigm. In some respects we are, by bringing these together separately from quantitative methods,

Box 5.5 Qualitative techniques particularly relevant to R&D

Technique	*Examples of use*	*Strengths*	*Weaknesses*
Observation The investigator watches, listens and records the unfolding events in a systematic manner; this is often called ethnography. The observations may be structured or unstructured.	1 To observe and document behaviour and arrive at insights explaining it. 2 To observe change as in the development of a service and learn how it may be effected more easily when rolled out elsewhere.	1 Findings not constrained by prior conceptions. 2 Does not depend on people being willing to participate actively in research (e.g. be interviewed). 3 It records events as they happen and does not depend on people's later recollection.	1 Units of study (e.g. workplace) limited by intensity and duration of observation. 2 Observer bias cannot be excluded. 3 The process of observing (if known to the subjects) may alter the behaviour of those being observed.
Participant observation Similar to the above but the observer is also a participant in the events being observed. Variants depend on whether or not the observer reveals his role to the group.	As in 1 and 2 above.	1 As in 1–3 above. 2 It is a powerful means of aiding the observer to understand the experiences of the subjects and their meanings to the subjects.	1 As in 1–3 above. 2 It is hard to form a detached view if one is an actor on the stage.
Unstructured interviews Individuals are encouraged to express their experiences, feelings etc. in their own words. The interviewer	Studies to understand people's perceptions about health services.	1 Helpful when exploring sensitive issues. 2 Opportunity to explore and probe in response to	1 Time consuming so number of subjects limited and issue of representation arises.

when necessary but does not work from a rigid script.

	Use	Advantages	Disadvantages
Focus groups These are unstructured (or partially structured) interviews with small groups of people. The people respond to each other and to the group leader. Typically the group will contain from five to fifteen subjects.	1 Useful for understanding people's perceptions of services. 2 A 'market research' tool when developing or implementing a service.	1 Group dynamics stimulate discussion. 2 Less labour-intensive than the corresponding number of individual interviews (at least at the data collection stage if not the analysis).	1 Dominating individuals may inhibit more reticent members. 2 People may not wish to be seen to be going against peer views. 3 Lack of confidentiality, which may inhibit responses on delicate topics.
Case studies These focus on a single instance or very small number of instances for in-depth scrutiny. Thus the study units could be people (e.g. service consumers), one or more clinics or the implementation of a service. Data may be gathered retrospectively, at a point in time or prospectively. Data may be observations, interviews and material abstracted from documents.	Useful at the exploratory stage of R&D. Help to gain insight into issues that may need to be explored in greater depth and taken into account during service development and implementation.	1 Relatively inexpensive. 2 Able to uncover detail in complicated situations.	It is unsafe to generalize from these studies.

Technique	Examples of use	Strengths	Weaknesses
Consensus methods These are used to establish the extent of agreement among experts when objective evidence is incomplete or inconclusive. They can also be used to develop consensus. Some methods use consensus panels of various kinds where experts are brought together. The Delphi technique uses an iterative series of mailed questionnaires using open questions.	1 In establishing the extent of agreed knowledge or practice and in identifying issues that should be subject to R&D. 2 In agreeing the research strategy for a particular issue. 3 In refining the research questions and methods for a particular study. 4 In agreeing and defining the implications for good practice ensuing from a programme of R&D.	1 They acknowledge the value of experience in supplementing objective evidence. 2 Winning the hearts and minds of key individuals who could be instrumental in promoting or blocking the proposed R&D and any subsequent development and implementation. 3 The Delphi technique permits anonymity among the experts which may enable some to be more open in their responses.	1 The outcome may be dependent on the choice of experts. The greater the uncertainty the more likely this will be. 2 There is the danger that a consensus opinion will be accepted too readily as a justification for practice when the state of knowledge is such as to require further R&D.

not operating wholly in the spirit of the new paradigm. However, the full integration of qualitative and quantitative research methods into a new whole forming the basis of methods for R&D will need more labour by us and others. Thus, for the time being we use the divide for convenience, while knowing that it does not really exist. Moreover, even within the context of the methods listed in Box 5.5 there is a coexistence of qualitative and quantitative approaches; it is just that the emphasis is towards the non-numerical. For example, case studies are not restricted to gathering qualitative data. In seeking to understand the case under scrutiny (e.g. the working of a clinic), the researcher may draw upon evidence from observation, testimony, written records and numerical material (e.g. workload and patient waiting time after arrival).

It is evident from Box 5.5 that there is a wide variety of methods available, and most of those, when explored in greater detail, will be found to have important variants of design, execution and analysis; it is beyond our scope to go into this in detail. Those commissioning qualitative research either alone or to complement a primarily quantitative study should bear in mind that just as much effort should be expended on setting the research questions and choosing an appropriate design as for quantitative research. This entails dialogue with the prospective researchers. It demands a clear understanding of what the chosen method can and cannot deliver. Further, because qualitative research is much less mechanical than quantitative research and inherently more subjective, much depends upon being able to place faith in the judgement of the researcher.

The role of consensus methods deserves special emphasis. R&D is done to diminish uncertainty. Yet uncertainty is not eradicable and thus must be managed. Consensus methods are a powerful and structured means to capture, use and direct (towards consensus) expert opinion. The process of seeking consensus, which might nevertheless not be attained, helps to make explicit what the issues are, as long as the known range of opinion is properly represented. Thus, it is a useful tool for generating research priorities, for refining study questions, for agreeing on appropriate methods and for agreeing actions that should flow from completed R&D. It is a more formal form of the wide consultation that was recommended in Chapter 4. Moreover, one should not underestimate the importance of the side-effect of consensus consultation: bringing on board influential individuals upon whose interest and goodwill the change management process may depend.

5.4 Evaluation: the concept

Referring back to Box 5.2, we observe that the first three broad areas of question that arise under the new paradigm concern evaluation. This

---

Box 5.6   Evaluating health services effectiveness

Definition
The critical assessment, on as objective a basis as possible, of the degree to which entire services or their component parts (e.g. diagnostic tests, treatments, caring procedures) fulfil stated goals.

Key elements
1 Reference to goals makes explicit that there is to be comparison of a service or procedure with some standard. That standard might be:
   • absolute (e.g. attaining 95 per cent pertussis immunization uptake);
   • relative (e.g. whether or not a new therapy is equal or better to existing therapies).
2 Objectivity is required so that findings are not based merely on opinion or trust and are open to scrutiny, criticism and attempts at replication.
3 There is an implicit requirement that there exist valid indicators of outcome to be compared with the goals. The goals must also be expressible in a measurable way.
4 It is implicit when evaluating the effectiveness of entire services that it is not sufficient to show that each of the component parts meets its goals. Clearly such is a necessary condition, but the effectiveness of the whole also depends on other factors, e.g.
   • the manner in which the service is managed (process);
   • its acceptability and accessibility to the client population (uptake);
   • its impact on overall population well-being (cost/benefit).

---

is so because each involves comparison between what is happening now and either an absolute goal or some other way of doing things. In the next few sections of this chapter we develop the concept of evaluation and outline the principles underlying some methods of evaluation.

In *Evaluating Health Services' Effectiveness*[1] we introduced a definition of evaluation in the context of health services. This is displayed in Box 5.6. Two key features are that, first, evaluation involves testing performance against goals (absolute or relative) and, second, it should seek to be objective and therefore (in principle) replicable.

It should be borne in mind that the concept of evaluation is much broader than its application to R&D. Box 5.7 displays a variety of uses. The first two instances (clinical trials and effectiveness studies) properly belong within R&D. The remaining instances are part of the routine management of health services (*for which R&D itself is a tool*). However, each of items 3 to 8 in Box 5.7 may itself be subject to evaluation (e.g. comparing ways of doing accreditation), and such evaluation is a legitimate element of the R&D programme.

Box 5.1 The Scope of Evaluation

Context of evaluation	Uses	Typical methods
1 Clinical trials	Efficacy of treatments, caring regimens and the like	Randomized controlled trials
2 Effectiveness studies	Judging the effectiveness of entire services	Randomized controlled trials, comparison of matched examples, before and after studies, case–control studies, mathematical modelling
3 Efficiency studies	Examining the use of manpower and financial resources	Observational studies, financial audit
4 Clinical audit	Determining whether clinical practice is meeting acceptable standards	The audit cycles, i.e. agree standards, measure performance, compare performance to standards, review practice
5 Quality assurance monitoring	Ensuring that services are delivered according to standards specified in a contract	Comparing easily measured outcomes (e.g. postoperative wound infection rates) against the specified standards
6 Accreditation of teams or institutions	Ensuring that the unit has the necessary expertise and other resources to be capable of delivering a product of acceptable standard	Setting and insisting upon acceptable minimum standards, e.g. of individual training, availability and maintenance of equipment
7 Accreditation of individuals	Ensuring that health professionals (including managers) have demonstrated the necessary knowledge and aptitude to function at an acceptable level	Rite of passage through examinations and, for renewable accreditation, regular systematic scrutiny of performance
8 Clinical governance	Overall responsibility to ensure that services meet high standards	Draws upon all the above instances of evaluation

5.5 Building blocks for evaluation

In this section two concepts are introduced which help in clarifying how evaluations may be approached. The first, due to Donabedian,[2] is to distinguish between *structure, process and outcome*. This is particularly valuable when one is considering the evaluation of services. The second concept is that of *levels of evaluation*. This is the identification of critical sub-units for evaluation within a complicated process, recognizing that the outcome from a service can be assessed at different levels.

Structure is the physical assets that enable the service to be provided, and how they are configured, e.g. people, buildings and equipment. Process is how things are done within the service, e.g. referral arrangements, clinic organization, decision pathways and flow of information within and from the service. Outcome is the effect a service has on its clients and the population from which they are drawn. These are illustrated in Box 5.8 with an example drawn from childhood immunization services.

The goal of an immunization service is to provide protection to individuals and (through herd immunity) to the community as a whole. If any components of structure, process or outcome are flawed then achievement of the goals may be hindered. At best the goals may be achieved but not in a cost-efficient manner. Box 5.9 illustrates the effects of flawed structure and process in the context of an immunization service.

When one is evaluating a complicated service the task might be simplified by the identification of critical elements and the relations among them. These elements may be evaluated separately. Indeed, it might not be necessary, or practicable, to evaluate in terms of the overall outcome from the service. Thus, in the case of a childhood immunization service, evaluation in terms of the ultimate outcome – morbidity – is extremely difficult. In the UK mortality from childhood infectious disease is so low that mortality statistics are in most cases a very poor proxy measure for overall morbidity (fatal and non-fatal). Routinely available infectious disease notifications are notoriously poor quantitative indicators, and are really only of use in identifying gross trends such as the occurrence of an epidemic. Building a robust surveillance system suitable for a rigorous evaluation of morbidity outcome would be very costly. Nevertheless, the outcome can be assessed at different levels. Box 5.10 illustrates this. Thus, if a vaccine is known to have efficacy in a given schedule it is necessary only to evaluate whether it is being appropriately delivered to the client population.

A consequence of the above is that when one is contemplating the evaluation of an existing service, or a proposed new one, time is well spent analysing the service in terms of its goals, the expected outcomes and the features of the structure and process which deliver those outcomes (see Chapters 2 and 3 in *Evaluating Health Services' Effectiveness*). Only after this is it sensible to embark on designing studies.

Box 5.8   Structure, process and outcome

Definitions	*Examples in the context of a child immunization service*
Structure The assets needed for there to be a service and their configuration • people, buildings, equipment	Management staff Clinical staff (doctors, nurses etc.) Support staff (receptionists, clerks, information technicians, cleaners) Computer systems and database of clients Service base and clinic sites (permanent, temporary, shared or mobile) Refrigerators Consumables (vaccines, syringes, etc.)
Process How the service is delivered • organization and management, day by day activity	Maintenance of database and scheduled invitation to clients Staff duty rosters Ordering vaccines and supplying to clinics Quality control on vaccine storage and expiry Collation of records from clinics and reconciliation with the database Staff training and professional development Audit
Outcome What the service delivers to individuals and to the population as a whole • promoting health, protection, reassurance, cure, disease control, amelioration, care	High degree of protection of individual children against specific diseases Reassurance of parents If uptake of service high (say 90 per cent) then general herd immunity damps down incipient epidemics of communicable disease and thus gives partial protection to the unimmunized

Box 5.9   How flaws in structure and process influence outcome in a child immunization service

	Examples of flaws	Consequence
Structure	Too few clinic sites or in wrong locations	Poor uptake of service
	Insufficient staff in key posts	Bottlenecks in service, errors through pressure, poor delivery, unfavourable perception by parents, reduced uptake
Process	Database incomplete or out of date	Eligible population not covered
	Poor quality control on vaccine storage and delivery	Vaccine of reduced efficacy if stored too long or at wrong temperature.
		Vaccine unavailable when required. Some parents will not bring their children back.
	Poor record keeping or slow collation of information	Database inaccurate about partially completed immunisation courses
		Management in weak position if negligence alleged
	Poor staff training	Mistakes, parents get unfavourable perception of service, reduced uptake, litigation
Outcome		Anything that reduces coverage, uptake or the efficacy of the vaccines results in fewer children being protected and less likelihood of benefiting from herd immunity

5.6 Some methods used in evaluation

In this section commonly used methods of evaluation are presented in overview. Some of these are examined in greater detail in subsequent sections. Box 5.11 presents a means of comparing and contrasting the methods.

The randomized controlled trial (RCT) is presented first because it is the technique with which the investigator has the strongest possibility

Box 5.10   Levels of evaluation for a childhood immunization service

Outcome	Comments
1 Vaccine efficacy – theoretical	This is an essential prerequisite. It may be established in clinical trials. The outcome measures may be in terms of morbidity. However, there is little point in long-term follow-up of morbidity unless it is first established that the vaccine evokes an appropriately strong immune response as may be measured by laboratory tests. Also important is establishing the most beneficial schedule of immunization – age of client, number of immunizations, interval between. If the vaccine is already established as efficacious then it suffices to evaluate a service at one or more of the levels below.
2 Vaccine efficacy – in practice	This raises issues such as how well the vaccine travels, i.e. how much mishandling it can withstand before losing efficacy. There is the question of whether the optimal schedule can be maintained in practice and the consequences of deviation from the schedule. To establish this it may be necessary to perform immunological tests on samples of the client population who have received immunization in a routine manner rather than as part of a rigorously managed clinical trial.
3 Delivery of vaccine	The degree to which an acceptable (if not optimum) schedule is being maintained in those who take up the service.
4 Coverage of the service	The accuracy of the eligible client database and the timeliness and quality of its updating. Clearly the potential population impact depends vitally on this even if the vaccine is perfect.
5 Uptake of the service	The degree to which eligible clients participate. Evaluation may entail exploration of client perceptions about the service and their ease of access to it.

Outcome	Comments
6 Immune status of the eligible population	This is influenced by both the immunization programme and naturally occurring immunity, the latter being a failure of the programme. See also 2 above.
7 Non-fatal morbidity	Usually difficult and costly to establish.
8 Fatality	An inappropriate outcome measure for most infectious diseases in developed countries. A useful measure in developing countries where mortality is often high. Its utility depends on the sophistication of death registration.

of eliminating bias from the findings. All the study designs, including the RCT, are subject to bias. This bias arises from unknown or unmeasurable characteristics of the study units (e.g. people) which have an influence on the outcome to be measured and are distributed differently among the interventions being compared. These characteristics are known as confounding factors. Clearly, if confounding factors are known and measurable they can be accounted for in the design of the study by, for example, stratifying (grouping) study units according to the values of the characteristic (e.g. male and female). This principle applies equally to randomized and to non-randomized studies. Confounding is an issue that is particularly important in the study of aggregate biological material such as humans and their institutions. Scientists in laboratories working with tissue samples from a strain of rats or with non-living matter have far less to worry about because their working materials are inherently more homogeneous. Entire human beings, particularly when viewed in the broadest context of their behaviours, interactions and lifestyles, are exceedingly varied and complicated. Their propensity to develop disease and their responses to therapies are influenced by myriad factors which investigators cannot hope to control. The problem arises because the combined influence of these factors upon outcome is sometimes of the same order of magnitude or greater than that of the effect being sought from an intervention.

As an illustration consider the example of a case–control study given in Box 5.11. The women may have been matched in terms of age. But what if other factors, such as social class and lifestyle, were ignored? Cigarette smoking is known to be statistically associated with the risk of developing cervical cancer. This may be a direct effect and/or it may be mediated through lifestyle factors (such as the number of sexual partners) which themselves directly increase the risk and are more likely in smokers than non-smokers. If the investigators had not troubled to take

Box 5.11 Methods of evaluation

Method	Application	Strengths	Weaknesses
Randomized controlled trial (RCT) Study units (people, GP practices etc.) are allocated at random among two or more different interventions. Follow-up measurements are made on the study units to enable comparison of the outcomes from the interventions. Within the umbrella of random allocation there are many variants of the RCT which seek to enhance the statistical precision of the comparisons while keeping the number of study units reasonable. One such is the factorial design, which, for example, allows the estimation of the effects of therapies alone and concurrently and of the manner in which they may interact to potentiate or diminish the joint effect.	RCTs are widely (but not universally) regarded as the only acceptable means of evaluating the efficacy of vaccines, therapies and caring regimens; particularly of innovations, where there cannot be any ethical objection to withholding a supposedly established procedure. They can also be employed to evaluate services (such as breast screening) and health promotion interventions.	RCTs are true experiments which in principle allow cause and effect relations to be imputed. The random allocation to interventions helps to minimize bias arising from characteristics of the study units, which are not known to the investigator, being distributed unevenly among the interventions.	Random allocation cannot guarantee lack of bias. RCTs of therapies are often conducted on people who conform to strict clinical criteria. Hence the findings do not always generalize well to routine practice employing those therapies. A way around this is to conduct pragmatic trials (see text). The further removed from study units of individual people the more costly and logistically difficult it becomes to conduct RCTs.

Method	Application	Strengths	Weaknesses
Use of historical controls The outcomes for prospectively recruited study units are compared to the recorded outcomes of similar study units which underwent an alternative intervention in some other trial or as part of routine practice.	This technique has been applied to therapeutic trials but most commentators now abhor the practice. This is because there is rarely an excuse not to randomize prospectively in a therapeutic trial and thus gain the considerable benefits mentioned above. The use of historical controls may be justified when the type of study unit makes it impracticable to randomize. However, a prospective non-randomized trial is preferable.	Less costly than an RCT. This design may be able reliably to detect dramatically large benefits, such as when penicillin was introduced. Such a 'breakthrough' is rare.	Despite the care taken in selecting historical controls it is impossible to know that like is being compared with like. Contrast this with the RCT, which through its design promises, on average, to deliver unbiased results.
Prospective comparison of matched study units The study units are assessed on all seemingly relevant measurable criteria and	If random allocation to interventions is not practicable then this is a	It maintains prospective comparison and thus minimizes temporal effects,	Control of bias depends wholly on the ingenuity of the investigator. The design

assigned to interventions in such a way that foreseeable bias is minimized.	good alternative. Its use is most justified when the study units are services rather than individual clients. When the number of study units is necessarily small this method may be preferable to random allocation, since bias is more likely to arise by chance in this circumstance.	as could arise from the use of historical controls.	is inherently biased, whereas the RCT is inherently, on average, unbiased.
Before-and-after studies These entail examining structure, process and outcome of a service, then making changes to the service and noting the effects. There may be multiple study units which could have been selected randomly from the population of potential study units. This random selection makes the selected units more likely to be representative but does not remove other potential biases.	This design is useful for evaluating service changes in circumstances when an RCT would not be practicable. It is not suited to the evaluation of therapies.	Comparison is maintained. This is usually less costly than an RCT.	It is difficult to eliminate coincidental temporal effects (e.g. changes in practice that were happening anyway) as explanations of identified changes.

Method	Application	Strengths	Weaknesses
Cross-over studies These are before-and-after studies in which some study units begin on intervention 1 and later cross to intervention 2, whereas other study units begin on intervention 2 and cross later to intervention 1. This technique can also be incorporated within RCTs.	When allocation is not random this design is applicable in the same circumstances as before-and-after studies.	Comparison is maintained. Temporal effects are likely to be less troublesome than in a simple before-and-after study.	If the study units are not randomly allocated to the sequences of interventions then the usual issues of bias arise.
Retrospective follow-up studies These are follow-up studies that start from events in time past rather than from the present. The data used have already been documented, perhaps within some routine information system. The sequence of events is reconstructed from this information.	This design may be used in the same way as prospective non-randomized follow-up studies.	Pre-existing information is put to good use. Such studies may be extended beyond the present into the future, thus increasing follow-up time.	Investigators have no control over what has been recorded or the quality of the data. However, if follow-up is to proceed beyond the present the investigator may influence future data collection.

Case–control studies (also known as case–referent studies)			
These are most easily illustrated with an example. In order to assess the benefit of cervical cancer screening investigators have identified cancer cases and matched them to similar cancer-free women. They looked back into the medical histories of both groups to identify the women's screening histories. From this they could establish that the cancer-free women were more likely to have taken part in the screening programme.	This design is a powerful means of imputing (but not proving) cause and effect relationships. It can be employed in circumstances when a RCT is impracticable or might be considered unethical (as many say is the case for cervical screening). Sometimes this design is nested within a prospective study.	It is relatively cheap. An index of risk – the odds ratio – is obtainable. This approximates to the relative risk which might have been obtained from a corresponding prospective clinical trial.	When using retrospective data there is always the possibility of differential recall etc. between cases and controls. Care has to be taken to ensure that cases and controls are either individually or as groups comparable. There is always the possibility that hidden confounding factors are present.
Opportunistic studies – natural experiments			
If a change to service configuration is already decided its effects may be	Some changes in health services configuration (e.g. the introduction of primary	Taking an opportunity that might not otherwise arise.	The circumstances are never going to permit a 'perfect' evaluation. However,

Method	Application	Strengths	Weaknesses
systematically observed. Before-and-after comparison should be possible. If the change is not to be universal immediately there should be an opportunity to make comparison between changed and unchanged units.	care purchasing groups in the UK) are more politically driven than by empirical evidence. Nevertheless, this need not prevent an attempt at evaluation.		resource managers live in the real world and must use imperfect data to best advantage.
Qualitative techniques Many of the techniques listed in Box 5.5 can be used as evaluative tools in their own right. In addition they should be used within the methods outlined above to enrich the inevitably restricted information provided by quantitative tools.	Whenever outcomes concern the knowledge, beliefs, attitudes, perceptions, satisfaction, quality of life etc. of clients, patients and workers in the system (i.e. humanistic elements), there is a clear place for qualitative tools. We believe that most instances of evaluation require the humanistic perspective.	See Box 5.5.	See Box 5.5.

Economic analyses

There are a number of economic techniques that can be used in evaluations alongside the methods mentioned above. These are summarized in Box 5.15.	Many evaluations arise from a desire to use resources effectively and efficiently. Hence the question of costs related to output cannot be ignored.	See Box 5.15. It should be noted that economic analyses in the absence of humanistic considerations are sterile.

Mathematical modelling

Mathematical models and computer-based simulations seek to abstract the key features of services and how these interrelate. This enables the doing of 'what if?' analyses and the identification of critical elements upon which the outcome of the service depends. Modelling relates closely to the discipline called operational research. It is also commonly used by health economists.	These methods have been used to evaluate options for health promotion and screening programmes. Models have been used to predict the spread of HIV/ AIDS and help to decide how to target preventive resources. In breast and cervical cancer screening they have been used to explore the optimum call– recall interval. Modelling is useful as an initial stage before deciding whether it would be sensible to commit resources to developing and evaluating a new service.	Use of modelling forces a careful examination of the goals, assumptions, structures and processes of services which is of itself beneficial. It is much less costly than real experiments and can be done in circumstances when other forms of investigation would not be practicable. Gaps in knowledge identified while constructing a model can be an impetus for well focused research.

A model can only be as good as the assumptions it is based upon. Many models are of such complexity that their end clients (resource managers) have to take the findings on trust. In our view a manager should be wary of employing techniques which he or she is not in a position to critically appraise at a basic level; in this respect all the other techniques listed here are accessible. It is not possible to include humanistic factors in models.

account of smoking in the design or the analysis of their study, it is conceivable, indeed likely, that smokers would be overrepresented in the cervical cancer group. It is likely that smoking goes along with attitudes, behaviours and socio-economic opportunities (e.g. its higher prevalence among the lower social classes in the UK) that make women unreceptive to screening offers. Thus the cancer group contains women who were inherently at higher risk of developing cervical cancer and at the same time less likely to accept screening. This may lead to a gross overestimate of the benefits of screening and a gross underestimate of other important factors.

The RCT promises that on average unknown or unmeasurable confounding factors will be evenly distributed among the groups being compared. It is important to understand what 'on average' means. Random processes can produce unlikely outcomes. Thus, although tossing an unbiased coin 100 times will *on average* produce 50 heads and 50 tails, that exact distribution will rarely happen and extreme distributions, such as 80 heads and 20 tails, will occasionally happen. Usually the vagaries of chance will produce a distribution that is not cause for concern but in any particular instance there is, with respect to unmeasurable or unmeasured characteristics, no way of knowing this. The larger the study population the better the prospects that common confounders will be sufficiently evenly distributed among the intervention arms (groups). The RCT, through its very design, gives a strong prospect (but no guarantees) that unmeasured confounders will be untroublesome; the same cannot be said for any of the other designs. They are inherently biased until proven otherwise and such proof is impossible. Nevertheless, steps can be taken to limit bias so that there may be reasonable confidence in the findings from non-randomized studies. These are pursued later in this chapter.

The RCT may be regarded as the 'gold standard' for evaluation. Whenever one of the non-randomized study designs is used it is helpful to identify potential causes of bias that might have been minimized in a corresponding RCT, and to ask oneself how far from that ideal the present study is likely to be. However, the RCT should not be placed upon too high a pedestal. To do so is to devalue falsely the ability of other study designs to answer important questions and to ignore the fact that the RCT is often impracticable or for other reasons not the design of first choice.[3] We regard the RCT as merely one among many *option appraisal* tools available to followers of the change-promoting paradigm.

It should be noted that we have included qualitative methods in Box 5.11 in two different capacities: first, as evaluation tools in their own right; second, as enriching concomitants to quantitative designs. Economic techniques are similar, in that they should not exist in a vacuum. Information about costs is usually of little use to resource managers unless it in some way relates to outcome. Thus, our listing of separate evaluative techniques, though convenient, is artificial. We envisage most individual evaluative studies, or at least programmes of evaluative research, as encompassing humanistic and economic considerations.

The final item in Box 5.11, mathematical modelling, might seem too detached from reality to be useful. It is one of the points where the new paradigm and the theory-enhancing paradigm of science overlap, and confusion of intent may arise. However, the interpretation of mathematical models differs between the paradigms. For us such models are worth considering only if they are likely be useful, in the pragmatic sense, to resource managers. The initial stage of attempting to model a service can be extremely valuable because it forces careful thinking about what is going on. Moreover, it may identify gaps of knowledge that should be filled by empirical research. Modelling is not wholly abstract because models require information (arithmetical constants, the nature of the relationship between some variables etc.), which has to be obtained from empirical observation. At the early stages of considering the introduction of a new service (e.g. asymptomatic abdominal aortic aneurysm screening for elderly men), modelling can be extremely useful for determining the cost and benefit *ball park* (e.g. an order of magnitude estimate of the cost per quality adjusted life year (QALY) gained) and a feel for factors (e.g. effect of differing uptake of the service) that might critically affect delivery of population benefit at acceptable cost. These considerations alone may be sufficient to deter resource-managers from encouraging further development of an idea. On the other hand, if modelling gives encouraging answers then it is essential that any new development be empirically evaluated according to the principles enunciated above. The results of modelling are dependent upon the validity of the underlying assumptions. If altering the assumptions fairly widely (sensitivity analysis) has little effect on the conclusions, then one may have greater confidence in the model than otherwise. Better is when models using different approaches give similar findings and each is insensitive to deviations in the assumptions. Unfortunately, modelling can be a black art. It can be difficult for anyone other than the modellers to develop an intuitive feel, as a basis for their own critical analysis, for what is going on. At the very least the clients of such models should insist that every assumption, and the reasoning or evidence behind it, is made explicit. If it is still incomprehensible, ditch it.

5.7 The RCT: an option appraisal tool

Here we shall discuss the RCT in more detail. We have already indicated that the RCT is the preferable, indeed many would say only acceptable, design for the evaluation (option appraisal) of new therapies, procedures and caring regimens. The reason for this is that when the study unit is individual patients or clients there is rarely any excuse (either ethical or logistic) for saying that an RCT is impracticable. Hence it is imprudent to base resource decisions on designs that are inherently more likely to be biased than the RCT. When the study units become aggregates of people or entire services then the RCT is still applicable, preferable in principle, but not always possible to realize.

Clinical researchers were slow to adopt the well established, powerful and bias-minimizing study designs that had been in use for many decades in other disciplines. The principle of randomized allocation to treatments was well established in agricultural research long before the first clinical RCT in 1948; the first RCT evaluated the efficacy of streptomycin for treating tuberculosis. From agricultural research (whose statistical heroes include the late Sir Ronald Fisher) come the names of a number of randomized designs employed nowadays by clinical researchers: for example, randomized block, factorial, Latin square, split-plot (the idea underlying modern multilevel analysis) and incomplete block designs. The introduction of the RCT to medicine is credited to the late Sir Austin Bradford Hill. It took many years for RCTs to come into widespread use. Figures such as the late Professor Archie Cochrane, author of a seminal work,[4] spent considerable time proselytizing the need for evidence to underlie clinical practice and the role of the RCT in this. In some respects this very necessary emphasis on the RCT retarded the development of a broader view of evaluation. The role of non-randomized designs was underplayed and qualitative methods were largely eschewed by clinical researchers. Moreover, the emphasis on the technology of RCTs and their being perceived as tools of science meant that the broader view in the context of change management was overlooked. To this day this seems to be a widespread perspective, enshrined in what may be called the Oxford school of thought: an emphasis on evidence-based practice through so-called *clinical epidemiology* (an oxymoron), the collation of databases on RCTs, and a passion for meticulous[5] systematic reviews and meta-analyses of RCTs, all of which are supposed to change practice largely through passive diffusion of knowledge from the experts downwards. Having established that RCTs and their priesthood need not be viewed with reverence and awe, we look under the bonnet of RCTs a little more closely.

Box 5.12 displays the key steps that would be involved in almost any randomized clinical trial. The preliminary steps are vital in determining the success and usefulness of the trial. They must involve collaboration between the commissioners and the researchers. This is explained in detail in Chapter 4.

After the protocol has been drafted, the next step is to gain ethical approval from whichever body oversees these matters. In the UK each health authority services an ethics committee that has health professional and lay membership. There are arrangements for large national studies being undertaken at many sites to be ethically reviewed by a central committee, to obviate the need for many local committees to

Box 5.12   Outline of a therapeutic randomized controlled trial

Procedure	Comment
Preliminary work • agreeing the questions • agreeing that a quantitative method is appropriate • appraised options indicate the advantage of using a RCT • agree on humanistic and economic measures required to supplement the clinical outcomes • preparation of protocol	Under the new paradigm these preliminary steps involve collaboration between the commissioners and the researchers. This is discussed in detail in the previous chapter.
Obtain ethical approval • submit full study protocol and copies of any non-standard instruments (e.g. questionnaires) that will be used to an ethics committee	All clinical trials in the UK and in many other countries require approval by an ethics committee. These committees may be local, regional or national. The committees consider the balance of inconvenience and risk to trial participants against the benefit to the community of the knowledge that might be gained. They are guided by various legal and general ethical principles. They also review the procedure for obtaining informed consent. Any proposed subsequent deviation from an approved protocol must be discussed with the committee.
Select eligible subjects • use preset inclusion and exclusion criteria	Inclusion criteria state the diagnostic information necessary for a patient to be considered. They may also specify age, sex, ability to speak the main national language etc. Exclusion criteria include factors which might make it inadvisable to take part in the trial (e.g. pregnancy) or ones which might confuse the outcome (e.g. concurrent illness or disability).

Procedure	Comment
Obtain informed consent • written description of what will be involved etc. • oral description and answer questions • consent form to be signed	Informed consent is an issue that ethics committees pay close attention to. It is generally not too difficult to devise ways of seeking consent from intellectually unimpaired adults. Studies involving children require special consideration and the consent of the parents or guardian is needed. Studies involving mentally impaired people are, in the UK, unlikely to receive permission unless the study is related to the impairment and offers some prospect of benefit. In the UK people in custody would not generally be deemed able to make a truly free choice.
Allocate to a study arm • use a truly random procedure	This is the defining feature of the RCT. Note that sometimes there will be restricted randomization to ensure equal numbers in the study arms.
Treatment and follow-up • all procedures are documented in detail • follow-up outcome measures are taken • interim analysis may be required	During treatment and follow-up there must be documented procedures for identifying subjects who are responding badly to treatment (e.g. side-effects). These would be withdrawn from the trial and treated in whatever manner seems in their best individual interests. Such subjects should not, if possible, be withdrawn from non-intrusive follow-up (e.g. if length of survival is an issue). Some trials require independent interim analyses to ensure that subjects in one or more treatment arms are not at an ethically unsustainable disadvantage.

Procedure	Comment
Analysis This entails combining information on clinical outcome with humanistic and any economic measures that have been taken.	The principal analysis will usually be on 'an intention to treat' basis thus follow-up information may be needed for withdrawn subjects. Other sub-analyses may analyse by the actual treatment received (which may have changed from that to which the subject was initially allocated) and may look at sub-groups of the subjects (e.g. older and younger subjects).
Dissemination	By diverse routes (e.g. publications, conferences) among relevant clinical and managerial professionals. That this is done effectively is every bit as important as getting the technical aspects of the RCT right.
Implementation	A change management task made more easy because the trial has been designed with the needs of resource-managers in mind. Initial efforts at implementation should be well documented (e.g. through action research) and analysed so that later implementers may benefit from the experience.

review the proposal in detail. Ethical approval does not just apply to clinical trials. It is required for any study (including those using wholly qualitative methods) that could harm, inconvenience or embarrass patients. It is not usually necessary for non-controversial population surveys such as might be undertaken in health needs assessment or for routine clinical audit. However, when in doubt it is wise to have a word with the chairman of the local committee. Adequate preparation of the study protocol is essential. The committee will wish to see the information that is to be given to the subjects and to know how informed consent is to be obtained. It will need to know exactly what will be done to subjects. Potential risks and how they are to be monitored must be documented. The committee will also need to be informed of measuring instruments to be used (including questionnaires) and of any steps that have been taken to evaluate new instruments. Although not strictly concerned with the detailed vetting of the methodological soundness of studies, many committees take the view that unsound studies are unethical because they waste the subjects' time (and perhaps needlessly expose them to risk) and waste resources. Thus it is not unusual for them to question aspects of the design such as the study power (see below).

The selection of eligible subjects must be according to agreed criteria stated in the protocol; it is the responsibility of the trial manager to ensure that deviations from the protocol do not occur. Thus, the potential subjects will have defined personal characteristics (e.g. age) and their diagnosis will have been reached through a systematic procedure common to all the participating clinicians. Some otherwise eligible subjects may be excluded according to exclusion criteria. This is because clinical trials usually seek to answer a question about the efficacy of a procedure in as direct a way as possible. Coexisting illness or disability may confuse the outcomes. Subjects might be excluded (e.g. pregnant women where pregnancy is not the main issue) because it would be unacceptable to expose them (or a foetus) to any risk, however small, even though they might consent. Hence, we comment in Box 5.11 that RCTs do not necessarily generalize directly to what might happen in routine practice. Routine practice is unlikely to involve the systematic and rigorous appliance of the inclusion and exclusion criteria of an RCT. So it might happen that the outcomes (and the cost–utility ratio) for routinely selected patients will be disappointingly worse than the trial indicates; this will be especially so where treatment is not restricted to specialist centres (e.g. for cancer) and may be administered by a variety of practitioners (e.g. for asthma). There are two ways round this.

The first is to provide usable clinical guidelines based as closely as is practicable on the trial criteria. This implies that the trial criteria should not be too esoteric or demanding for ordinary practice. The problem with this is that practitioners who live in the real world rather than that of clinical trials will inevitably, in seeking to do their best for their patients, expand the criteria. Strictly, such expansions should be the subject of further trials, but this is expensive and rarely happens.

The second way is to base the trial as closely as possible on likely real world practice. These are the so-called pragmatic trials. In Chapter 3 we discussed studies of Irritable Bowel Syndrome (IBS). IBS is a notoriously ill-defined condition. Although it is possible to devise criteria (e.g. the Rome criteria) for use in IBS research, these are much more restrictive than those employed by a general practitioner confronted by a patient troubled by persistent bowel symptoms of no apparent cause. Therefore, it was decided to conduct a pragmatic trial based on relaxed Rome criteria and to analyse the findings both for the whole group of patients and for the sub-group strictly eligible only by the unrelaxed criteria. Even in this case there would have to be strict exclusion criteria.

Unfortunately, the issue of strict versus pragmatic trials is difficult to resolve. There are many circumstances when careful selection of patients for trials is sensible. Pragmatic trials would be less necessary if practitioners were more consistent among themselves. However, uncertainty forces them to use professional judgement based on evidence moderated by experience – the art of medicine. Uncertainty is the reason for clinical trials in the first place. Perhaps the best that the commissioners of clinical trials can do is to be conservative about the level of efficacy (and cost–utility) that a strict trial must deliver before they would consider introducing a new procedure into routine service, e.g. to demand 50 per cent improvement over current procedures from the trial in the expectation that in routine practice 30 per cent improvement will be delivered and worth paying for. This certainly demands more sophisticated resource management than at present, but this is what the new paradigm is about.

When trials are proposed it should also be borne in mind that potential clinical collaborators may not be in a position of equipoise with respect to the treatment options to be evaluated. Although the commissioners and researchers may believe that there is sufficient uncertainty to warrant a clinical trial, it should not be taken for granted that all practising clinicians share this uncertainty. Thus, it may prove difficult in some centres to find enough clinicians to recruit patients into the trial. Rather than expecting treating clinicians to be equally happy with the, say, two arms of a study, it might be possible to assign patients randomly to centres willing to offer one or the other arm, if not both. There should be no ethical dilemma for the clinicians, since the referral decision would not in routine practice have been theirs anyway. However, they must still be comfortable with the idea of employing the treatment acceptable to them according to an agreed protocol, and with the other disciplines imposed by a clinical trial.

Informed consent is sought from eligible subjects. Essentially, subjects must be made aware of what they are letting themselves in for, the possible benefits and the possible inconveniences or hazards. They must be informed that they may withdraw themselves from the study at any time, that in such a case they will be offered the most suitable of currently available therapies and that this will not affect their relationship with their therapist. We do not discuss this further other than to emphasize its importance legally and ethically. In some trials subjects who have given consent may undergo further confirmatory diagnostic procedures. These would be procedures (e.g. invasive procedures such as biopsy) not routinely necessary for all patients outside the context of a trial, which therefore could not ethically be undertaken before recruitment. As a result of these further tests, some subjects may be withdrawn from the trial.

'Randomization' has to be random and not merely haphazard, or allocating patients alternately to one or other of two treatments. Proper randomness is easily achieved using computer generated pseudo-random numbers: if generated by a suitable algorithm these are undetectably different from supposedly truly random numbers, as might be observed in sub-atomic events. Any experienced medical statistician will be able to advise on setting up a protocol for the random allocation of patients in a clinical trial. It should be borne in mind that random allocation does not guarantee equal numbers of subjects in each of the intervention arms (e.g. treatments) in the trial. Usually this does not matter. When it does it is possible to set up a restricted randomization which balances the numbers and is unlikely to introduce bias. Sometimes the allocation may be made at the site where the subjects are recruited (e.g. sealed envelopes opened in sequence by the investigator) or by contacting the trial's central office, registering the subject and requesting the random allocation.

All major contingencies during the subject follow-up period should have been anticipated in the protocol. These include data collection and their quality control, handling subjects who choose to withdraw, taking decisions to withdraw subjects because it may be in their best interests to do so etc. It is very important that, as far as is practicable and ethical, outcome information is obtained for subjects who have been withdrawn. For instance, if survival after entry to the trial is an outcome measure then it may be easy, especially in the UK, to arrange to receive automatic notification of deaths and cause of death for a defined group of people (e.g. subjects lost to contact in the trial) from central government sources. This entails no intrusion on the subjects or their relatives. To ignore such subjects during analysis is to invite serious bias (see below). If a trial carries the risk that subjects in one or more of the study arms might be put at serious hazard or disadvantage compared to those in other study arms, the protocol should have provision for interim analysis. This would be planned for one or more points during follow-up after sufficient subjects had been recruited and followed for long enough to detect grossly worrying deviations of outcome among the study arms. Such interim analyses should be performed by statisticians not otherwise involved in the trial or its final analysis. Generally, these findings would be reported to an independent oversight committee with the power to halt the trial if there is an ethical imperative so to do.

How a trial is analysed depends on its design. Thus, for example, the analysis of a factorial RCT will differ from that employing random allocation to single distinct procedures (the most usual kind). The details do not concern us here. The general principle is that estimates will be made of the effects of each procedure (e.g. therapy), and these compared among the study arms. The indices of comparison may take various forms, such as difference in proportion of subjects pain-free after a stated interval and/or odds ratio (an estimate of the ratio of chances of being pain-free at the end of the interval on a therapy compared to a baseline therapy, e.g. standard therapy). Statistical considerations (outlined below) determine whether the observed differences or ratios are of such a magnitude as to warrant the conclusion that they represent differences in treatment effects rather than chance artefact. It is good practice for findings to be reported showing the estimated differences, or ratios, along with margins of error (confidence intervals). Further analyses may explore the effects of known confounding variables, how outcome is influenced by presumed prognostic factors and sub-groups of the subjects of particular interest. However, the analysis upon which major decisions about efficacy are to be made is that looking at the principal outcome measure – as defined in the protocol – over the study population as a whole (after any necessary statistical adjustments).

Rarely does a clinical trial proceed so smoothly that all subjects remain on their allocated treatment and none gets lost to follow-up. It is tempting to ignore patients who withdraw from treatment or are withdrawn by the investigators. To do so risks serious bias. For one cannot be sure that withdrawals are not influenced by the treatment. Subjects withdrawn by the investigators may have had adverse side-effects of the treatment. Those withdrawing themselves may have found the treatment too unpleasant or otherwise onerous. If there are differential numbers of withdrawals among the study arms and/or differential reasons for withdrawal then exclusion of withdrawals can bias the findings for or against treatments. For instance, if on putative wonder drug 'A' 90 per cent of subjects show worthwhile benefit, while on standard therapy 'B' 50 per cent show similar benefit, then, all other things being equal, there is a case for introducing drug 'A'. However, if the withdrawal before final assessment were 50 and 10 per cent respectively for drugs 'A' and 'B' then one would have to reassess the indications for using drug 'A'. More particularly, if the withdrawals were a consequence of serious side-effects, and if there is no way of predicting in advance of treatment who will get side-effects, then drug 'A' has limited, if any, use in routine practice. The pragmatic way of dealing with this problem, and the one which we commend to resource-managers, is to 'analyse by intention to treat'. That is, the follow-up results are grouped by the initial treatment to which the patient was allocated, regardless of whether that patient subsequently received that treatment or stayed on it for the full course. If there are side-effects (however minor) or other reasons that lead to patients withdrawing or being withdrawn, then analysis by intention to treat more nearly reflects what would happen in routine practice and also reduces the bias in the trial. The alternative, which may be a subsidiary analysis upon which resource decisions should not depend, is to analyse on the basis of the main treatment the subject actually received. This 'on treatment' analysis, particularly when withdrawals are high, does help to answer the 'scientific' question of whether the drug can produce any benefit at all. The answer to this should not dominate the issue of whether to introduce the drug routinely, but might be helpful to the drug's developers in seeking to improve it. Loss to follow-up poses risk of bias for similar reasons. We have already remarked that steps should be taken during data collection to maximize the amount of information held on these subjects. Commissioners should be concerned if there is large differential loss to follow-up among the study arms and no circumstantial evidence to allay the fear of serious bias.

The discussion of analysis thus far has been rather traditional. The new paradigm, which encompasses Peckham's[6] extended trial protocol, demands that clinical trials answer more than questions about technical efficacy. There are the humanistic issues (e.g. acceptability and quality of life) and cost–benefit or cost–utility matters. These are not merely optional extras but key factors in the decision about whether the innovation should be funded and implemented on a routine basis. Thus measures of the humanistic and cost–utility elements should be built into the protocol with every bit as much care as the clinical components. Humanistic measures may be accomplished through well validated questionnaires and some of the qualitative methods discussed earlier. The humanistic findings should be presented alongside the clinical findings. They may be in part quantitative, e.g. the percentage of subjects findings the procedure acceptable, and in part qualitative, e.g. insights into the subjects' perceptions distilled from a mass of testimony. The economic component would involve the careful monitoring and documentation of resource use throughout the trial. Ideally, it would have been broader than just looking at health service costs; there would be consideration of financial (e.g. travel costs and lost earnings) and social costs (not always easy to translate into money) incurred by the subjects. The economic component should be juxtaposed with the clinical and humanistic components so that one may see what has been achieved by each unit of money spent. This can then be compared among the treatment arms. Combining financial and clinical outcomes can lead to measures such as the cost per year of life gained, the cost per year of remission, the cost per pain free year etc. Humanistic measures, such as the QALY, may be combined with financial measures to give indices such as the cost per quality life year gained. Some of these measures are discussed further below. Finally, the robustness of the findings should be tested through sensitivity analysis. Clearly, the drawing together and interpretation of these elements cannot be left to some backroom technician. All the investigators, the participating clinicians, the commissioners and external advisors will have skills and insights to contribute. All too often 'scientific' studies pay lip service to these considerations (for example, most cancer efficacy trials include some sort of index of well-being), but because they are not what really interests the researchers, and because there are no decision makers requiring or influencing assessment, they contribute little to the knowledge of the humanistic and cost–utility components of different interventions. Our paradigm bridges this gap.

The foregoing account presents the bare bones common to most clinical RCTs. There are many refinements and variants which we cannot detail here. However, Box 5.13 summarizes some common variants. Here, we discuss the hierarchy of clinical trials. Box 5.13 shows that drug studies may be placed into one of three research categories, phase 1 to 3 studies, and one of post-marketing surveillance, phase 4 studies. Obviously, the pharmaceutical industry has an important role in this. The underlying science will have been conducted in-house by the companies or with associated university departments. Phase 1 studies usually take place outside the NHS, though ethical approval is sought from NHS ethics committees. Phase 2 and 3 studies in the UK require access to NHS patients and cooperation by NHS management. Phase 2 studies, and most phase 3 studies, are funded by the industry, though the NHS bears routine treatment costs. This raises issues for far-sighted resource managers. With cooperation in phase 2 and 3 studies, there is an implicit expectation that if the new therapies are beneficial the pharmaceutical industry will be able to market them to the NHS and elsewhere. While the NHS cannot direct pharmaceutical company R&D programmes it can set ground rules for what happens when that R&D impinges on the NHS. Pharmaceutical companies are obliged to satisfy national licensing requirements for new products. These no longer merely seek evidence of safety but also, nowadays in the UK, demand evidence of efficacy. However, evidence of safety and efficacy is but a small part of what resource managers need to know if they are to make wise decisions. Further, once evidence of efficacy is presented it proves very difficult to curtail the introduction of a product that does not meet NHS priorities and will inevitably lead to robbing Peter to pay Paul. Viagra is, at the time of writing, a case in point.

Viagra (a trade name for sildenafil) is a drug that helps to induce erections in impotent males, extends the strength and time of erection in potent males and seemingly increases the clitoral pleasure of females who take it. Clearly, there are four potential markets: impotent males who wish to procreate; impotent males who wish to return to consummated sexual relationships; potent males who want a recreational drug to enhance their pleasure; and females whose erotic experience is also enhanced by the drug – all very worthy and no doubt great fun for those who partake. Unfortunately, Viagra is expensive. The first market is undoubtedly within the remit of the NHS and not very large. The second is also within the remit of the NHS to help to restore people (e.g. men suffering from diabetes) to normal functioning but, perhaps, not as high a priority as the first. The third and fourth markets seem to lie beyond the remit of the NHS. Indeed, given what people are prepared to spend on a good night out, the cost per tablet is but a small component of the whole. Private prescription would bring happiness to the sybarites, increase the income of the morally nobler members of the medical profession (such as rent consulting rooms in Harley Street, London) and enrich the manufacturer's shareholders. Viagra has (assuming that no nasty side-effects creep out of the woodwork) created a tremendous and

Box 5.13   Some variants of the clinical trial (not necessarily mutually exclusive)

Variant	Comment
Multicentre trials Trials conducted at more than one centre. Subjects at each centre are randomly allocated among study arms.	With less common conditions it is not feasible to recruit sufficient subjects at one centre (e.g. hospital) over a reasonable time. Thus, several centres (possibly internationally) will be involved. Multicentre trials require particularly good management to ensure adherence to the protocol.
Blinding A bias reduction technique. Single blind: subject only. Double blind: subject and investigator. Triple blind: subject, investigator and analyst.	Blinding involves the patient, investigator and/or statistical analyst being unaware of which treatment the subject is receiving. This reduces bias resulting from the response or interpretation being influenced by the individual's prior expectations. Blinding is not always feasible. Clearly, when there is double or triple blinding some independent person must be able to break the treatment code if the possibility of withdrawal arises.
Sequential trials Trials analysed repeatedly as subjects' responses to treatment accrue.	In most trials the total number of subjects is set in advance based on statistical considerations. In conditions when the outcome is rapid following treatment it is possible to perform a sequential analysis of the results as they accrue. Statistical stopping rules determine when the trial has reached a conclusion and may be stopped. Such trials may allow an earlier conclusion to be reached than the fixed number design, and hence subject fewer people to inconvenience or risk.
Placebo treatment A dummy (pretend) treatment.	In instances when there is no treatment of proven worth to test an innovation against, it is desirable to use a dummy treatment rather than none at all for

Variant	Comment
	the comparison group. This is because people respond positively to inert treatments for psychological rather than physical reasons – the 'placebo effect'. Thus, if the innovation is useless there may still be a placebo response, the nature of which is revealed by comparison with a real placebo.
Techniques to increase statistical precision	A variety of techniques are available in special circumstances. For instance, in some eye conditions the patient may act as her own comparison by using different treatments in each eye. This removes the statistical variation arising from the fact that different people respond differently. Some other techniques include factorial designs, Latin squares and cross-over designs. They are beyond our scope to discuss further.
The hierarchy of drug studies Phase 1: exploratory studies Phase 2: small-scale RCT Phase 3: definitive RCT Phase 4: monitoring routine use	*Phase 1* studies are concerned with drug safety, pharmacological action and optimum dose levels; they are usually on small numbers of healthy volunteers and are rarely RCTs. *Phase 2* studies are small studies on carefully selected patients looking at circumstantial evidence of efficacy (e.g. tumour size reduction) and quantifying common side-effects. Ideally these should be RCTs. Nevertheless, evidence from phase 2 studies alone (however many) should *never* be taken as justification for routine implementation of a therapy. *Phase 3* studies should be definitive RCTs looking at true outcomes (e.g. survival and quality of life). *Phase 4* studies are observational post-marketing exercises aimed at quantifying less common side-effects. The UK 'yellow card' scheme of reporting suspected side-effects by clinicians serves a similar purpose.

continuing demand. It is an extreme example. It was so extreme that the UK Department of Health (DoH) finally came to realize that it could not, as usually is the case, devolve the decision about introducing the drug on the NHS to its regional outposts and individual health authorities. For once licensing did not mean an automatic market in the NHS. Thus the DoH placed a moratorium on NHS, but not private, prescription of Viagra to give a breathing space for the consideration of how Viagra might be available on the NHS and for whom. An important side-effect of this action is to give the manufacturer pause for reconsideration of its UK pricing structure for Viagra. Doubtless a better deal will be struck eventually. The guidelines that emerged from the DoH sensibly did not try to ration Viagra alone. Instead they place limits on the frequency of prescription of all erection potentiating agents and allow each patient, under his doctor's advice, to select the one which best suits his needs.

The danger we allude to is that once a drug is licensed and a demand for its use is generated it is very difficult for individual health authorities to stem the demand. Moreover, it is hard to persuade people that a decision should await further trials to elaborate on the humanistic and economic issues. Thus, in so far as the phase 2 and 3 trials are taking place within the NHS, which seems not to have been the case for Viagra, they should be forced to conform to protocols that meet the needs of NHS resource managers. Hence, there is a need for commissioners to collaborate closely with the pharmaceutical (and equipment) industry and not leave such matters solely in hands of clinical researchers. Perhaps it is time to review the way in which clinicians receive payment (directly or indirectly) for collaborating in clinical trials using NHS patients. There is a need for greater national coordination of if, how, when and to whom new drugs are issued. Hitherto this is something the DoH would have resisted, as politicians wish to distance themselves from these contentious, politically sensitive and often emotional issues. Seemingly a solution may come through the creation of some national prescribing authority to which emotional flack may be diverted away from politicians. How this should relate to the recently established National Institute for Clinical Excellence is not clear. However, it would be a pity if the latter follows the 'dreaming spires' model of being detached from the reality of resource management decisions.

We return to phase 2 trials with a word of warning. We have experienced the intense pressure that clinical researchers can place on management for the routine introduction of a therapy on the basis of phase 2 trials alone. This happened to be in a field of cancer chemotherapy. The phase 2 RCTs had primary end-point measures of radiologically visible tumour regression. A whole series of related trials on a number of variants of a drug were put forward as compelling evidence that these drugs should be routinely paid for by the health authority. The clinician researchers were powerful academics with honorary NHS consultant contracts. The professional managers had little understanding of clinical trials technology and certainly did not feel in a strong position to gainsay the academics. Fortunately, they did seek 'counsel's opinion' from a public health physician and the pressure was resisted. The phase 2 trials did show tumour regression. An absence of tumour regression would have indicated that the drugs lacked efficacy and that it would not be appropriate to proceed to a definitive phase 3 trial. The presence of regression, even if dramatic, says nothing about the broader clinical effectiveness of the drug. Resource managers need to know whether the drugs prolong life sufficiently to justify the financial cost and whether the patients feel that the costs to them of an unpleasant therapeutic regimen justify their gains (if any). These questions can only be answered by a phase 3 trial with adequate follow-up time of survival, and including the necessary humanistic and economic measurements. If on the basis of a phase 3 trial the evidence suggests gains over conventional therapy but these are insufficient to justify the cost, then that need not be the end of the matter. It remains open to the pharmaceutical company to continue developing and improving the drug at its own expense; the NHS is not obliged to pick up each incremental improvement. R&D resource managers in pharmaceutical companies should be following their own version of the change-promoting paradigm when deciding which potential products to back.

RCTs are not just for drugs or esoteric procedures. Seemingly technologically simple nursing and caring procedures equally require evaluation. In some (we suspect many) instances these simpler procedures may have greater impact on a patient's feeling of well-being than biomedical science-based therapeutic procedures. Increasingly, the nursing, other paramedical and caring disciplines are questioning hallowed practice[7] and subjecting new procedures to evaluation.[8] This should be encouraged and R&D funding should be available not only to finance appropriate studies in these areas but also to promote the acquisition of evaluation skills. To this end, resource-manager R&D commissioners must maintain dialogue with all professions involved in promoting health and in healthcare delivery.

The discussion thus far has been about clinical trials in which each study unit is a person. Study units may also be groups of people or institutions. For example, two health promotion techniques may be tested on workplaces. We are assuming that the techniques are aimed at people en masse (e.g. leaflets and talks) rather than through individual counselling. Participating factories may be randomly allocated to one or other technique. The outcome might be the proportion of workers who change their lifestyle in a positive way (e.g. drink red wine instead of beer and spirits[9]) and sustain that change for a year. A point to bear in mind is that in deciding the size of study needed to give a clear result it is the number of factories that counts and not the total number of people in the factories. An analysis of individual people might appear to give an enormously powerful study, but this would be erroneous. The people within each factory cannot be regarded as being independent of each other in their responses. The culture of the workplace and the interplay between individuals will partly determine who responds to the message. To clarify the matter, consider another design of RCT. Let us assume that the intervention is targeted at individuals and that there will be little contamination of one individual's response by that of another. In this case we might choose a set of factories and within each randomize individuals to one or other intervention. The study units would be individual people and the factories would be strata like centres in a multicentre trial. The analysis would be individual-based within strata. Even in this case there is likely to be some degree of contamination. Statistical techniques of multilevel modelling have recently become popular as a means of allowing for the so-called intra-class correlation. However, if intra-class correlation is expected to be small and the study size is made somewhat larger than the minimum necessary (to allow for the dilution effect of intra-class correlation), these niceties may be ignored and a more straightforward (and intelligible to lay people) analysis performed. This point illustrates another feature of the new paradigm: the emphasis is on acceptable usefulness and intelligibility of results rather than methodological purity.

It should now be clear that there are no theoretical obstacles to extending RCTs to aggregates of individuals and to institutions. Difficulties arise because of the logistics and the cost.

5.8 Non-randomized prospective studies

Picking up on the theme of acceptable usefulness (above), it is better to have a carefully executed non-randomized intervention study than none at all. Although many might quibble with that statement in the context of clinical trials it is certainly defensible in circumstances where RCTs are impracticable, e.g. sometimes when looking at entire services. Nevertheless, one should not too readily assume that RCTs are impracticable; for example, several variants of the RCT were used to evaluate mammographic screening services for early breast cancer.[10]

The principles underlying non-randomized studies do not differ greatly from those for RCTs. The fundamental element, common to all evaluative studies, is that of comparison either to an absolute standard or to the outcome from a different way of doing things (relative standard). In the RCT the comparison is always relative, i.e. among two or more options, one of which is usually the currently known best practice (or treatment). We explored the use of absolute standards in the context of evaluating a childhood immunization service. Non-randomized relative comparisons can follow many of the variants of the RCT (e.g. cross-over studies), and differ solely in that random allocation of study units to trial arms did not take place. The main issue in the design is to try to ensure that the study units to be compared are as alike as possible and that appropriate measurement is made of known or likely confounding variables. Study units can be made alike in one of two ways.

The first is to 'match' each study unit, to which the intervention is to be applied, with a similar comparison unit (often a control to which no change is being made). The matching is on the basis of known confounding factors or other issues that might confuse the interpretation of the findings. For example, if a change in admissions policy for general medical patients is being evaluated it would be sensible to compare units similar with respect to size, case mix, type of hospital (e.g. district general) and socio-economic mix of the catchment population. Thus each pair would be compared and differences among the pairs in outcome could be explored with respect to the characteristics of the pairs (e.g. pairs having catchments with much social deprivation versus pairs with well off catchment populations – this might show whether the new admissions policy reduces bed-blocking more in well off areas than poorer areas).

The second is to try to ensure that the intervention and comparison groups overall represent a similar range of potential confounding variables but not to match individual study units. The comparison in the case would be between some average outcome from each group (e.g. the difference between the comparison arms in the overall average of weighted average length of stay in each medical unit for some fixed time period; the weighting might be related to the size of the medical units).

A different approach, which can also be used with either of the first two, is to try to disentangle the influences of the measured variables using statistical modelling techniques (e.g. multiple regression analysis). These methods may also be used in the analysis of RCTs to elucidate some of the more subtle relationships among the data.

When comparison is not possible prospectively in time with another study unit, a before-and-after design becomes useful. This entails gathering baseline data before a change in service configuration and following the consequences of the change over time. As noted in Box 5.11, it might not be possible to disentangle the effects of the intervention from events that might have occurred anyway with the passage of time.

5.9 Case–control (alias case–referent) studies

Studies that gather data prospectively follow the arrow of time, in that causes precede their effects. The RCT and observational studies are examples of prospective studies; the same is true of retrospective follow-up studies (see Box 5.11) because these still follow previously documented events forwards in time, even though the starting point is in the past. In an RCT the 'causes' are the interventions and the 'effects', if present, are the outcomes. Similarly, in an observational study chains of possible cause and effect are followed forwards.

Box 5.14 The arrow of time: case–control studies deduce cause from effect and prospective studies deduce effect from cause

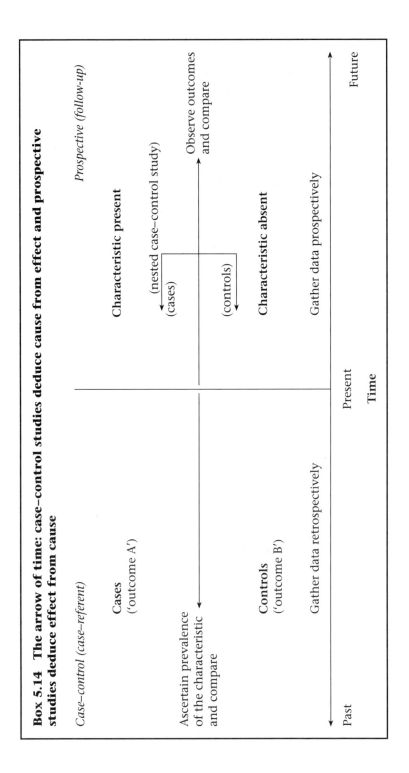

Case–control (also known as case–referent) studies follow the arrow of time backwards. They start from the 'effects' and look into the history of the pre-identified affected study units to identify whether the putative cause was present. Thus, in the example given in Box 5.11 the two 'effects' are having cervical cancer and not having cervical cancer. Delving into the histories of the two groups of women reveals the numbers in each who had undergone cervical screening. If the presence of a screening history is greater among the cancer-free women than the afflicted women then that is suggestive of screening having a beneficial effect. Thus, in Box 5.14 outcomes 'A' and 'B' may be identified with the presence and absence of cervical cancer respectively, and the characteristic being compared is screening history. The theoretically ideal[11] prospective approach would start with the presence and absence of the 'causal' factor and follow up women to see whether they developed cervical cancer; women would be randomly allocated (as individuals or in groups) to a screening programme or not to a screening programme.

Case–control studies are widely employed in aetiological epidemiology (seeking to understand the cause of disease). However, that, being a theory-enhancing activity, is of no concern here. Thus, we are going to eschew terms such as risk factor (for the causal agent) and talk generally of study units rather than people, though, as in the example of cervical cancer services, the study units are often people. Further, the word 'case' should be construed as an identified attribute of a study unit which is believed to be an outcome of the causal factor, rather than as a sufferer from disease.

Box 5.14 displays a variant of the case–control study known as a nested case–control study. This can be incorporated into a prospective follow-up study; ideally it is designed into the follow-up study but sometimes it is possible as an afterthought. The follow-up study would have recorded baseline characteristics of the study population and observed events as they occurred. It would be designed with sufficient study power to enable a convincing comparison of the incidence of specific (and relatively common) events among groups of the population with baseline characteristics putatively 'causal' to those events. Less common events which the study was not powered to examine prospectively but which may nevertheless be interesting can be studied for possible causes via a nested case–control study. At some point in the course of the study (not necessarily the end) all study units to which the event occurred would be identified, as would a group (sub-sample) of study units similar to the former but to which the event had not occurred. The presence or absence of the suspected causes would be ascertained for each case and control from the baseline data (and/or subsequently recorded information). From thereon the logic of the nested design is the same as for a retrospective case–control study. An advantage of the nested design over retrospective case–control studies is that the investigator gathers the information on the risk characteristics prospectively (rather than relying

on records or recollection) and can ensure that this is done in a consistent manner for all the study units, whether or not they later become
cases or controls.

Discussion of the nested variant has brought forth an important
feature of all case–control studies. They are a powerful tool for seeking
cause and effect relations leading to comparatively rare events: events so
infrequent that an enormous (large number of study units and/or long
follow-up time) and, perhaps, prohibitively expensive prospective follow-
up study would be needed to explore the same issue. An example where
the case–control approach has been valuable is in exploring the relation
between factors such as sleep position of infants and the risk of sudden
infant death syndrome. For more common events the case–control approach is also useful because it is generally cheaper and gives more rapid
results than prospective studies. However, case–control studies give less
reliable evidence of cause and effect than adequately powered prospective studies, and of these only the RCT truly intervenes in an experimental
manner in putative cause and effect relations. Even if a prospective follow-
up study is feasible, one or more case–control studies is useful first to
establish whether the size of the effect being sought is likely to justify
the expense of a follow-up study.

As in all the non-randomized study designs, a key issue for the investigator is minimization of bias. Investigators do not have the prospect, as
in the RCT, of chance being on average on their side. There are three
major considerations. First, the cases should be representative of all cases
and the controls should be representative of all non-cases. Second, how
cases and controls are juxtaposed. Third, the quality of the information
gained about the history of exposure to the supposed causal factor should
not be influenced by whether the study unit is a case or a control.

The importance of having representative cases and controls may be
exemplified by looking at an obviously biased study. Suppose that in our
example of evaluating cervical cancer services the investigators had picked
their cases (cancer patients) from hospital records and the controls similarly from hospital patients not suffering from cervical cancer. It is
arguable that almost every cervical cancer sufferer comes into contact at
some time with hospital services and hence hospital records may be an
acceptable way of identifying sufferers. If asthma were the condition of
interest this would not be true, and hospitalized asthmatics are not
typical of all asthma sufferers. The controls definitely are not typical of
cervical cancer free women. They are all (apart from women in labour),
by definition, ill. Most of the population outside hospital is not ill. The
mere fact that they have a history of illness may bias their likelihood of
having undergone cervical cancer screening compared to the general
population of eligible females. There may be other subtle effects: for
example, hospitals deal with a lot of smoking-related illness and thus the
prevalence of smoking among a hospital control group may be greater
than in the general population; earlier in this chapter we explored smoking

as one of the confounding factors in studies on cervical cancer. Thus, ideally cases are selected, preferably at random if not all are to be studied, from a complete list of cases and controls from a complete list of non-cases. This can be hard to achieve (except in nested case–control studies) and the investigator is obliged to think through possible sources of bias, their likely magnitude and how they might influence the findings.

There are several approaches to juxtaposing cases and controls. At one extreme each case is individually matched with one or more controls; at the other extreme the cases as a group are compared with the controls as a group, and in between cases and controls may be stratified into sub-groups (the cervical cancer patients may be stratified by age and/or smoking habit) and compared within them. Individual matching is just an extreme form of stratification. Stratification is a technique common to most of the designs we have discussed. The strata serve two purposes in analysis: to make explicit allowance for known confounding variables and to increase the precision of statistical estimates within strata that are more homogeneous than the entire set of data. Individual matching entails selecting for each case controls which share several important factors (for confounding or for homogeneity) with the case; if the study units are people these are commonly age, sex, ethnicity, smoking habit and socio-economic status. Thought must be given to the choice of matching variables for several reasons. Matching on many variables is tedious and may exhaust the potential population of controls. Matching on inappropriate variables adds nothing to the precision of the study or to the control of bias. Overmatching results if a variable strongly related to the characteristic under scrutiny ('cause') is chosen. In the example of cervical cancer screening there would be overmatching if a history of vaginal bleeding were used, as it is very likely that those women would have had investigative cervical smears. Thus, those sets of cases and controls in whom vaginal bleeding had occurred (admittedly few) would contribute little to determining whether screening contributes to the control of cervical cancer.

Individual matching attempts to take care of confounding and precision in one step. Stratifying groups of cases and controls or taking the cases and controls overall leaves part or all of those issues to the analysis. Regression techniques[12] enable the influences of all the variables to be explored and in our view lead to a more informative analysis than individual matching. The use of more than one control for each case increases the precision of the comparison (e.g. narrower confidence interval for the odds ratio – see below). Diminishing returns set in rapidly for more than about five controls per case. Given a choice of expanding the number of cases or expanding the number of controls per case, the former is the better option, but cases are sometimes in short supply.

The final major issue is ensuring that information of similar reliability is obtained about the histories of cases and controls. For example, the records of the cervical cancer patients are likely to have been collated and checked, and to make explicit reference to whether or not screening had been done in the past. The medical records of the controls are likely to be scattered and reference to screening history may not have been recorded consistently. Similarly, asking the women may evoke differential recall of events; perhaps the cancer sufferers are now more aware of the significance of the question to them and search their memories more thoroughly.

The findings from case–control studies are usually presented as an odds ratio. This is an estimate of the ratio of the probability of the effect occurring if the 'cause' was present to that of it occurring if the 'cause' was absent. These numbers should be presented with a confidence interval to give a feel for their precision. Thus, for example, we might say that unscreened women have twice the risk of developing cervical cancer of screened women, and give a range of values around two. Note that the absolute probabilities of the effect occurring given presence or absence of the 'cause' are not usually individually estimable. An exception is when the sampling fractions of cases and controls are known (e.g. in a nested study).

5.10 Economic measures

We have repeatedly stressed that R&D can fulfil its purpose only if it is led by the agenda of resource managers and if it produces findings that aid their decision making. Resource managers need to know more than whether treatments, procedures and services produce measurable benefit for individuals. They need to know whether they are effective in serving the wider population of individuals who might benefit and how they contribute among the broad range of possible services to promoting the health of the population as a whole. Clearly, how much you get for what you pay is a central issue for anyone commanding resources. The 'how much you get' element has several facets.

1 How much positive outcome is gained for individuals per pound sterling spent on a treatment or procedure? This relates cost to efficacy. The outcome can be any of the measures we have discussed hitherto: symptom relief, years of life gained, quality of life gained etc. It may be presented in an absolute or relative manner, e.g. cost per year of life saved or additional cost over current best practice per additional year of life saved. This is the kind of information that RCTs on individual drugs or procedures can produce. One would wish to have at least some of this information in a form that allows comparison of cost with efficacy across the range of treatments or procedures available for patients/clients under consideration.

2 How much overall (population) effect[13] is gained per pound spent on a service? Remember that a service consists of the structure and process necessary to deliver treatments and procedures to eligible consumers.

A broad service (e.g. surgery) may be disaggregated into sub-services such as vascular surgery or even further to services to meet a particular problem, e.g. dealing with abdominal aortic aneurysms. Each of these levels may be evaluated for this type of cost-effectiveness. The effect is not merely whether some individuals can be shown to benefit but rather whether or not the targeted population is benefiting. This information may come from RCTs of the whole service (e.g. of mammographic breast screening) or through a combination of many of the evaluative techniques outlined above.

3 Cost-efficiency is an important consideration, i.e. whether the same could be delivered at lesser cost or more could be delivered at current cost. A service may have components that have high cost-efficacy but not be delivering in a cost-effective manner because its structure or process (including financial management) is weak.

4 Comparative cost-effectiveness (and cost–utility) across a range of diverse services (e.g. breast cancer screening for women versus abdominal aortic aneurysm screening for men) is necessary for taking global decisions about the configuration of services.

In order to answer these questions there must be information on costs. It is beyond our scope to discuss how costs may be obtained. However, we shall make some general remarks. First, defining and gathering costs can be a complicated task – every bit as difficult as performing the clinical component of an evaluation. Second, it is not necessarily something that people with accountancy skills, such as NHS trust finance officers, are good at in a research setting, though their collaboration is invaluable. The reason is that costs may be defined in diverse ways and those needed for evaluation purposes may differ in how they are defined from those for financial management and audit purposes. Third, health economics – the discipline central to these considerations – is, despite its quantitative nature, not an 'exact science'. There can be genuine dilemmas about which form of costing is most appropriate in given circumstances. These need to be understood and discussed by the R&D team as a whole (especially commissioners), as they have a bearing on the interpretation and generalizability of the findings. Further, some health economists have a (seemingly unthinking) habit of discounting future costs and benefits at an arbitrary discount rate. Whether or not this is appropriate will depend on circumstances and must be decided by how resource-managers will use the information coming from an evaluation. Fourth, costs are best obtained concurrently during an evaluative study, rather than retrospectively or from other sources. In this manner it is possible to ensure that the actual kind of cost required is collected, that it actually bears on the circumstances of the evaluation and that the quality of the information is acceptable. Finally, when one is making cost-projections in the development stage of a service it is important to translate the costs determined by the evaluation into the procedures of income and expenditure used in health services ('write off' decrements and times for equipment, wage incremental drift, capital charges etc.). These considerations reinforce our view that a person with health economic skills should be consulted at the earliest stages of a R&D programme and maintain a link throughout. It also reinforces our notion that those involved in R&D (commissioners and researchers) should become multipotent across the disciplines because there are so many issues where there are choices with no right or wrong answers, and thus they should not be delegated solely to experts.

Box 5.15 lists some health economic approaches useful to R&D. Between them these techniques can provide the information sought in the list of four items above. Cost-effectiveness and cost–utility are used more often than cost–benefit analysis. This is because the last is much more difficult to do convincingly, though it does provide more directly useful answers for health resource policy decisions at the global level. One of its strengths is, in terms of putting its information to use, also one of its weaknesses. Cost and benefit need not be restricted to the jurisdiction of health services. Thus it could be found that a costly health service intervention provides considerable benefits which more than recoup the costs by returning people to work in the economy (through patients going off welfare and paying income tax). Unless some of the benefit reaped in other sectors of the state is used to reimburse some of the health service costs it may not be feasible for health planners to fund it from their budgets. Thus, unless government departments are able to collaborate effectively there is little incentive for health planners to open cans of worms by commissioning wide-ranging cost–benefit studies. Cost–benefit studies may also lead to conclusions which, if implemented, might be inequitable. For instance, setting the cost and benefit net widely and not valuing life appropriately might establish that caring for the elderly or the mentally incapacitated is not good value for money. Thus, when using economic tools in health planning one must be aware that they and/or those deciding what to measure contain hidden assumptions (about who and what is valued, and how).

This concludes the overview and commentary on the most important study designs. In the remaining sections of this chapter we comment on miscellaneous issues having a bearing on the design, execution and analysis of R&D studies.

5.11 Sampling

In most studies it is neither necessary nor feasible to make measurements on all potential study units. Thus a sample of the study units must suffice. If the findings from the study are to be in any sense (quantitatively or qualitatively) generalizable, then the sample members should reflect the distribution of characteristics among the wider population

Box 5.15 Commonly used economic techniques

Technique	Strengths	Weaknesses
Cost–effectiveness analysis This relates cost to a single outcome when comparing procedures or services having the same aims. Cost is given per unit of effect e.g. life year gained. This can be inverted to give life years per pound spent.	A straightforward comparison among options seeking the same outcome. Allows incremental analysis of the change in costs and outcome in moving from one service specification to another.	Choice of an appropriate single outcome may be problematic. There is usually an assumption that a do nothing outcome does not exist and choice will be made among existing options. The do nothing option may not be tangibly worse than the existing options.
Cost–benefit analysis This is not restricted to a single outcome. It values all costs (e.g. treatment, travel, social) and benefits (e.g. restoration of function, earning) in monetary terms and relates one to another. Services should only be implemented if benefits exceed costs.	This may take into account a wide range of costs and benefits which need not be restricted to health service costs or to benefits to individual patients/clients. Thus more general costs and benefits to society as a whole may be calculated. It can give a measure of absolute cost and benefit.	Not all costs (e.g. inconvenience) and benefits (e.g. pain relief) can readily (or convincingly) be stated in monetary terms. The findings from the analysis may be sensitive to how widely the net is cast for costs and benefits. Going beyond health services costs does not always lead to a realistic scenario with respect to health budget use.

Technique	Strengths	Weaknesses
Cost–utility analysis This relates the cost of an option to a measure of the usefulness of the outcome (utility). Utility, is the underlying worth or value of a given level of health status. For example, scaling life years gained by a measure of their quality for the patient (QALY) places gains on a common basis. Thus ten years at half quality is deemed equivalent to five years at full quality.	This provides a means of comparing alike (e.g. two ways of dealing with mental illness in the community) and different (e.g. mammographic breast screening with screening for prostatic cancer) options in a common currency which is not just monetary. It is a useful tool for service specific and global health policy decisions.	The various scales (e.g. Rosser & Kind, EuroQol and SF36) are not without controversy. Going for a disease-specific scale may be prudent but that loses the advantage of being able to compare unlike options. It is not good for addressing issues of equity of health care or matters other than the maximization of health gain.
Cost–efficiency (cost–minimization) analysis In essence this is a search for the least cost way of delivering a service to stated levels of outcome and quality of care. It may entail comparison of options (e.g. day case versus inpatient surgery) or analysis of potential inefficiencies in a given option followed by observing the effects of changes.	A useful tool for assessing structure and process.	This cannot be used when the outcomes differ among the options being compared. It implicitly assumes that the outcomes are identical (something the investigator must check).

from which the sample was drawn. Very small samples can represent only coarse features of this range, and as sample size increases finer detail may be perceived. How one decides the size of sample required is discussed below. Here, we concentrate on methods for obtaining samples. Box 5.16 summarizes the most commonly used methods.

The methods portrayed in Box 5.16 fall into two broad categories: those that rely on a sampling frame and those that do not. A sampling frame is merely a list of all the potential study units, e.g. a list of hospitals, a general practice age–sex register and the national list of state registered nurses. Those requiring a sampling frame are also the ones better suited to quantitative research where it is the intention to extrapolate the findings in a numerical manner from the sample to the population of study units from which the sample was drawn. Those techniques that employ simple random sampling[14] – either as the entire procedure or as part of multistage or cluster sampling – are the least likely to give biased findings and are those most compatible with the standard (frequentist) tools of statistical inference. When a sampling frame is unobtainable it is possible to obtain quantitative findings (e.g. using snowballing), but these should be treated with great caution and regarded as semi-quantitative: that is, putting an order of magnitude gloss on mainly qualitative findings (e.g. it would be of interest to know that most drug addicts in a large snowball sample used clean needles). The numerical findings should be presented simply and statistical inference (e.g. significance tests) should not be attempted.

Qualitative research is not restricted to non-random sampling. Indeed, in circumstances where representativeness by proportion (e.g. getting a feel for what is most common) is required, in addition to coverage of the range of main characteristics in the population of potential study units, then random sampling methods are optimal for qualitative research. Theoretical sampling[15] (Box 5.16) might be more efficient, in terms of subjects needing to be seen, than random sampling in meeting the qualitative aims of the investigator. The commissioners of research must be satisfied that whatever methods are to be employed for sampling in the qualitative and quantitative components of a programme of R&D are justified, and not merely a result of laziness or ignorance on the part of the investigator (as can sometimes be the case for, respectively, choosing samples of convenience or systematic samples).

The validity of samples drawn from a sampling frame depends on the quality of the sampling frame. Sampling frames can be inaccurate because not every potential study unit gets registered (e.g. some people are not registered with GPs) and because they get out of date (e.g. GPs' patients' changes of address or moves to other practices take time to be notified). In inner cities, GP age–sex registers and the electoral roll may be markedly deficient in some groups of people, e.g. young adults.

Another influence on the validity of inferences drawn from samples is the response ratio.[16] This is the proportion of the study units in the

Box 5.16 Sampling methods

Technique	Strengths	Weaknesses
Simple random sampling (SRS) Pseudo-random numbers are used to identify a sample from a sampling frame. Sampling is usually without replacement, i.e. a unit cannot be selected twice.	It is the best technique for minimizing bias. Samples are easy to draw from computer-based sampling frames. SRS is also straightforward manually. Most widely used statistical procedures for drawing inferences from sampling assume SRS.	This technique has the fewest weaknesses of all. Randomness promises but does not guarantee representative samples; small samples can by chance be highly unrepresentative. This last is true of all the methods outlined below.
Systematic sampling Starting from an arbitrary point near the beginning of the sampling frame every *n*th unit is taken so that a sample of requisite size is obtained.	Simple to do, but in these days of computer-based sampling, frames are not noticeably easier than SRS. Simpler manually than SRS.	Potential for subtle biases arising from cyclical patterns in the sampling frame. Although statistical procedures assume SRS this in practice makes no difference.
Multistage sampling This applies to any sampling method that uses a sampling frame but for which a unified or fully informative frame does not exist. Thus, to sample hospital ward cleaners one might first sample hospitals from a list and then from each obtain a list of ward cleaners and sample again (two-stage sample). A second	Promotes the objective of drawing samples in an unbiased way. It can also be more economical than constructing and using a unified sampling frame because study units (as in the first example) may be clustered and therefore more readily accessible.	Can be time consuming. Analysis of findings is more complicated if one seeks to make proper allowance for the effects of the sampling strategy on the statistical properties of quantities estimated (intra-class correlation). In practice, this refinement often makes little difference and would

example is to sample from the electoral register (which does not contain ethnicity) and construct new sub-frames by ethnic groups and then sample within these.

apply to the first example but not the second.

Cluster sampling
This is similar to the first example of multistage sampling above. Instead of sampling patients across a city (as could be done from age–sex registers), one might first sample primary care practices and then patients within these.

Even though it may be possible to draw an SRS from a sampling frame of study units it may be more convenient to access these units physically in clusters via the geographical area or institutions in which they reside.

Intra-class correlation may need consideration.

Quota sampling
For example, preset quotas of people having various characteristics (e.g. of age or ethnicity) may be approached at an outpatient clinic and their views sought. Sometimes there may be two stages in that at the first approach it is confirmed that the characteristic is present.

Convenient when a suitable sampling frame is difficult or impossible to construct. Has proven to be a useful technique in market research and opinion polling. In the health context it is a useful means of identifying samples for qualitative and semi-quantitative research.

Requires experience and skill to do properly. Large bias is possible and its extent in part depends on the choice of quotas. Quantitative findings based on analysis using the assumptions of SRS may be faulty.

Convenience sampling
Recruiting units (usually people) that are near at hand, easy to recruit and likely to be cooperative.

A straightforward means of recruiting people into exploratory qualitative studies which themselves may precede a more structured qualitative or quantitative approach.

Potential for bias is considerable. Findings are unlikely to be generalizable except in the sense of giving insights to guide more structured research.

Technique	Strengths	Weaknesses
Purposive sampling This is similar to quota sampling in that units (often people) with particular characteristics are deliberately recruited.	If random sampling is not practicable then this method does ensure that presumably important characteristics are studied. It is useful in preliminary qualitative studies to refine research questions, and for designing and piloting questionnaires.	Some bias is very likely but this may not matter much if the method is used solely for developing research tools and not as an attempt to give definitive findings.
Snowballing An initial group of respondents (purposively sampled) identify further subjects who are then approached by the researcher and so on.	A powerful technique if a sampling frame does not exist or cannot be constructed. Populations such as drug addicts can be sampled in this way.	There is no guarantee that the initial respondents link into all the networks needed to characterize the population. Quantitative findings must be treated with caution as they do not relate to a sampling frame.
Theoretical sampling Starting from initially chosen subjects the (purposive) recruitment of further subjects is determined by the issues and insights emerging as the study progresses and continues until nothing new of interest arises.	This is a useful tool for qualitative research seeking to generate insights and hypotheses. In principle, this method could lead more quickly and more cheaply to the desired results than slavishly working through a simple random sample in which some issues may be replicated by many subjects.	This is not a suitable means for generating quantitative findings, though its findings may lead to a better informed and focused quantitative study.

sample from which information was gathered. Response ratios generally do not include study units in the denominator if they were phantoms from a defective sampling frame. Such phantoms will be noted and recorded separately as they have a bearing on the quality of the sampling frame. Taking the study units, by way of example, to be people, it is usually the case that those who do not respond (or are otherwise inaccessible) to surveys differ in various respects from those who do respond. The ways in which they differ often have a bearing on the objectives of the study. For example, surveys on health needs might underrepresent currently sick or disabled people because they may be less able to respond. A 100 per cent response is the gold standard and figures close to it can be attained if the investigators are able to invest enough resources. For example, a postal questionnaire might involve repeat mailing to non-respondents and visits to the home by field workers. Other steps, such as offering a small inducement (e.g. a pen or entry in a prize draw), ensuring that documents are written plainly in an appropriate language and with an attractive layout and making sure that respondents will not be put to much inconvenience, help the achievement of a good response. Pragmatically, one might ask what an acceptable response is. There is no universal answer. It depends entirely on the purpose of the study. Thus, if one is looking at overall patient satisfaction, 40 per cent response gives some basis for identifying serious problems, which themselves remain as valid problems no matter how large the response; however, it might seriously under- or overestimate the prevalence of negative (or positive) feelings depending on whether dissatisfied (or satisfied) patients are more or less likely to respond to such a survey. Forty per cent response in the context of a population health status survey can be so hopelessly inadequate as to make the findings not worth reporting (except as an internal NHS political ploy or a public relations exercise). Generally, if there is a choice between placing more resource into getting an acceptable response or into increasing the number of study units in the sample then the former will usually be the better option. This is because no amount of statistical sophistication during analysis can correct biased information consequent on poor response. Non-response should also be of concern in qualitative studies, as it might be from these 'difficult' people that unusual and important insights arise. Sometimes it is possible to find out something of the characteristics of non-respondents without their cooperation. For example, when sampling people from age–sex registers one can easily find out their age, sex and residence; moreover, further information about their family circumstances and health may be obtained by going to their medical records. The characteristics of non-respondents (or a sample of them) may be compared with those of respondents. From this comparison insight can arise as to the likely direction and magnitude of bias, e.g. the non-respondents might tend to live in less affluent areas and to be sicker.

5.12 Theory, measurement, validation and scales

For the purposes of R&D we have eschewed theory-enhancing 'scientific' research in favour of a pragmatic[17] approach to costing and appraising resource use options. Thus our readers might be surprised that we now dwell on theory. However, there is a distinction between research aimed at enhancing theory and the use of theory to enhance research. R&D takes place in neither a moral nor an intellectual vacuum. We have alluded to value systems elsewhere. The intellectual sub-stratum of R&D concerns the theory of evaluation and its role in change management (which is what much of this book is about) and the theoretical under-pinning of turning well posed questions into usable answers (an issue common to all research). We have already discussed the properties and relative merits of various research designs. Thus it is the role of theory underlying measurement that remains to be discussed here.

Measurement is the means by which answers to questions are cap-tured. The answers may be textual descriptions of what was seen or heard, or they may be entities bearing various of the properties of num-bers (e.g. order and magnitude). We have stressed that only well posed questions can have usable (meaningful) answers. Thus theory comes in at two levels.

First, there is our understanding of the systems about which we are posing questions. If we do not have some, however crude, insight into the systems then we do not even have a language in which to start posing questions. The language concerns the components of the system, how they interrelate and how this is to be expressed. Thus, this level concerns the theory of the system. This theoretical basis can be very complicated and may be a concatenation of diverse theories from vari-ous disciplines. For example, when one is evaluating a drug the follow-ing (at least), each with their own theoretical basis, will be involved.

- What is known and understood about the disease process in anatom-ical, physiological, biochemical terms etc.
- Diagnosis.
- What is known about the prognosis and factors influencing it.
- What is known about the pharmacological properties of the drug which also relates to potentially efficacious dose regimens and tolerance.

From this understanding will arise potential markers for the success of the drug, e.g. biochemical changes, physiological changes, physical signs, survival, pain relief, quality of life and satisfaction. Similarly, something as apparently mundane as comparing inpatient with day case surgery requires an understanding of a complicated system. One has to under-stand the structure, processes, dynamics and constraints on surgical ser-vices. There has to be clarity about how costs accrue and what might be amenable to change. The human dimension in terms of those who work in the service and its recipients has to be understood if there is to be any hope of later change management. Potential outcome markers such as cost, patient satisfaction, staff morale and surgical success might arise from this theoretical understanding as suitable means of comparing the different service configurations.

The second level of theory concerns translating the desired markers of outcome into measurable entities. Surgical success and patient quality of life can each be measured in different ways. There has to be selection (or sometimes design) of instruments of measurement. The properties of these instruments must be known; in particular, how closely the end-results of the measurement process truly portray the marker sought. This process, known as validation, concerns both the theoretical congruence between the measures and that being measured and, for numerical measures, the statistical properties (e.g. repeatability) of the measures.

An instrument of measurement is an objective procedure for obtaining a measurement. For example questionnaires, sphygmomanometers and biochemical tests, together with the procedures for operating them, constitute instruments. Objectivity, in this context, means that suitably trained operators would come to similar findings in similar circumstances. Even measurements which have a highly subjective content (e.g. assessing the amount of glandular tissue in mammograms or identifying themes from focus group discussions) can be made objective in this sense: that is, agreed procedures (sometimes involving duplicate independent measurements) can minimize the likelihood that operators will behave in an eccentric manner.

Instruments of measurement usually have an underlying theoretical basis that is independent of the system they are being used to make measures within. This will influence the degree to which measures will be congruent with the underlying entity (marker in our terminology) being measured. We will elaborate level 1 and level 2 issues in the context of blood pressure. After Harvey's discovery that blood circulates it soon became apparent that the properties of the circulatory system (blood pressure, vascular muscle tone etc.) have a bearing on the health of the individual. Thus the risk of stroke is strongly related to the level of blood pressure. If we are testing a blood pressure reducing drug then we have to be clear about what it is we wish to achieve. Not necessarily incompatible aims might be to reduce the frequency of peaks and troughs in blood pressure, to reduce the pressure differential between peaks and troughs, and to reduce the overall daily average blood pressure. Suppose that it is average blood pressure that is to be reduced. Unless continuous monitoring is to be undertaken (which is costly on large numbers of subjects), the average blood pressure will have to be inferred from samples of a patient's daily blood pressure profile. Part of the measurement process, regardless of the physical instrument used, is to have an agreed sampling strategy. In deciding on this, one also has to consider the properties of the physical instrument employed as well as the physiology of blood pressure. The sphygmomanometer measures blood pressure indirectly and non-invasively. A cuff surrounding the upper arm is inflated to a higher level than the systolic (the higher pressure pulse) blood pressure and then slowly deflated while the operator listens through a stethoscope applied to the skin above the brachial artery and below the cuff. When heart beat sounds appear this corresponds to the lateral pressure of the cuff being just insufficient to occlude the artery; this is read off a mercury column and taken as the systolic blood pressure. The operation of the sphygmomanometer itself is predicated on the following: the physics of fluids in the airbag and mercury column, the properties of tissue in transmitting the lateral pressure, the physics of the stethoscope, the ability of the human ear to discriminate faint sounds, the ability of the human eye to read off the manometer column accurately. All these properties, and the theory underlying them, determine how well a sphygmomanometer and its operator are able to capture the true instantaneous blood pressure. These considerations are summarized in Box 5.17.

The point is that level 1 and level 2 considerations apply to every measurement process. A decision has to be made as to what markers of outcome are desired: this relates to the theory of the system being studied and to the utility of the given marker as an indicator of the state of the system. A second decision is needed about what measurement instrument will give an adequate measure (qualitative or quantitative) of the marker. Demonstrating that a marker is useful and that an instrument to measure it is adequate is known as validation. Essentially, the point of this section is to show that this is a complicated matter, more so than many researchers realize, which involves recognition (at least implicitly) of empirical knowledge and theoretical perspectives that have little direct bearing on the problem being studied. Validation at its heart impinges on deep epistemological matters about what we can know and how. Moreover, any measurement has meaning and utility only if that is demonstrable within the theoretical understanding of the system under scrutiny. Thus, a well operationalized procedure may be constructed such that it can give consistent and replicable results but those results may be meaningless and useless unless that kind of measure has been validated for the context of its proposed use. This point is illustrated in Box 5.18. The curved shape can be measured for length from point A to point B in two ways: along the shape or with a rigid ruler from A directly to B. Both are legitimate measuring processes. The first is valid to help to determine the length of material needed to make a replicate of the shape. The second is valid for working out the base dimensions of a box to contain the shape. Neither is valid for the other purpose. Validation determines the degree to which an instrument measures what it purports to measure, and, very importantly from our point of view in R&D, it determines whether it is a useful measure to make. Box 5.19 summarizes validation under conventional headings.

The matter of the validity of measurements should not be delegated wholly to the researchers. We are not saying that the commissioners

Box 5.17 The issues and diverse theoretical considerations underlying the measurement of blood pressure

Content

Level 1

The utility of blood pressure as a measure	The properties of the cardiovascular system as modelled using the principles of fluid dynamics etc. The empirical and theoretical understanding that the level of blood pressure predicts the risk of stroke. The understanding that reducing blood pressure decreases the risk from stroke.
The characterization of blood pressure	Whether it is pressure extremes, pressure differential between extremes or an overall average blood pressure that is at the heart of what should be measured and of what it is sought to control through therapy.

Level 2

Options for the measurement of blood pressure	Comparison of the properties and utility of direct measurement via a cannula or indirect measurement using a sphygmomanometer.
The sphygmomanometer	The physics of fluids in airbags and columns. The physics of pressure transmission through tissue (which has a bearing on cuff size). The physics of sound transmission.
The operator	Human auditory and visual discrimination. The psychology of numeric recording, e.g. digit preference leading to patterns of rounding that can introduce bias.
The process	Deciding the frequency of recordings required to characterize 'average' blood pressure. This depends on knowledge about physiological variations and their determinants. In addition, statistical considerations arise with respect to measurements at each sampled time being repeated to average out non-systematic error inherent to the sphygmomanometer and its operator.

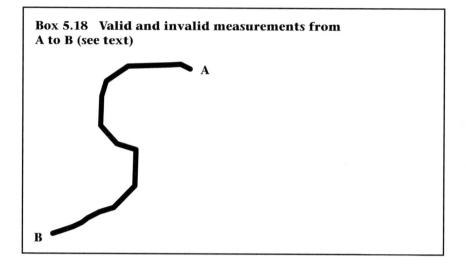

Box 5.18   Valid and invalid measurements from
A to B (see text)

need to get bogged down in the technicalities of validation, but they must ask pertinent questions. From the foregoing it should be clear that the selection of measurements and of the corresponding instruments is not simple. Rarely is there a perfect instrument. Choices have to be made and these will have a bearing on how the study findings may be interpreted and used. An instrument must be validated in the context of its use unless other work has already done so. Even if an instrument has apparently been validated for use in the same or closely similar circumstances that evidence must be scrutinized carefully and not taken at face value. If necessary, resources should be directed towards validation of an instrument that really measures what the commissioners want rather than taking some compromise instrument off the shelf. That effort will not be wasted because, first, the main study will stand a better chance of meeting the commissioners' requirements and, second, the newly validated instrument is likely to be usable again in similar areas of study.

We end this section with a brief commentary on the properties of the measures made in quantitative studies. Although the general properties of numerical measures may seem a little abstracted from the concerns of resource-managers, an understanding of them is vital to the commissioning and use of R&D. The properties of quantitative measures are displayed in the list below. Descending this list of scales of measure leads to stronger numerical properties.

1 *Nominal scale.*[18] This uses the weakest of the properties of numbers – classification and grouping. Observations are placed into mutually exclusive and collectively exhaustive categories, e.g. type of hospital: district general, teaching, maternity, community and other. The categories have no inherent order. The measurement process assigns each

Box 5.19 Validity and related properties of measurements

Type of validity	Comment
Face	This is an informal assessment of whether or not an instrument is getting at relevant matters. For example, whether the questions in a questionnaire are relevant and appropriately constructed.
Content	This is an evaluation of the degree to which an instrument captures the important properties of the underlying entity being measured. For example, whether or not a quality of life questionnaire actually encompasses the things that people regard as important to their quality of life.
Criterion	This is an evaluation against a criterion: another instrument of known properties or a 'gold standard' if there is one. There are two variants of criterion validity. 1 Concurrent validity: the criterion and the measurement refer to the same point in time, e.g. a sphygmomanometer can be validated against direct measurement of blood pressure using an arterial cannula. 2 Predictive validity: the measurement predicts the criterion, e.g. cardiac enzymes (indicative of infarction) rise a few days after the initial electrocardiographically recorded events. This is a very powerful indicator of overall validity because when a measure predicts some aspect of the system under study it has clear utility.
Construct (convergent and discriminant)	This looks at how the measurement relates to the system to which it is to be applied. For convergent validity the measure is shown to correlate with related variables. For discriminant validity it is shown not to correlate with unrelated variables.
Miscellaneous properties	
Precision	The smallest change in an attribute the instrument can detect.
Repeatability	The degree of similarity of findings when tested in circumstances which predict similar findings.
Bias	Whether or not there is a systematic bias. This may be correctable.
Random error	This is the error inherent to the instrument and the operator.
Inter-operator variation	This may be reduced by clarifying the operational procedure and by training.
Sensitivity	The ability of a screening instrument to correctly detect cases.
Specificity	The ability of a screening instrument to correctly identify non-cases.

observation of the relevant variable into one category. Thus, one might end up with the numbers of hospitals in a region that fall into each of the categories of type. Categorization is such a fundamental property that it also applies in qualitative measurement.

2 *Ordinal scale.* Observations can be placed in order: first, second, third etc. The comparisons between observations may be 'equal to', 'greater than' or 'less than', but not how much greater or less. Preferences are usually measured on this scale.

3 *Interval scale.* Observations are represented as numbers with magnitude (e.g. decimal form such as 3.2). The zero point of the scale is arbitrary (as with °C or °F). Thus, it is not useful to observe that one value is twice that of another. However, the ratio of two intervals on the scale does have meaning. Many scoring systems (e.g. psychometric measures) result in values that are alleged to be interval scale.

4 *Ratio scale.* Observations are represented as numbers with magnitude, and there is a fixed zero point. The ratios of these numbers (as well as ratios of intervals) have meaning. Thus, it makes sense to say that one person weighs twice as much as another or that one hospital has twice as many staff as another. The ratio scale has the strongest numerical properties and includes all those of the lesser scales, e.g. ratio scale values can be ranked or grouped if desired.

The scale of measurement is important for two reasons. The first relates to the properties of the underlying marker. If this is on a ratio scale then it would be good to have an instrument that produces measurements on that scale because it has so many useful properties. Perhaps it is not feasible to produce an instrument that measures on the ratio scale, and an ordinal scale has to suffice. In this case, although the investigators might have liked a ratio scale, they have to content themselves with ordinal properties and certainly should not draw inferences from their findings as if they were based on a ratio scale. The second reason why the scale is important has to do with statistical analysis. For each scale of measurement there are appropriate statistical techniques to aid inference. Use of a technique suited to a scale with more numerical properties than the scale actually has can give rise to wholly misleading findings. It is acceptable to reduce the properties of a scale (from, say, interval to ordinal). By doing so information is lost, but this sacrifice might be necessary because the data do not satisfy all the properties required (e.g. statistical distribution) for statistical methods applicable to that scale, whereas they can be analysed legitimately on the less demanding scale.

Measures such as height, weight, temperature, order of preference, categorization and cost are straightforward to comprehend, probably because they relate closely to everyday experience. Numerical entities arising from scoring systems (pain, quality of life, psychometric measures etc.) generally do not have immediate intuitive meaning. Consider an intelligence quotient (IQ) standardized to a mean of 100 units and to a standard deviation of 15 units (the population distribution will be a bell-shaped curved like the one shown in Box 5.20, but centred on 100 and such that fewer than 5 per cent of the population fall either above or below 100 + 30 (i.e. 2 × 15) units. This is an interval scale, so it will not be helpful to observe that one individual has twice the IQ of another. However, it does have meaning to ask what difference seven additional IQ points make (though the effect of this addition may vary depending on the starting point). This might be relevant to a consideration of whether it is economically worthwhile (given other social priorities) to reduce the exposure of young children to lead in the environment. It might be possible to design a study with sufficient statistical power to detect a difference of five IQ points between children brought up in a lead-reduced intervention environment compared to the ordinary environment. But what would increasing the average IQ of the intervention group from, say, 100 to 105 units mean? Is the gain spread throughout the population, or confined only to a sub-group already scoring quite well? Most people have no intuitive feel for the effect of one unit of IQ. Unless one is happy to rely on the opinion of experts that five units are a worthwhile gain one ought to ask some pertinent questions. Can the experts state what five units mean in terms of educational achievement, job opportunities etc.? In these terms, which everyone can understand, a rational decision about the use of resources can be made. The same considerations apply to scores on quality of life etc. It is not sufficient to show in a study that the scores can be improved by a certain amount, even though the scoring system is purportedly validated. If the experts are unable to show convincingly that given changes in their scores will reflect otherwise tangible and worthwhile improvement then they should be sent back to the drawing board. The translation of scores into comprehension is a crucial aspect of validation that can too readily be overlooked.

5.13 Statistical inference

Most studies are conducted so that the findings may be extrapolated to the population from which the study units were sampled, i.e. generalizable. In quantitative research the values of the measurements[19] obtained are taken to be estimates of the values that would have been found had the entire population of study units been examined. If many repeated random samples of the study units had been subjected to the investigation then one would expect different values for the estimates on most occasions. These repeated values could be portrayed as a frequency distribution that would approximate ever more closely to the bell-shaped 'normal' (Gaussian) distribution as the sample size increases. The mean (average) of these estimates would, for unlimited repeat sampling, coincide with the 'true' population value that was being estimated. The width of the normal distribution of repeated sample estimates is influenced by the

Box 5.20   The bell-shaped curve of the Normal distribution

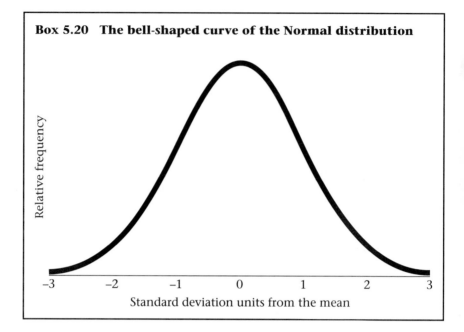

Standard deviation units from the mean

size of the sample of study units employed in each repeat study (assumed to be fixed for any series of replications). As the size of the sample increases the width of the distribution (in units of the measurement) decreases, reflecting the fact that larger samples give, on average, more precise estimates. Box 5.20 illustrates a normal distribution. The horizontal axis is in dimensionless units known as standard deviations from the mean. In real data any actual deviation from the mean can be transformed into this dimensionless unit by dividing it by the observed (estimated) standard deviation. We will not go into the calculation of this quantity (which is very simple but irrelevant to our purposes), but comment on its properties. For any normal distribution about 95 per cent of the observations will lie with plus or minus two standard deviation units from the mean; almost all the observations will lie within three standard deviations from the mean.

In real life there will be only one actual realization of a study – not a set of all possible replicates. However, from the observed data, estimates of the population mean and standard deviation can be made. On this basis it is possible to infer something of the properties of the hypothetical distribution of all sample estimates for the given sample size. This leads to the construction of significance tests and confidence intervals. These two concepts are closely related, and we discuss them from the point of view of their interpretation rather than their construction. The latter is the job of the researchers, but their correct interpretation is everyone's business.

A significance test is a decision-making tool. At the completion of a study there will be values for the end-point measures. In a clinical trial one such might be the proportions of subjects in each of the two arms of a trial who are symptom-free after one year. These proportions are more likely to differ than to be identical. The question that then arises is whether the observed difference represents a real difference in benefit between the treatments or is merely owing to the vagaries of chance. The logic of a significance test is as follows. A null hypothesis[20] is constructed: this is usually that no effect has been observed (which is why it is called null), e.g. that there is no real difference in the efficacy of the treatments. The alternative hypothesis is that there is a real, rather than chance, difference. On the assumption that the null hypothesis is true, the probability of obtaining the observed difference or greater by chance alone is calculated. If that chance is quite high, say 30 per cent, then one is inclined to the view that nothing unusual has been observed and accept the null hypothesis. If that chance is small, say 1 per cent, then one may reason as follows.

A difference as large as that observed is a rare event if it has been brought about by the effects of chance alone. Rare events, by definition, occur rarely. I prefer to think that I have not observed a rare event. Rather, my assumption underlying the calculation of the probability – that is, the null hypothesis – was false. I will reject the null hypothesis and accept the alternative hypothesis that a real difference has been observed.

All decision tools are subject to error. Significance tests have two types of error: type 1 when the null hypothesis is wrongly rejected, and type 2 when the alternative hypothesis is wrongly rejected. The type 1 error corresponds to the significance level chosen: that is, the probability deemed small enough to warrant rejecting the null hypothesis. Thus, if a null hypothesis is rejected at the 1 per cent level of significance there is a 1 per cent probability that the observed difference really was a chance effect and a mistake has been made. As with all decisions, the relative costs of making the various mistakes have to be balanced. For example, if introducing an innovation as a result of a clinical trial is going to be more costly than staying with current practice, then one is likely to be very conservative and demand a high level of statistical significance (i.e. low type 1 error). Similar considerations apply to type 2 errors that have a bearing on the power of a study to detect a real difference if it exists. Power is discussed below.

Another consideration is the direction of the difference of interest. If any difference is of interest then a two-tailed test is used. This would be the case in circumstances when it is as important to demonstrate relative harm as relative benefit. If changes in only one direction are deemed important then a one-tailed test may be used. A one-tailed test will have greater power for detecting this unidirectional difference than a two-tailed test. However, the logic of significance tests demands that the choice between one- and two-tailed tests be made before the data are gathered. If in doubt, use a two-tailed test.

Sometimes a dataset requires many separate comparisons, each involving a significance test. If 100 independent such comparisons are made at the 5 per cent level of significance then, on average, five of those comparisons will yield a statistically significant result just by chance; that this is so follows immediately from the definition of type 1 error. To reduce the risk of erroneous conclusions investigators can reduce the nominal significance levels[21] of these tests from 5 per cent to, say, 1 per cent. That is, each comparison is regarded as statistically significant only if the probability value is less than 1 per cent, but its type 1 error is still assumed to be 5 per cent. Often, multiple comparisons arise because the investigators lack clarity about their aims. This should not arise in evaluative research. However, if multiple comparisons are known to be unavoidable the matter of nominal significance levels should be decided at the study design stage.

Significance tests are concerned only with making a decision about whether or not a real difference has been observed. They are silent on whether that difference is of such a magnitude as to be important. Thus, findings that are presented solely in terms of statistical significance are unlikely to be useful to resource managers. These considerations have led to the increasing demand for the presentation of confidence interval around estimated quantities.

Confidence intervals are constructed from the same kind of information that leads to significance tests. They are based on the hypothetical sampling distribution outlined above. Ninety-five per cent confidence intervals (CIs) are interpreted as follows (the logic is somewhat convoluted).[22] If for each of the unlimited number of hypothetical replicates of the study a 95 per cent CI is constructed, then 95 per cent of those intervals will contain the mean value of the outcome (e.g. a difference in efficacy) of the population of studies. Note that 5 per cent of the intervals do not contain the true mean. In real life only one study is done. Its 95 per cent CI for a value either does or does not contain the true value; one hopes that it is one of the 95 per cent of all possible intervals that does actually contain the true value. If one wishes to be more certain of getting an interval that contains the true value one may construct a 99 per cent CI. Greater certainty comes at a cost: 99 per cent CIs are on average wider than 95 per cent CIs and will always be so in the context of a single study. A 100 per cent CI is obtainable at the cost of being useless, as the interval will cover every possible value for the measure. Informally, people like to interpret a 95 per cent CI as a range of precision around an estimate. This does little harm as long as it is remembered that there is a 5 per cent chance that the true value will not be in that interval at all. It should be clear that CIs convey far more information than significance tests. They show the magnitude of the estimate together with a range of values around it which indicate the precision of the estimate. The link with significance tests is simple. Suppose that a two-sided significance test on a treatment difference gives a probability value of < 5 per cent under the null hypothesis. The corresponding 95 per cent CI will not include zero difference in its range of values around the estimated difference. If the significance test does not lead to rejecting the null hypothesis at the 5 per cent level of significance the corresponding 95 per cent CI will contain zero treatment difference but will be more informative than the significance test.

The most important messages for managers and research commissioners are twofold:

- decide the confidence interval before embarking on the study;
- feel comfortable about the risk of either missing a 'real effect' or erroneously concluding there is significant impact, according to your other considerations (cost, politics, change that might be needed).

These messages are developed further in the section on study size.

In the analysis of data it is important to bear in mind the population of study units from which the actual study units were drawn, for it is only to these that the findings are generalizable. Sometimes that population is more hypothetical than real. For example, an RCT of therapy generalizes to the population of patients present and future who have the same inclusion criteria and lack the exclusion criteria of the trial; usually there does not exist any list of this population akin to a sampling frame. Sometimes there may be no obvious population to which to generalize quantitatively, in which case it is hard to justify using significance tests and confidence intervals. For example, consider an audit of aspects of the school health service in South Manchester.[23] Among other things this looked at the provision of visual and auditory screening facilities meeting given standards. Many of the findings were presented in tables showing the percentages of schools by categories meeting various levels of the standards. The authors eschewed using significance tests or presenting CIs. The reason was that the study aimed to show things as they were at that time and in that place. Moreover, South Manchester schools could not be considered to be a random sample of either Manchester schools or those in the UK. It would also make little sense to consider South Manchester schools to be a sample from their own historical time line. Nevertheless, many insights, issues and problems arose which in a qualitative sense would be applicable to those organizing school health services elsewhere; hence the justification for the study findings being published.

In general, when one is considering the need for statistical inference it is necessary to think through the levels of variation that contribute to the measurements that are being presented. Consider a hypothetical study of the distribution of blood pressure among adolescents.[24] This might be done in one of two ways. Either blood pressure measurement is taken on samples of adolescents from a single geographical area (e.g. South Manchester) or it is taken from samples from many randomly chosen areas within the UK. In the first case inferences would not necessarily be generalizable to the UK; in the second they would. However, in both cases it would be useful to present CIs for the mean blood pressure. The reason is that there are several levels of variation that lead to imprecision in the measures. These are listed below.

1 Variation in (average) blood pressure geographically in the UK.
2 Variation in (average) blood pressure among adolescents in any given area.
3 Sample variation.
4 Variation in blood pressure value from time to time throughout the day in each individual around their own average.
5 Random measurement error consequent on the properties of the instrument of measurement.

Thus, the estimated average blood pressure in a single geographical area has uncertainty introduced by levels 2 to 5, and hence a CI is a useful indication of the precision of the estimate.

Variation is always additive. In principle, as illustrated above, it can be analysed into components arising from the different levels. Thus, in the planning for an investigation consideration should be given to identifying critical levels of the variation that might be reduced by an appropriate design. For example, it might be found that paying greater attention to reducing error in the measurement instrument yields a more cost-effective solution than increasing the study size in an attempt to compensate for this. One way of reducing random measurement error is to take the mean of repeated measurements on the same study unit.

5.14 Determining study size

It is crucial for the commissioners to take an active part in the determination of study size, for the study size is a critical determinant of the ability of the study to answer the questions posed. Major components of the cost of a study will be roughly proportional to study size. Study size is a consideration for both the quantitative and qualitative aspects of R&D programmes. In qualitative research there are no algorithms to help set study size. Nevertheless, experienced qualitative researchers have a feel for how many subjects are required for specific purposes. Theoretical sampling (Box 5.16) is a useful approach if there is some flexibility of resources.

For quantitative studies there are several ways of approaching the issue.

1 Setting the size such that a given observed difference in a key outcome variable will be statistically significant at, say, the 5 per cent level (e.g. treatment outcome difference be significantly different from zero).

2 Setting the size such that a critical CI (e.g. for treatment outcome difference) will be of a predetermined width.
3 Setting the size so that a predetermined minimum real difference in outcomes (e.g. treatment outcome difference) will be detectable by the study with a given probability.

All three methods require some knowledge of the statistical properties of the outcome measures in the context of the study population; depending on circumstances these might be the mean and standard deviation of some measure in the group being conventionally treated, the proportion of individuals who survive one year on standard therapy etc. Slightly better than order of magnitude approximations usually suffice. These can be obtained from published work on similar study units or, if necessary, from a special small observational study or a pilot of the main study. We will not discuss the first two methods further, as they are not in the spirit of change-promoting R&D. The third is in that spirit because it forces one to state the minimum effect one is interested in detecting. This minimum should have been determined during the early commissioning discussions about what magnitude of effect would be worth researching and worth implementing through routine service (and at what cost). This is a discussion that should involve researchers and relevant health professionals, as their experience will help in the identification of an appropriate primary outcome measure.

In the previous section the type 1 and type 2 errors of significance tests were raised. The type 2 error is the probability of wrongly concluding, on the basis of a significance test that does not reach significance at some stated level (e.g. 5 per cent), that there is no real difference even though such a difference of a specified magnitude exists. The probability that the significance test will be significant at the stated level if a real difference of stated magnitude exists is called the power of the test (i.e. 1 – type 2 error). Thus, one might ask what study size is necessary for there to be 80 per cent probability (power) of detecting 15 percentage points difference in survival at one year and using a significance test at the 5 per cent level of significance. Given some information about the likely percentage survival of patients under the conventional therapy, it is very easy for the investigator, using an appropriate formula, to estimate how many subjects would be needed for the two study arms. The number of subjects required increases as the power increases and as the significance level decreases. That is, to get smaller type 1 and 2 errors costs resources.

Researchers applying to grant-giving bodies commonly design their studies to a power of 80 per cent at the 5 per cent level of significance. Neither of these numbers has magical properties. Researchers are under pressure to keep costs down. Many patrons of research specify maximum awards within which researchers have to budget. Others, all else being equal, might give preference to two less costly applications than one very costly one. The figures of 80 and 5 per cent are what the research community itself seems to have come to regard as an acceptable minimum and maximum respectively; it is mainly members of that community that determine the distribution of traditional grant awards.

Commissioners should be more sophisticated. They should weigh the costs of type 1 and type 2 errors in a study against the knock-on effects of those errors in the decision as to whether or not to implement a service change. A service change that might be cost-effective to implement if a real difference is detected would probably not be if the decision to implement were influenced by a type 1 error. Bear in mind that implementation may take place on a long-term basis throughout the healthcare system. Similarly, a decision not to implement influenced by a type 2 error may have long-term and widespread knock-on effects in terms of costs and/or denying people access to a worthwhile procedure. Thus, each resource decision based on R&D carries a financial and humanistic multiplier to the broader service that must be weighed when one is deciding acceptable levels of error.

In principle, decision theory techniques[25] can aid consideration of these matters. What should be clear is that change management associated with R&D involves much more than the technical issues of producing sound research designs. The research question should arise from the concerns of resource managers (or at least be consistent with them); the effects worth detecting and potentially running with as service developments should be worthwhile in terms of cost, benefits and broader strategic considerations; R&D work should be prioritized within its resources; and the resources devoted to any particular project or programme should be decided in the light of the long-term consequences of right and wrong decisions. Obviously, the decision analysis will be different for each programme. However, until such analysis becomes the norm it might be prudent for commissioners to take 90 per cent power at a 1 per cent significance level as their routine values, even though this might mean funding less R&D.

There is more to study size than power considerations. There is the matter of representation and generalizability. It might be thought that power calculations take care of that along the way, but they may not. We have already discussed the problem of the study population in many clinical trials being a highly selected sample of the patients with that condition who would be encountered in routine practice. There is the separate matter of whether a relatively small sample of study units can reflect important aspects of the diversity in the population from which it was drawn. This may become particularly noticeable when samples are as small as fifty study units. It does not appear prudent to allow strong evidence from a single adequately powered but small study to determine resource use policy. This situation may arise when the effect being sought is large. There are two options. The first is to regard the initial study as a pilot and to reinvestigate on a much larger scale. This has the attraction that it enables the impact of a potential service development to be examined in its broadest terms (including management issues) over a longer time scale. It is a monitored implementation (which we recommend anyway) that still carries the possibility of leading to the recommendation to terminate the service and not allow its implementation elsewhere.

The second option is to replicate the study elsewhere. This has the advantage of making sure that the apparent benefits will emerge in different circumstances (location, client population, personnel etc.) and should always be considered when the initial study, no matter how large, took place in a single centre. Bear in mind that in the initial study there may have been plenty of subjects but there would have been relatively few health professionals and support staff involved. The enthusiasm and dedication of that clinical and investigative team might have been a significant contributor to the outcome and might not be easily replicable elsewhere. This is also a reason why clinical trials and other studies should not concentrate solely on clinical outcomes; the dynamics of the process leading to that outcome might be just as important as the procedures being tested. While this replication is being done there is no reason why the sites of the initial study should not be funded to continue on a small scale and be further evaluated. This preserves the expertise and goodwill, and will speed the process to full implementation at those sites if the go ahead is given. In essence, we are proclaiming the need for planned programmes aiming at possible implementation and routine use, rather than relying piecemeal on particular studies, however statistically powerful they may be.

When either of these options is followed it is important to ensure that the clinical staff, the investigators and, sometimes, vocal members of the client population are aware that a decision to implement the development is not a foregone conclusion and also aware of the criteria that remain to be satisfied before that conclusion is reached. It may be very difficult to withstand the clamour from professionals and their clients/ patients to introduce what seems on the basis of the existing evidence to be a good thing. Nevertheless, it is feasible if nationally R&D is adequately coordinated and linked into resource management concerns, and the leaders of a health service (political and otherwise) defend a rational approach to resource decisions.

5.15 Statistical presentation

The results of studies should be presented as simply as possible. The quantitative findings upon which resource decisions are to be based should be portrayed in tables and charts intelligible to resource managers, health professionals and others; similar considerations of intelligibility apply to the presentation of qualitative findings. These consumers should receive the information in a form that allows them to make their own judgement of what may be concluded. Thus, the authors of such reports must eschew the temptation to impress their peers, and baffle their real audience, with statistical legerdemain. The onus lies on the investigators to express their findings and the discussion leading to their conclusions in a manner accessible to the intelligent lay person. In effect, we are saying that the technical machinery of statistics (apart from simple notions like CIs) should not be apparent, other than, perhaps, in appendices. If the import of the findings (bearing in mind that the subject at hand is primarily evaluative work) is mainly dependent upon sophisticated statistical analysis, then those findings should be regarded with suspicion. Resource managers are generally asking the straight question of how much may be got and at what cost. There seems no reason why they should not receive a straight answer (which includes 'don't know', rather than obfuscation and special pleading because the study was inconclusive). Those who commission R&D are in a strong position to demand straight answers under the principle of 'he who pays the piper calls the tune'.

Although the main findings should, so to speak, hit one between the eyes through a simple presentation, there is a place for more sophisticated analyses. Statistical modelling (e.g. regression analysis) helps the analyst to sift through the relationships among variables and adjust for known confounding variables in a more subtle manner than tabulation. These analyses may be used to confirm that what is presented in simple summary tables is not misleading because of the influence of confounding variables. The analysis helps in selecting the most helpful and revealing tabulations. Further, modelling facilitates the exploration of fine detail and of interesting issues that might be secondary to the main study aims. The commissioners and consumers of R&D do not need deep expertise in statistical modelling. However, if they are to keep their wits about them and to be in a position to ask pertinent questions they need an appreciation of the logic of modelling. This is partly because it is a good thing in its own right for them to be able to look critically at all aspects of a study and partly as protection against ill-used modelling. These days the mechanics of modelling is easy by virtue of powerful personal computer software packages. This makes it readily available to researchers and it is all too easy for them to go beyond their depth. Ideally, a professional statistician will be associated with each programme of quantitative work, but this will not always be the case. In the next section we introduce the logic of statistical modelling in a non-technical way.

5.16 The logic of statistical modelling

In the previous sections of this chapter we gave a commentary on study designs applicable to R&D and introduced the ideas underlying simple methods of statistical inference. In this section these notions are placed in a more general setting to aid the introduction of modelling. In many respects the concepts of statistical modelling provide a unifying framework for much of statistical inference and provide a strong link with study design.

Biological entities and social systems are inherently complicated. Hence, any assumed understanding of them can be only partial. No theoretical perspective or experimental procedure yet devised can hope to include or control all the influences that determine the response of biological and social systems. Therefore, attention is initially directed towards identifying major determinants of response and seeking to understand the relationships between them; as understanding increases finer detail can be absorbed into theory and experiment.

When the major influences on a system have been identified it is usually found that the combined influence of myriad small (unidentified or deliberately ignored) determinants of response behaves as though it were a random perturbation[26] from what would be expected from the major influences alone. This random behaviour can be characterized by an appropriate probability distribution. Indeed, the common occurrence of the normal (Gaussian) distribution in quantities measured on an interval or ratio scale[27] is partially explained by the central limit theorems.[28]

Hence, statistical inference is like trying to see important structures through a fog which distorts their position and magnitude. The properties of the 'fog' are described in the language of probability theory. As far as possible the obscuring and distorting effects of the fog are quantified, so that bounds of error may be placed upon the measurements of the structures so dimly perceived.

Statistical design should precede data gathering and inference. The purpose of design is to maximize the efficiency of data gathering so that the questions posed in a study have a good prospect of being answered. Within the resources available, the aim is to minimize the effect of 'fog'. Design leaves its mark on data. It introduces relationships between data items/categories, i.e. it creates *structure*. Structure must be taken into account during data analysis.

There are many books on aspects of 'data analysis' but fewer on design and on the context within which the statistical enterprise takes place. There is a danger that data are perceived as being entities of independent existence that serve as fodder for statistical analysis. It should be apparent from earlier sections of this chapter that data are the end-product of measurement. Measurement arises from experiment or observation. Experiment and observation should flow from questions posed within some *theoretical* (see above) context. It is theory that determines what is of interest and *measurable*. Theory determines the properties (e.g. measurement scales) of what is measured. The validation of any instrument of measurement rests ultimately with the theory which specifies that such a measurement will have *utility*.

The mathematics of statistical modelling[29] has been developed independently of the theoretical contexts within which the models will be used: the application of the models must not be. In developing the notion of structure we shall see why this is so.

Structure

The individual items making up a collection of data are not independent of one another. There are relationships among them, which are here termed *structure*. Moreover, this structure is obscured by the 'fog' or, as it is more commonly termed, random error. Structure is of two kinds: fixed and presumptive. Fixed structure arises from two sources:

- experimental design (including the way an observational study is organized);
- theoretical and *a priori* necessity.

Presumptive structure arises from:

- study hypotheses (theoretically contingent);
- incidental influences being controlled.

Fixed structure

The contribution of experimental design to structure is the most easy to see. We illustrate it through some examples.

Example 1
Consider simple random samples taken from two populations. It would usually be meaningless to pool the samples into one. The structure here is almost trivial: the data values within each sample have something in common with each other which they do not share with the other sample.

Example 2
Consider a randomized controlled trial which uses each subject as his or her own control, e.g. two topical drugs for the treatment of an eye condition (present in both eyes) are randomly allocated to the left and right eyes of subjects. When analysing the results of the trial, a prudent investigator would take account of the fact that the left and right eyes of each subject have more in common (e.g. genetic origins) with each other than either has with the eyes of other people. Hence, the analysis would be based on within-subject comparisons of treatments.

Example 3
Suppose that a study identifies families with children and divides them into two groups, which receive differing dietary interventions; all members of a family receive the same

intervention. An analysis of responses to intervention should take account of a rather complicated structure: members of each family have more in common (genetic, social and cultural) with each other than members of other families receiving the same intervention; children within each family are more closely similar to each other than to either parent; parents within each family are likely to be more similar (assortative mating) to each other than to adults in other families etc. Note that some of these expectations of similarity derive from theoretical (Mendelian[30]) genetic considerations. Thus, the distinction between design influences and theoretical necessity is not absolute.

In general, experimental design imposes structure through the manner in which study units are grouped, through the relationships among study units within and between groups and through specifying what happens to the groups. *Theoretical necessity* and other *a priori* considerations lead an investigator to impose structure on data. That is, certain relationships among data items are known to exist before the data are gathered (and are not themselves the subject of the present investigation) and must be taken into account for a valid analysis and interpretation of the data.

Example 4
The genetic considerations in example 3 above give prior theoretical reasons why certain responses from related people are likely to be more closely correlated than responses among unrelated people; this leads to the statistical concept of intra-class correlation.

Example 5
The analysis of anthropometric data should explicitly recognize the geometric relationships between lengths, areas and volumes.[31]

Example 6
In a cross-sectional study of lung function related to various factors it would be prudent to record the ages and heights of subjects even though those may not be the measurements of prime interest. It is well documented from prior observations that FEV_1 (a measure of lung function) is related to height (for plausible anthropometric reasons) and to age. Thus, including these variables in the analysis recognizes their capacity to contribute structure to the data. Explicitly taking account of this structure during the analysis reduces the random error associated with estimates of other relationships.

Presumptive structure

Study hypotheses generate presumptive structure. A study is designed to test specific hypotheses which are expressed in terms of relationships that might be expected to be found among the data. Confirming the presence or absence of this structure is the purpose of the study. In some circumstances the predicted relationships may be very precise. In clinical science and epidemiology theoretical predictions are usually semi-quantitative (e.g. 'risk of myocardial infarction is positively correlated with saturated fat intake') and the study may not only confirm the relationship but help to quantify it. In many cases this structure may be perceived dimly and only after due account of other structures inherent to the data has been taken. Evaluative research is primarily interested in quantifying outcome effects. Resource managers are unlikely to be interested in effects that after due analysis remain heavily enshrouded in fog.

Many observational studies do not at first sight appear to fit this mould. Indeed, the extreme case of the 'fishing expedition' is to be deplored.[32] Nevertheless, observational studies usually have some prior expectations, although sometimes they are not explicitly stated, and they may not be easy to articulate precisely.

Incidental influences is our term for a collection of variables each of which is believed to have some possible influence on the response of the system under study, but whose precise role need not be theoretically understood. These include confounding variables. They are used as *covariates*[33] in an attempt to control for the influences they might exert. This is a *post hoc* procedure during analysis.

The four categories of structure are not always easily differentiated. In the design of a study there is a choice whether various influences on outcome should be incorporated in the designed structure (e.g. as strata) or allowed for less formally during statistical analysis (compare the comments about case–control studies in this chapter).

Formulating models

The discussion that follows is loosely based around regression models; the general principles apply universally to statistical modelling.

In a highly abstract form a regression model may be formulated thus:

outcome variable = fixed structure + presumptive structure + fog

The equals sign in the pseudo-equation should, at this stage, be interpreted very broadly as reading 'is predicted by'.[34] The plus sign joining the fixed and presumptive structures merely means that they are linked in some way, which, when the model is fully specified, may include addition and multiplication of components of the structures. The final plus sign indicates that the prediction will be imperfect and there will be some fog. In standard terminology, the variable being predicted by some combination of the other variables in the dataset is called the dependent variable. The variables making up the structure are called independent variables, though they may not actually be independent of each other. Loosely speaking, the fog can be equated to the difference, for each study unit, between the outcome variable as empirically recorded and the values predicted for it by the other variables in the model.

The construction of models entails formulating a fairly flexible type of mathematical relationship among the independent variables, such that it may be used to predict the dependent variable. This relationship will have unknown values (parameters) that will be estimated by finding the combination of parameter values that gives the best fit (i.e. the least fog) of the model to the data. With few exceptions, there will be one and only one set of parameter values, from the infinite possibilities, that provides best fit.

The simplest, and most commonly used, relationship among the dependent variables is linear in the parameters (coefficients). For example, one may try to predict the forced expiratory volume in one second (FEV_1) of adults from other variables in a data set thus:

$$FEV_1 = A + B \times age + C \times height + D \times age \times height + E \times race + F \times race \times height$$

Linearity in the coefficients means that A, B, C etc. appear once each and are not subject to any more complicated relationships than shown above. It is worth persevering a little further with this example, as it illustrates many of the main features of regression analysis.

The coefficients A to F are estimated from the data through the process of model fitting. Coefficient A is an overall mean value for FEV_1. The linear combination of the other coefficients with values for age, height etc. represents the deviation from the average of an individual of the given age, height etc. Coefficients A, B, C and D are numbers with the properties of the ratio scale. Their units of measurement are those of FEV_1. Coefficients B and C represent the separate individual effects of age and height respectively on FEV_1. So if coefficient B had the value of -0.5 it would mean that, on average, in the data set FEV_1 declines by 0.5 units for each year of adult life. Coefficient D represents the joint effect of weight and height over and above their separate effects. This is called an interaction term.[35] It allows for the possibility that the joint effect is greater or less than the sum of the individual effects. It is analogous to synergism between drugs.

The variable 'race' is a measurement on the nominal scale.[36] Individuals would have been placed into groups according to their racial origins, e.g. Caucasian and Mongoloid. The coefficient E is not really a single coefficient but a set of coefficients relating to the racial categories.[37] In essence, the value of each of these component coefficients is an offset to the overall mean FEV_1, representing the average effect of being in one or other of the racial groups. Similarly, the coefficient for the interaction between race and height is a set of coefficients relating to the racial categories. This term in the model allows for the possibility that the effect of height on the predicted FEV_1 differs among the racial categories for, say, genetic reasons.

This example illustrates how some structure in the data has been accommodated. Rather than treating the study population as a homogeneous group of people, explicit recognition has been given to the possibility that racial origin may be a predictor of FEV_1, though this relationship was perhaps not of prime interest to the investigators.

Selecting and fitting models

Modelling is a way of handling *structure*. It is mandatory that known *fixed* structure be included in a model. Dealing with the *presumptive* structure is as much art as technology. The analyst must explore different ways of specifying presumptive structure and how it relates to fixed structure. In essence, the art is in using the variables, factors (nominal scale variables), derived variables etc. to specify a model that is informative. Occam's razor[38] is the guiding principle. This demands that one settle for the simplest satisfactory model.

Every set of data has a fixed total information content. An important statistical concept, which is a correlate of information content, is that of *degrees of freedom*. The maximum degrees of freedom equals the number of study units (e.g. persons on whom measurements have been made). Each structure imposed on the data (or quantity estimated) uses some of the degrees of freedom. That is, once a structure has been imposed it leaves less room for manoeuvre in imposing further structures. This is analogous to designing a house. The position of the outside walls and internal supports places constraints on the size and positions of the rooms. Once the size and shape of one room is decided it places a constraint on the sizes and shapes of all other rooms on the same storey. The position of the staircase places constraints on the sizes and shapes of rooms and corridors on all storeys. As the plan progresses there are ever fewer remaining choices.

Any statistical model has two functions: the first is to elucidate structure; the second to allow inference in a world of uncertainty. It is *always* possible to specify a model that uses all the variables, together with many high-order interactions among them, such that every value of the dependent variable is explained *exactly*. Such a model (known as *fully saturated*) would use all the degrees of freedom. In that circumstance it is impossible to draw inferences about the sampling variation of the parameters that specify the model. All that has been done is to express the original data in a different form. Moreover, there is no unique combination of variables and interactions that leads to a saturated model. Thus, why should one have any reason to believe that the particular saturated model selected is any more informative than the infinity of other (quite different and, in terms of apparent meaning, often contradictory) saturated models that could have been formulated using the same data?

In order for there to be statistical inference, degrees of freedom – the more the better – must be left over to specify the random error, or probability, structure. In fact, the random error can also be thought of as consisting of discarded variables and/or interactions: those whose possible 'existence' is compatible with being a chance effect. However, most of the discarded interactions will never have been considered in the first place. For one proceeds by fitting simple models and adding complexity only if it can be shown to enhance the model. Thus, one would never contemplate using a high-order interaction between variables (or a high-order polynomial in one variable) unless the next lower order interaction (or polynomial) had been shown to be useful.

When one is fitting a model, candidate variables or groups of variables (including interactions) are discarded if it is shown that their inclusion does not explain (i.e. reveal structure rather than fog) any of the remaining random variation. Explaining random variation entails showing that the greater homogeneity of variation produced by structures exceeds in worth the consequent reduction in the degrees of freedom for the random error. In the case of a single variable being considered for adding to a model this is equivalent to saying that it will be retained only if its coefficient is statistically significantly different from its null value (usually zero). Consequently, because all statistical tests are decision tools with the possibility of error (type 1 and type 2), there can never be certainty that the right choice has been made. The best that can be done is to specify error levels that are acceptable

Traditionally, the aim of statistical modelling is to find the most parsimonious model: that is, the one with the fewest independent variables that satisfactorily predicts the dependent variable. In other words, adding further variables to the most parsimonious model does not, beyond chance effects, reduce the discrepancies between the actual and predicted values. This process can be automated using procedures called the forward and backward elimination of variables. The use of these procedures alone in the analysis of evaluative studies is to be discouraged, because it is not just the most parsimonious model that matters. It is through the process of reaching it, guided by the human intellect, that important insights into the data arise. Investigators who have a clear notion of the various components of fixed and presumptive structure can approach modelling systematically to explore the effects of key variables. For example, it is much better to look at the various known potential confounding variables explicitly than just to assume that because they do not appear in the most parsimonious model they do not matter. Some of the independent variables will correlate with each other and hence may individually or in combinations substitute for one another in alternative parsimonious or near parsimonious models. It should also be noted that an individual variable may drop out of a model because its coefficient is not statistically significantly different from zero, but it does not mean that that variable has no bearing on the interpretation of the data; indeed, the non-significant coefficient could still have appreciable magnitude and it is prudent to ask what this would mean if there had been a type 2 error.

Elsewhere in this chapter we have mentioned mathematical modelling or simulation as a tool to aid evaluation. There is an important distinction between that kind of modelling and statistical modelling. Mathematical modelling is akin to a theoretical exposition of the system under scrutiny. It identifies presumably important elements of the system, posits relationships between them and on this basis makes predictions about the behaviour of the system. Within these models the various mathematical relations expressed are assumed to be isomorphic with those occurring in the real system. The relations portrayed are assumed to be cause and effect. It is possible to add a random element to these models (stochastic models), but this is a device to introduce uncertainty in order to represent the cumulative effect of many, presumably lesser, variables that have not been identified or included explicitly in the model.

A statistical model, even though its underlying representation is mathematical, is mainly atheoretical. The mathematical relationship represented by the variables and the coefficients in the model is merely an empirical entity for the purpose of predicting one variable from others within the dataset. The process of selecting the prediction model gives insight into what are important influences on the outcome. It helps one to see the effect of key variables after the effects of covariates have been taken into account; alternatively, it can be used to 'adjust' key variables in the light of the apparent effects of covariates. Statistical modelling rarely gives insight into a mathematical representation of how the system behaves. Nevertheless, as the discussion of different types of structure shows, statistical modelling should be approached logically and with due regard to known or presumed statistical associations. The consumers of R&D should satisfy themselves that in any given instance the investigators have given a logical account of their approach to statistical modelling and taken due steps to ensure that the statistical assumptions underlying their model (and thus essential for the validity of inferences flowing from it) have been checked.

5.17 Systematic review: virtues and vices

Commissioning R&D and making resource decisions about implementation should not take place independently of the corpus of existing knowledge. In recent years the manner in which literature is reviewed has been systematized in an effort to ensure consistency, minimization of bias and the reduction of the necessarily partially subjective judgements in the conclusions. An important influence on this has been the International Cochrane Collaboration. It seeks, through a network of Cochrane Centres, to maintain databases of all RCTs (in progress, published or unpublished) relating to the various clinical fields. The motivation for this is the belief (with which we partially concur) that changes in practice should be driven through evidence and that the RCT must underpin such decisions. Systematic reviews derived from Cochrane databases strive to apply common standards to the assessment of the methodological aspects of RCTs. By actively seeking unpublished studies and including them in the systematic review it is hoped to reduce publication bias. This is a bias that arises because studies with 'negative' or inconclusive findings, such that the end-point effects are not statistically different from zero, have, hitherto, had less chance of being accepted for publication. Thus, if unpublished studies are not taken into account, and bearing in mind type 1 errors, there is a risk that the published material assessed will give a falsely optimistic glow. These principles are also being applied more widely by workers outside the Cochrane Centres to systematic reviews that include evidence other than that from RCTs.

In association with these developments there has been the increasing use of a statistical technique called meta-analysis. This seeks to give a more objective and quantitative overview of the evidence than traditional reviews. There are two major variants. The first seeks to find a common outcome measure for all the eligible studies.[39] This might be an odds ratio for success on competing therapies. Putting all the findings on to a common basis entails either reinterpreting the published data or going back to the original data source and reanalysing. The odds ratios, with their confidence intervals, for all the separate studies are then displayed graphically and a visual comparison can be made. This is a helpful technique to which few would take exception. Meta-analysis can be taken further by calculating a summary odds ratio for the entire set of studies. This can be done in one of two ways: first, a weighted average (with confidence interval) of the separate odds ratios; second, a formal reanalysis of the primary data, treating each separate study as if it were part of a single multicentre study and leading to a common overall outcome measure.

We do not seek to deny the overall value of databases of studies and systematized review. However, we have reservations. The Cochrane and systematic review industries may be too detached from the practical issues that exercise resource managers. At present, they largely set their own agenda and their values appear to be those of science. This is natural because until the new paradigm is fully implemented resource managers will not have the means or confidence to wrest the helm. Moreover, many of the concerns of the systematic review and database technicians seem irrelevant to the needs of the service. Is it really a worthwhile use of resources to track down unpublished and grey literature[40] in order to avert the theoretical risk of publication bias? Pragmatically, should one not assume that most material that has not reached the light of day has probably not done so for good reason and is best left alone? Moreover, much of the published material, which is pre-new paradigm, is wholly insufficient to meet the needs of resource managers (the broad questions about cost-effectiveness, cost–utility and humanistic issues). Any view that places the RCT on a pedestal and refuses to value other sources of evidence (such as qualitative research) must be suspect in the light of the points we have made elsewhere in this chapter.

Our greatest reservations concern the use of meta-analysis, primarily the sort that seeks to present an overall summary outcome. We are not alone in our heresy.[41] First, we are wary of claims that the studies brought together in meta-analysis can be sufficiently alike to treat them as if they were centres in a multicentre study. In a real multicentre study all the centres should be working to a rigorously enforced common protocol with regard to patient recruitment criteria, treatment regimens, outcome measurement etc.[42] Second, meta-analysis seems against the spirit of independent replication of findings by studies each designed to have acceptable statistical power to answer its study questions. It is becoming almost an excuse for not designing studies of sufficient power. The notion of experimental replication (and confirmation) comes from science and seems equally applicable under the change-promoting paradigm. Replication in slightly different circumstances (different catchment populations of patients, different health professionals and perhaps minor variants on the treatment regimen) is a powerful way of helping to decide what the impact would be in routine service. In these circumstances the individual studies need to be compared and contrasted and not mechanically combined. Third, if some of the studies included in a meta-analysis can *post hoc* be shown to have been inherently lacking the power to have a reasonable chance of answering the study question unequivocally, then that casts an overall doubt about the competence of those conducting the studies and perhaps they should not be included in the corpus of knowledge.

The question arises as to the circumstances in which a systematic review should form the basis for changes in practice and resource allocation decisions. The problem at present is that the systematic reviews are mainly of studies that have taken place in a poorly coordinated way and are not usually able to answer all the questions that resource managers should pose. In this circumstance systematic reviews should, except where non-contentious changes are proposed, not be accepted as a basis for resource decisions. This is especially so when few or any of the reviewed studies give clear answers in their own right and when the supposedly compelling evidence only emerges from summary statistics (with confidence intervals) from a meta-analysis. However, they can inform R&D policy and commissioning. As R&D becomes better managed and more focused on the needs of resource managers, the need to review vast quantities of literature should diminish. The value of databases of research proposed, in progress and completed will remain. To these should be added a growing literature on the lessons learned from implementing specific changes and manuals to assist implementation.

The left-hand side of Box 5.21 displays a widely used categorization of evidence.[43] The right-hand side of Box 5.21 is our addition and offers examples of the management actions the given levels of evidence justify, and hence makes the categories useful within the new paradigm.

Box 5.21   Categories of evidence and the decisions they support (an extension of a table from the US Task Force on Preventive Health)

Evidence	*What the evidence supports*
A There is good evidence to support the use of the procedure	General introduction of the procedure through monitored implementation if it is proven cost-effective and accords with resource use priorities.
B There is fair evidence to support the use of the procedure	Modelling and decision analysis to assess likely costs, benefit and impact of the procedure, followed, if it seems worthwhile, by commissioned R&D to improve the evidence.
C There is poor evidence to support the use of the procedure	If the procedure looks potentially useful and 'poor evidence' means lack of evidence rather than evidence against then commission R&D. Otherwise do nothing.
D There is fair evidence to support rejection of the use of the procedure	If it is not already in use prevent its introduction. If it is in use commission R&D and discourage further spread of the procedure meanwhile.
E There is good evidence to support the rejection of the procedure	Use change management skills and control of resources to withdraw the procedure.
Quality of evidence	
I Evidence obtained from at least one properly designed randomized control trial	Supports the introduction of most procedures including therapeutic and caring regimens. If the innovation is likely to have large overall resource implications it is preferable to have evidence from replicated studies, which may need to be commissioned.
II-i Evidence obtained from well-designed controlled trials without randomization	Supports changes to management and process procedures. Insufficient for the introduction of therapies but may justify commissioning R&D.

II-ii	Evidence obtained from well designed cohort or case control analytic studies, preferably from more than one centre or research group	As above.
II-iii	Evidence obtained from multiple time series with or without intervention. Dramatic results in uncontrolled experiments (such as the results of the introduction of penicillin in the 1940s) could also be regarded as this type of evidence	Such evidence may be indicative of something worth pursuing through R&D but does not justify changes to organization or practice. Even if another 'penicillin' were discovered there ought to be a formal assessment of its indications for use, cost, benefits and disadvantages.
III	Opinions of respected authorities based on clinical experience, descriptive studies or reports of expert committees	It may be sufficient support for policy and organizational changes. It may also point to fruitful avenues for commissioned R&D.
IV	Evidence inadequate owing to problems of methodology (e.g. sample size, or length or comprehensiveness of follow-up or conflicts of evidence)	If evidence from well designed studies conflicts then it is prudent to take no resource decisions until the matter is resolved (perhaps through R&D if a priority area is concerned). If the inadequacy is due to methodological deficiency then the evidence should be rejected and there should be no attempt to resurrect it within a meta-analysis.

6

USING RESEARCH

KEY POINTS

A series of recommendations is made in this concluding chapter.
R&D useful to change management requires all the players
(researchers, health service resource managers, clinicians, etc.) to be
interlinked in a mesh of multi-way communication, fostering mutual
respect and support. The top-down model of researchers setting their
agenda and passing down their wisdom as they see fit should be
abandoned in favour of a 'virtuous circle' wherein the commissioners
of research, the consumers of research, and the research community
each contribute to setting the priorities, formulating and refining the
research questions, and integrating findings into practice. The social
and practical complexity of incorporating desired innovation into a
health service is more easily handled if that service has the culture of
a 'learning organization'; the move towards clinical governance within
the NHS will provide leaders to nurture this. Nationally funded R&D
should set the right example for others to follow by expecting good
research to be multi-interest, by funding only that which directly
addresses management issues, and by ensuring that the 'virtuous circle'
is in place. The process of adopting and applying the 'new paradigm'
should be documented (for example, through action research) so that
examples of good change promotion practice may be systematically
implemented throughout health services.

6.1 Preamble

The whole purpose of this book is to ensure that health services research
is both useful and usable. To this end we have set out our arguments
largely within the context with which we are most familiar and which
has stimulated our concern: the NHS in England and Wales and the
history of R&D in that health service. From this we have expanded what

we call our new paradigm: a model of research that is inseparable from the context it seeks to influence. To make this a practical reality we have then drawn out what we see as particularly important components of this process of ensuring that health services research is useful. The process starts with commissioning, which we have explained at length because it is so important, and will be unfamiliar to many readers, as well as being a complex process in itself, requiring considerable high level skills. From that we have moved to a more conventional precis of research methods and advice on project management, largely because this book is concerned with practical realities, and we feel that our readers should be quite comfortable about how research methods, which can be explored in more detail in other texts, could ease in to our new paradigm.

This final chapter looks at using research. We have labelled the new paradigm as change-promoting, so ways of using health services research must be compatible with recognized ideas about change management. All students of change will be familiar with some of the concepts that are seen to underlie successful change management, such as innovation, ice-breaking, leadership, change drivers and refreezing. Successful use of health services research will depend partly on how well the earlier stages in the research process have been managed, which we have already described, and partly by acknowledging the contribution of sound research to decision making, to the decision makers' understanding of their context, to some change management dilemmas and to the model of change management outlined above. So, unashamedly, we see using health services research as inextricable from management responsibilities, regardless of the discipline, speciality or organizational size of whatever the manager manages.

Consequently, we have structured this final chapter in terms of a series of change management topics, using each to illustrate the benefits of our approach. First, however, we reiterate our belief in the richness of multidisciplinary involvement, by expanding on the concept that underlies much of what we advocate. Then we look at the decision process, initially in terms of a four-stage model, and the opportunities it offers for mutual benefit for managers and researchers. We then examine the decision context, and the mutual insight that managers and researchers can gain by collaborative work, especially in understanding their organization. This is followed by a section illustrating how change-promoting research contributes to resolving five well recognized dilemmas of change management. Part of the resolution involves the culture of the organization. The earlier sections describe the value of research in understanding the local culture of the organization. Now we put forward the model of a 'learning organization' within which change and research are less likely to arouse xenophobic antibodies than they would in stable or ossified cultures. Finally, we apply features of change management theory directly, summarizing the responsibilities of all players, and then draw all this together in our conclusions.

6.2 Holding it all up: the safety net

In this book we have repeatedly emphasized the importance of collaboration in making health services research useful. Here we introduce the analogy of the safety net, to illustrate how essential, in our view, is the underlying idea of many people of different backgrounds and different skills working together to ensure that health services research is really useful. Many readers will be familiar with the idea of networking, now part of our conceptual jargon, a 'scientific' way of legitimizing what many successful people have always done well: communicate with each other. But here the communication we advocate is in all directions, with individuals and groups hitherto unseen as part of an appropriate peer group; furthermore, we suggest a deliberate seeking out of those different from ourselves because of what they can contribute to the overall purpose of R&D and change management. Hence the safety net analogy. Isolationists in ivory towers are dismal failures in terms of change management and really successful health services research; so too, we would argue, are ill-informed activists. It is the combination of intellectual rigour and the creative energy of the different people concerned with health services research and change management that makes the warp and weft of the net, and the strength of the determination to continue the links that make it safe. If people from apparently opposite sides of an intellectual or behavioural gulf actually function in ways which mean that they are inextricably knotted together, they will provide not only threads of continuity of purpose, which never doubts its origins, but also multinodal opportunities for other links. The more people involved, the more threads of communication there will be and the stronger those individual threads; the more cross-links and knots there are, the closer the mesh, the greater the safety in terms of the adventure we suggest and also the greater the opportunities.

What does this all mean in practice? Our idea of this safety net analogy developed because we felt that implementing our new paradigm required two main types of activity: the sharing of ideas and the sharing of change management practice. While one might be seen as very much on the research side of health services and the other as very much on the managerial side of health services, it is ensuring that there are well constructed links between the two which makes the success.

First, the sharing of ideas. As already described in the chapter on commissioning research (Chapter 4), conventionally the dissemination of ideas follows a hierarchy of respectability, with, at the lowest level, casual conversations, working up through round table discussions, then meetings, then conferences, then website pages and finally peer reviewed scientific journals. This is the hierarchy developed by and for the theory-enhancing researchers. It seems to us ironic that although all dissemination routes matter, and there is no one single perfect answer (any more than there is a therapeutic silver bullet for most health concerns), success in terms of influencing practice and bringing about change is almost inversely proportional to the scientific status of the route by which ideas are shared. Thus, an informal corridor exchange may lead directly to far more happening than, say, a leader in the *New England Journal of Medicine*, although, of course, one might in any event have fed into the other.

Alongside this hierarchy of intellectual collaboration is a hierarchy of the ways in which change management practice is disseminated, although the ranking here may be far less explicit than in the research community. None the less, it should be clear to all observers that the process of change management, and the dissemination of change management practice, is hierarchical: it requires leadership, trained and experienced senior staff who can itemize the tasks to be done and delegate responsibilities to motivated and committed subordinates. And, like the scientific hierarchy, we all know that the apparent managerial hierarchy can be overturned. Change management induces resistance in many participants, and those who are apparently the most junior can at times be in a position to jeopardize major strategic change, and in fact invert the conventional power structure in a determination not to meet whatever fate it is they fear.

Our argument is that all the different levels of intellectual dissemination, and all the different levels of change management practice, need to be brought together. The understanding of science, as well as the practice of change management, varies for us all, according to our proclivities and experience. By networking, and by remaining linked together rather than insisting on a purist elitism (untouched by either 'real life' for academics, or 'irrelevant experts' for active managers), the net acquires tremendous strength. And the more skills there are the better. Literacy and numeracy are fundamental, but important too are economics, social sciences, epidemiology, leadership, communication and team working. The more give and take there is in the networking, the greater the elasticity of the relationship, and its durability and strength in testing times.

6.3 Improving the decision process: an opportunity for mutual benefit

There are numerous management and other texts which set out a range of different approaches to decision making, each of which will claim various advantages and disadvantages. Here we have drawn on a four-stage model[1] which approximates to our experience, although quite clearly each decision situation will be unique, and could be represented with a varied balance of factors. The model, which is essentially chronological, involves the following stages:

1 Defining the question and gathering the relevant information.
2 Creating alternatives and tolerating waste (that is, jettisoning data or ideas or even documents which are non-contributory).
3 Attempting to predict the future consequences, and planning for contingencies.
4 Making the decision by balancing probabilities, risks and rewards.

The model is very similar to decision analysis in its concepts, but we have not labelled it as such because such terminology implies a rigorous modelling approach which is not often applicable in the complex web of day-to-day events. There certainly are bold claims for decision analysis in the field of R&D, both in terms of using research results and in terms of deciding research priorities.[2] Here, however, we simply describe the general ideas underlying the model.

Defining the question

Readers will instantly detect an echo here of what we have already said about the role of the researcher in our new paradigm. It is not, conceptually, a difficult model to believe. However, often so-called researchers simply collect data, and do not concentrate on defining what the real question is. And the same is true of managers, who may feel safer surrounded by statistics, even if that barricade is, in reality, non-contributory.

So, in this context, there can be a major contribution from skilled researchers, who can not only help to provide the data, but also support the decision maker distilling out the key issues on which answers are sought.

Examining alternatives

All decisions involve choice, and the choices are often competing. Even doing nothing has to be recognized as an option, and should explicitly be part of any manager's approach to decision making.

Change-promoting research cannot necessarily provide a balanced list of options. However, the process of question refinement and relevant data collection necessarily means that there has already been some selection of what really matters, and that non-necessary matters have thereby been excluded. In addition, commissioning research may well have involved bringing together superficially disparate groups whose ideas and collaboration have enriched both the research question and the data collection, so that not only might there be a wider range of options than was thought possible, but the knowledge about the options is greater than it would have been otherwise. For example, the previously quoted paper bemoaning the absence of costing data from an assessment of anti-depressive pharmaceutical interventions illustrates this. The suitably enriched questions and answers are not just 'does this work?' or 'is this safe?', but also 'how much might it cost?', and the financial implications are a great incentive for creating alternatives. The trick is therefore to recognize useless information in this context. Hitherto, it has been all too easy to reject most research data as irrelevant, incomprehensible or out of date. Now, with our new paradigm, the options and the alternatives that could be followed should emerge with far greater clarity.

Here, the contribution from decision theory to change-promoting research is to ensure that the range of contributions is meticulously documented. This should happen anyway with good quality research for the purposes of, for example, elucidating possible models. Recognizing the complex web of interests from which the research has emerged is part of the decision-making process, and so highlights the importance of doing this particularly well.

Possible consequences

Logical and mathematical thinking (such as decision trees with their probability branches) attempt to package this difficult stage into something that can be controlled and made somehow more straightforward, less contaminated by unforeseen circumstances. However, health care is largely about people, be they givers or receivers, and people do not always behave in neatly predictable patterns. It would be naive to assign probability weightings to personal relationships.

None the less, this is where we would argue, again, that the involvement of managers in the research process has much to contribute. It takes little imagination to see how, for example, the process of clarifying the research question will of itself identify the consequences the manager may most fear or desire, and hence why the research is so important. The future might not be as forecast, but what we today think might be the key factors for tomorrow will have to be explicitly set out in the process of asking what the research is all about. Thus, again, engagement in the research process should help the decision maker, and not simply by producing 'research' answers.

A balanced decision

This stage is the most difficult, the most political, often the least 'scientific' in many ways. As discussed above in relation to the problem of being a health services manager, there are fluctuating political expectations, issues that might suddenly enter the public domain, risks that are current this week but were not envisaged last week and often no clear guiding objectives that we can use to map a way through. This might therefore seem to be the most skilful domain in the decision maker's repertoire.

Researchers may well find this one of the most difficult areas. There might, apparently, be little logic, at least none that can be presumed from a scientific conclusion. As a result, many people feel uncomfortable with this stage, the sense of heading for the finishing line, and this may well be one of the main skill differences that separate senior managers from researchers.

There is a great deal to be learned from observing this skilful balancing act, on a personal basis, and also in terms of the research repertoire, not least in terms of the ways research reports are presented and written. Close collaboration with senior managers will help researchers to understand at a quite different level from the normal academic expectations the importance of how their results are conveyed, the use of graphics and tables, and live discussions. Close collaboration from the start will enable this to be the most fruitful process. As a result, the researcher can learn a great deal from the manager. Thus, overall, we feel that looking at the decision process in this way outlines clear opportunities for both managers and researchers to learn a great deal from each other.

6.4 Improving decisions: the decision makers' context

Hitherto we have discussed the mutual benefits to managers and researchers from their combined involvement in the research process, and have also shown how research can support a model of decision making. Here we look at the complex environment in which health service managers, of all disciplines (including clinicians) make their decisions, and the role of research in clarifying that context.

In doing this we are quite explicitly subscribing to 'modernity' as the governing ethos. That is, we see a contribution from health services research to decisions and change management because we believe, like many scientists too, that it is possible to make progress through the application of rationality.[3] This point may seem so obvious that it is hardly worth making. However, this belief is relatively recent in our history, having had its roots in Francis Bacon, taking off in the seventeenth century through Isaac Newton in science and René Descartes in philosophy, and reaching its peak in the eighteenth century (the Age of Enlightenment). Thus mankind, not just a distant deity, can control its future, and its future contains a 'truth' which harmonizes all the complex areas of life that affect us – morality, religion, philosophy, art and science – with many little truths eventually compiling to make a coherent whole. The steady gathering in of objective 'facts' is our contribution to this ultimate goal.[4]

The point is laboured because in more recent times there has emerged a system of values and an approach to life now labelled as 'postmodernity.' 'Truth' for postmodernity is something constructed, not discovered. Its reality is not a distant overarching understanding to which we are all adding bit by bit, but the senses of today: health, beauty and other 'feel good' factors. So we judge everything in relative rather than objective terms, we place a high value on pleasure and we are deeply cynical because we have seen so many 'truths' come and go that we cannot believe in their permanence – support for any ideas is, at best, provisional. Change depends on fashion, it is not interpreted as progress and observers redescribe medical objectivity as veiled self-interest.

It is not the place of this text to argue for or against the value of 'postmodernity' or 'modernity'. But given the social context within which our readers exist, it is only fair to point out that, at times, they may feel a tension between what we advocate and what they feel is happening elsewhere, and to emphasize our belief in the importance of a change-promoting paradigm, which stems from our support of a notion of progress, and that contributions from a wide range of expertise can help to achieve harmonious comprehension – a truth of sorts, both sufficient for and necessary to successful decisions and change management in health services.

So prevailing attitudes may induce cynicism regarding the value of any sort of research. This feeling might be strengthened further by the view that whatever politicians may throw at it, the health service in the UK seems remarkably stable: few behaviours have changed.[5] Research examining the impact of the 1991 reforms concluded that neither the radical transformation predicted by the government nor the opposition's prophesy of imminent disaster actually occurred. The essential core of this massive organization went on as before. There were, of course, very many changes to individual behaviours and sub-organizations (such as health authorities, hospitals and groups of GPs) but, overall, the NHS continued undented. But, as currently managed, evaluative health services research, from which we could learn so much of what did and did not work beneath the skin of the mammoth, is not sufficiently funded, well organized or timely to contribute to the thinking of policy makers, and thus change management at a national level, let alone in smaller, more local, health services communities. This, we feel, makes a strong case for our paradigm. Only the engagement of researchers and managers (including politicians) together with the work of commissioning, doing and using research will address the problem.

Roy Griffiths's analogy of the NHS as a mobile comes to mind.[6] The relevance here is the contribution of well conducted health services research to decision makers' insights into the context within which they work: is this organization really as ill-defined and structurally loose as might be thought, or, at the other extreme, is it so frozen in its rigidity that it will crack and fall apart at the first attempt to remould it? It has been said that 'the most important characteristic for successful decision makers is that they do not approach decisions unprepared', and that part of this preparation is understanding the organization within which decisions are to be taken.[7] In this approach it can be said that understanding the organization has three main components:

1 Understanding the basic beliefs and the culture of the organization.
2 Understanding the goals and the vision of the organization.
3 Understanding what the organization is doing – its activities and the plans that guide them.

Here 'the organization' can refer to a small team of, say, half a dozen people, or the whole national system, or a number of different groupings, depending on the position of the manager.

It is possible to do a 'culture inventory' to assess the first aspect (beliefs and culture), by, for example, examining the relative salience of effectiveness, efficiency and support to do a job well, as well as innovation and enjoyment in the context of attitudes such as respect for people, the importance of personal growth, opportunities for reward, openness of communication and fairness. Much of this will be understood intuitively by good managers who have spent any time in their organization. It should be clear that without their insight the utility of health services research, in terms of being used to change services for the better, will be sadly diminished. This knowledge of organizational culture is a major contribution to successful change by managers. It would not be surprising if at times they required good research to help them investigate and understand the culture of their organization. When everyone is so busy and wrapped up in the pressures of a demanding job, exploration of local culture by, for example, social scientists can provide a refreshing slant on what may at times seem too overwhelmingly familiar.

As regards the vision of the organization, its goals and its sense of direction, the responsibility for setting this often falls to senior managers, and is part of our expectation of good leadership. It would not be surprising if change management were resisted more than usual if the results of research were conceived as incompatible with an organization's vision. The skilled manager can ensure that the results are presented in a way which fits the direction and the vision, and this requires early involvement, because even if the findings of the research necessitated a complete change of practice, there is less likelihood of immovable resistance where the manager has already fed in a sense of what this organization views as its future. Of course, that vision may have to change dramatically as a result. As will be discussed, the skilled manager can use such an opportunity to provide the energy for much needed change, and that is all part of effective change management. But such results are best used knowingly, ideally anticipated and subsequently incorporated into the new vision, which is most likely to happen, we argue, if the whole approach of the research has been in the spirit of 'change-promotion'.

An illustrative case study

The 1998 NHS reforms included increased devolution of power and responsibility to primary care groups – that is, general practitioners and other primary care workers – organized on a basis compatible with local perceptions of certain localities and with a responsibility for ensuring the most appropriate health care for that local community, either through commissioning the care from secondary providers or by improving local primary and community care to meet those local needs. Health authorities were charged with the responsibility for developing and monitoring these primary care groups. Prior to the publication of the government's White Paper, South Staffordshire Health Authority had already done some preliminary thinking around this issue, and had come up with some early ideas. Senior management commissioned an evaluation of these early ideas from the Health Services Management Centre in Birmingham. The results clearly showed that while many of the ideas within the early policy development were valued, the health authority's organization was perceived from outside as being unduly centralist and inappropriate for the modern era.

As a result, not only were the senior managers given greater insight into the basic beliefs and culture of their organization (which, understandably, wished to retain a somewhat centralist and controlling approach), but as a result of the research it was possible to develop an alternative strategic vision for the organization (as empowering and developmental) and hence to decide what the activities of the health authority should be.[8]

6.5 Managing change and change-promoting research: the resolution of dilemmas

So far, in terms of using the results of research, we have shown the mutual benefits for both researchers and decision makers of their close collaboration, and we have indicated the contribution of researchers to managers' understanding of their organizational context with a local case history. Here we summarize briefly how some of the key dilemmas of change management can be resolved by using our new paradigm.

If health services research is to be really useful, researchers need to be aware of what have been described in some of the change management literature as some of the 'key dilemmas' of change management.[9] It is no longer appropriate to picture learned scientists undertaking work of great worth that is then passed down to others to use as they see fit (illustrated by model A in Box 6.1). Rather, our approach inverts this (illustrated by model B in Box 6.1) and converts it into a virtuous circle, rather than a one-way hierarchical flow.

The first model assumes that the most important aspect of research is an investigation of efficacy and effectiveness, presumably almost springing from nowhere, with that research then being subject to review and scientific criticism. Ultimately the results can be converted to policy or guidelines, thus leading to change management through a variety of

Box 6.1   Two models for the role of R&D in change management

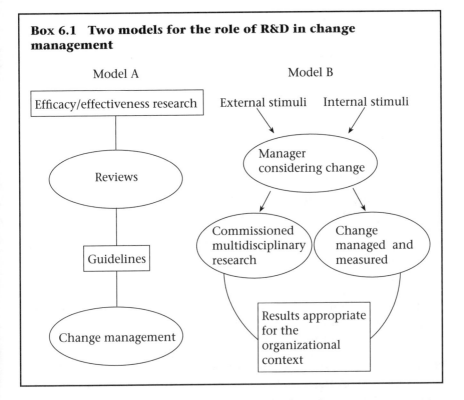

processes such as management action, education and work practice.[10] In contrast, the approach we advocate begins with a managerial interest in change. Here the 'manager' may be of any discipline. The manager may have been stimulated by reading about research findings from elsewhere – their value should not be dismissed. But there may be other valuable sources which are internal, such as wanting to do better or to make complex resource decisions in the face of competing demands. The manager is then engaged with the research team, which is multidisciplinary, and produces results appropriate to the organizational context. The commitment and involvement of interested parties from the start helps the implications of the research to be managed as a joint endeavour, using necessary techniques, including measuring change, to implement those decisions and to keep feeding back the results, ideally 'owned' (to use the jargon) by key participants.

This implies, as has been suggested elsewhere,[11] that part of asking the right questions, the *sine qua non* of good research, involves doing developmental work first. That is, understand the context, the implications of the decisions, the key players and what they really seek and what they really do – issues covered in our discussion of understanding the organization and using research, often qualitative, to gain useful insights.

Assisting the process, we envisage a notably powerful role for our paradigm in informing five key dilemmas:

1 A need for experimentation versus a need to be right.
2 Powerful leadership versus empowered followers.
3 Managing the present versus managing the change.
4 Handling the environment versus building the internal organization.
5 Simple beliefs versus complex issues.

Each is discussed in turn, and fitted into our virtuous circle.

Experimenting or being right

It is singularly unfortunate that this dilemma still exists. As will be pointed out, experimenting (appropriately) as part of the process of learning *is* being right. The concepts are not polar opposites. Instead they are integral to an organization that is continually improving and learning, and creatively using the change process in order to sustain success.

In health services the gulf between researchers and managers perpetuates the myth that 'experiment' and 'being right' are separate territories. By continually working together both researchers and managers learn, and help the organization to do so too. This is not just applicable to the Western world and the pressures we face from high technology. A fascinating case study on the topic of Chagas disease (a parasitic disease) in South America illustrates the point beautifully.[12]

Chagas disease affects mainly poor rural areas in developing countries; traditionally these areas receive little or no political priority. Unlike many other parasitic diseases, it can be controlled by eliminating the becta insect that transmits it, mainly by using insecticides and improving housing. Field trials carried out in 1948 showed that there was a group of insecticides which were particularly effective in this context. However, although the disease was common, little action was taken, apart from isolated examples between 1950 and 1975.

Suddenly things changed. From 1984 there was a succession of annual meetings involving scientists, research managers and policy makers, meeting to discuss science and public health. The meetings helped to transform research into action by sensitizing scientific and public opinion, and stimulating decision-making. The close involvement of researchers with policy makers opened up new perspectives, and radically changed governmental priority-setting mechanisms. Today Chagas disease is close to being eliminated as a public health problem in Latin American countries. The initiative came from researchers and policy managers desperate to make something happen. The important lesson here is the continual engagement and commitment of researchers as part of the policy-making forum, not just remaining splendidly isolated in laboratories. Their contribution to the improvement in health cannot be overemphasized. If they had remained isolated in their laboratories they would have been safely right, from 1948 on. But the organization of healthcare effectively dealing with Chagas disease would never have happened. The dangerous experiment of working with unfamiliar groups of people was their brave step, and absolutely essential in this context. So it is not just senior managers who have a responsibility to encourage their organization to experiment and learn from experience;[13] ideally researchers with important messages should be similarly engaged.

Powerful leadership or empowered followers

Change initiatives need major and sustained commitment from the top of the organization if they are not to flounder. This is well recognized in management science and in the business sector, and we have illustrated the point in this text with the NHS reforms of the early 1990s, which, we have argued, only happened as smoothly and rapidly as they did because there was senior policy-making and management drive, and because what was happening was regularly monitored.

Powerful leadership is both essential and necessary. There are also management models of the sustainability of change, which show well that there is a need for emotional as well as intellectual commitment from subordinates required to deliver the change.[14] We have shown that vague notions of empowering (for example, with published guidelines), while deliciously correct politically, have not proved demonstrably successful in achieving desired change in clinical practice.

That approach is well meaning, but atheoretical, and has not been thought through – at least not hitherto. For example, a survey of GPs found that they did not want to explore all the research evidence themselves, unsurprisingly, but did feel that the way to move towards evidence-based general practice was by using evidence-based guidelines or proposals *developed by colleagues*.[15] The health technology assessment programme publishes lists of reports available to support this type of process.[16] The NHS Executive has published a guide to good practice in using guidelines.[17] There seems to be a view that somehow clinicians are passively grateful recipients of good advice, which will be followed quite happily. We know this is not enough. An alternative approach to 'empowering followers' is to explore ways of ensuring continual learning, a concept that fits with the answer to the previous dilemma and recognizes the complexity of sustainable change. We discuss this idea of a learning organization below.

In practice, the clinical changes that do occur are often dependent on:

- the complexity of the innovation;
- the relative advantage of the innovation over existing practices and procedures;
- the opportunity to observe the innovation in use before adopting it into practice;

- its compatibility with other similar products and procedures already in the professionals' practice;
- an opportunity to try the innovation before adopting it.

In addition, motivation to change occurs if a doctor, for example, experiences anxiety because what is already known or done does not match what ought to be. The relevance of the notion of continual learning here, and thus of 'empowered followers' is the belief that this learning, this improvement in practice, is best based on a self-directed curriculum with opportunities for learning in groups, and, essentially, *being part of a learning organization*.[18] Learning organizations gather and process information and feedback, thus creating some of the standards that govern practice and modifying other specific local problems and needs. This in turn means that the leadership of the organization must create the opportunities for such standards to be agreed, and to be monitored, and that the leadership cares about continual improvement. Change requires powerful leadership *with* empowered followers, and this is exactly where our new paradigm comes into its own.

The NHS of the twenty-first century will incorporate the concept explicitly as part of the structure: clinical governance is now a major management responsibility. Chief executives of health care providers, not just the clinical professionals, will be accountable for the quality of clinical care. A primary task of the new primary care groups is to identify a lead clinical professional responsible for clinical governance.[19] We feel that for these leaders to nurture learning organizations there has to be close involvement between those managing resources and those researching the best use of those resources. In other words, it should be impossible to separate research from the organization for which that research may be intended. The whole process of our model will empower leaders with knowledge of research, will empower followers with the questions to which answers can feasibly be implemented and should result in a greater sense of corporate ownership of the driving of good quality improvement continually, rather than fear of change.

Some professionals can be immensely helpful, or incredibly obstructive, in this process, so it might well be helpful to share some ideas about 'professional intellect' in this context. Professional intellect can be defined as having four main characteristics: cognitive knowledge (a basic mastery through training and certification); advanced skills (translating the book learning into effective application in the real world); system understanding (a deep knowledge of the web of cause and effect relationships, and an ability to solve complex problems, sometimes thought of as highly trained intuition); and self-motivated creativity (professional intellectuals will often outperform groups with greater physical or financial resources, often because they are extremely competitive).[20]

Useful levers for change with this group (relating directly to the empowered followers concept) include: boosting their abilities (say, by

capturing their knowledge in systems and software); developing incent-
ives that encourage the sharing of information, rather than allowing per-
petuation of the 'knowledge is power' idea (merit awards for nationally
acclaimed publications are one example); and organizing around the
intellectuals (that is, do not emphasize productivity, but value the ability
to develop customized solutions to an endless stream of new problems).
The implications of this approach are greatest for those middle managers
playing a supporting role between the notional top of an organization
(chief executive) and the field workers (professional staff), because it is
their ability to translate, stimulate and motivate that is crucial to success,
and, of course, they too need to feel empowered.

Managing the present or managing the change

The previous dilemmas have been looked at more as opportunities for
managers to bring together what might been seen as polar opposites,
using our new paradigm, so that the integration of the senior manager
with the health services research process is a means of making change
and harmonizing the apparently dissonant. This may seem less easy for
this third dilemma. This is partly because of the contrasts between managing the present and managing the change. For example, managing the
present is often more about stability, bureaucratic structures and a heavy
reliance on good administration. Managing change is often more about
uncertainty and ambiguity, success depending on structures that are
innovative and collegiate, and needs leadership rather than administration. The picture is further complicated because we support the conten-
tion that in fact there is a third aspect to these management challenges:
managing transition.[21] Going back to the original model of change management, with which we opened the chapter, while the turbulence of
change may provide useful innovation and ice-breaking, and so suit
learning organizations that are continually evaluating and researching,
the final resolution has to involve some element of refreezing, calling on
the skills and structures that may best suit good management of the
present.

We contend that our approach to health services research is most
useful in the context of transition management, which should be part
of the repertory of senior managers. Transition management can use a
number of different approaches, which may involve leaving everything
to one general manager, having a project manager or having teams
formed from representatives of groups most involved in the change. The
teams can be formed from 'diagonal slices' through the organization
(that is, building on the strengths of natural leaders, not just those
who happen to occupy positions of seniority). We have already shown
how our model can clarify the question that is really being asked, and
ensure that directly usable data are collected to answer the issue. This in
turn draws on a collegiate approach to problem solving, much as the

approaches to transition management suggest. Thus, having a learning organization, where senior managers and researchers collaborate on practical as well as research-based change, feels like transition management always happening somewhere in the organization. The skills of administrative bureaucrats will be necessary as stability is agreed in some parts of the organization, those which are being refrozen, but there also needs to be room for a perpetual roving team of experienced researchers and decision takers, minimizing the danger of harmful ossification.

Thus, our advice in relation to this dilemma is to acknowledge the range of skills required, and suggest that they need to be available for use at different stages along the organization's evolutionary path. Transition management as an explicit part of managing the organization provides not only a home for the researcher–manager collaboration, but also a continual reminder to the rest of the organization that learning and change, not just stability, are facts of life.

Handling the environment or building the internal organization

We would never, in any way, wish to suggest that managers should neglect the internal organization. They do so at their peril. Good clinical care can happen only if there is good internal organization, including good communication and exchange of information.[22] Patients will suffer otherwise.

Yet political influences on the health service in any country are unavoidable, part of the job, meaning that managers have to cope with a wide range of ideas. These include legislation, models of care, patterns of disease, information systems and so on. Managers may feel overwhelmed by the complexity, and attempt to cope by operating in a reactive manner, dealing with the problems as they arrive. However, effective, innovating organizations keep in touch with their environment, and engage with it, attempting, at least in part, to shape it to their needs. The most benefit comes from deciding which aspects of the environment can be exploited most beneficially for the organization. Thus, identifying relationships that are already satisfactory, aspects of the environment that can be safely ignored (if temporarily) or external colleagues whose neglect would jeopardize any change we contemplate, and understanding what 'outsiders' expect of us, will all help senior managers to assess the key domains of the external environment that are especially relevant to the change being considered.

Many senior and experienced managers probably already do this on a day-to-day basis without realizing it. Where there are difficulties we would suggest that familiarity with research techniques can, at least, help managers to think about these conflicting demands. An ideal model, which has researchers as part of a senior management team, would do even better. The discipline and rigour of effective research can elucidate the value to be ascribed to the various external influences, and in which domains. For example, there might be mounting public demands for a new wonder drug. Researchers who are used to reviewing literature prior to embarking on any research process can help to assess the true value of the drug, the inadequacy of the research so far and the potential positive and negative impact. This will then be part of the mutually beneficial decision processes already described in terms of, for example, managers' decisions regarding such external pressures.

In day-to-day terms the internal building must take priority. This is because it is the shared vision of a better future that is the powerhouse of change. 'If everyone is pointing in the same direction it is magical; then nothing seems impossible.'[23] Visions need to be shared; one person alone cannot bring about change because the energy of the one person can be dissipated too easily. The energy is more likely to be available if there is already a sense of the core purpose of the organization – what it is as well as what it is not. The role of researchers in achieving a detailed understanding and evaluation of the purpose has already been illustrated.

Are the two parts of this dilemma really opposites? An organization sure of its purpose will react coherently to external pressures, and researchers, in our model, can help both internal and external relationships, not least because, as researchers, their objective views may be especially value added, while as team members they can contribute their insights in ways that are useful to their colleagues.

Simple beliefs versus complex issues

A clear vision for the organization has been mentioned. It will often be stated in relatively simple terms, and sufficiently broadly to be unarguable. The achievement of the vision may, however, be horrendously complex, dealing as it does with internal and external cultural issues. We have shown the contribution of our new paradigm to this. Together, managers and researchers can make better informed decisions, understand their organization, learn safely, inform (empower) participants in the change process, energize the engine room of transition management and cope with the environment. There will always be a temptation to lose sight of the overall goal of some work in order to attain some immediate gratification and tangible results. The discipline of research, and senior management, ensures that methods and research fit the original research question and task to be achieved. So it is here. The synergy exemplified in resolving the earlier dilemmas should mean that yet another balancing act is safely achieved.

It is clear from all the above that change management and, for that matter, research are more readily and productively and successfully part of the business if they are part of a 'learning organization'. The terminology is slick and slips easily off the tongue. Next we define our understanding of this important contribution to management theory and illustrate how well it fits with our paradigm.

6.6 Learning organizations

Learning organizations share the following characteristics:[24]

1 They are not just a collection of individuals who are learning. Learning occurs simultaneously and often collectively at different points and in different units within the organization.
2 They have a demonstrable capacity for change.
3 They can accelerate the learning capacity of individuals, but also redefine organizational structure, culture, job design and mental models.
4 They involve widespread participation of employees, and often customers, in decision making, dialogue and information sharing.
5 They promote systemic thinking and the building of organizational memory.

This means that 'learning' is not something applicable only to isolated disciplines and specialities, such as complex surgical techniques for surgeons, or dense managerial theories for managers. Rather, there is a sharing approach to the whole learning process, and thus a shared benefit, and a respect for all participants in the process. There is also no stop and start to the learning process. The learning organization learns continuously, and continuously transforms itself. The learning is integrated with, and runs parallel to, work. It enhances organizational capacity for innovation and growth. There are systems throughout the organization to capture and share such learning.

In many ways, this feels very much like our new paradigm for change-promoting health services research. There are also links with another idea with which readers may be be familiar: action research (a form of participant observation; see Box 5.5. This grew out of the belief that people take more effective action by collecting and analysing data together. It is an integrated process of intervening, collecting data on the effectiveness of the intervention, reflecting on the results and designing new interventions. In this way it is not dissimilar to the audit loop, but has an emphasis (which audit so often lacks) on the link between research *and* action. Data gathering, analysis and diagnosis lead to action planning and action implementation. Action research teams frequently learn well together during the research phase (although this is not always the case) because they share a commitment to solving a problem which they all believe is important. The research requires them to open their minds to new viewpoints. The team members may have to reframe their initial understanding in the light of new data. However, action research groups get stuck when they test their conclusions with others in the organization who have not shared their journey. This is partly because others may not see their findings as clearly or judge them to be as compelling, or because the findings may threaten those in power or challenge existing norms. Action research is not a natural, intellectual process, as the name might imply. It needs leadership and it needs time, and it needs a range of skills. Thus, as we have already outlined, really useful health services research requires the commissioning and methodological skills discussed in earlier chapters.

If our paradigm is followed, will this result in a learning organization? It is possible to 'audit' an organization for its capacity to be a true learning organization. Unfortunately, the characteristics for which one audits are stuck with the alliterative imperative that seems to be at the heart of most management texts! None the less, we think that they are useful markers.

- *Continuous*: that is, *not* selective, involuntary and time limited, but related to real work problems and issues and the opportunity to learn from mistakes.
- *Collaborative*: this means cooperative participation with others and learning from each other.
- *Connected*: this means that in a real sense people are working towards a longer-term goal, and a feeling of being linked to a larger environment of suppliers, customers and society at large.
- *Collective*: this is the shared learning of individuals or teams, able to learn across the normal boundaries across any organization, to understand the range of perspectives and to be able to cope with the challenge of new ideas and assumptions – very much the new paradigm.
- *Creative*: this means a sense of delight in innovations that will please, no matter how trivial they may appear to be at first sight, as well as frequent good ideas. These good ideas are needed as much in terms of doing successful research as in terms of delivering a successful service.
- *Captured and codified*: this includes having procedures for debriefing colleagues regularly when key decisions have been made, as well as opportunities for 'how was it for you?' sessions within both the research and the day-to-day service environment.
- *Capacity building*: this means big and little R&D, and a continual willingness to develop other skills, rather than a fear that our own jealously guarded territories will be invaded.

It can be seen that the learning organization has much in common with how we envisage using research as a result of our approach.

To achieve all of the above, to ensure that research is undertaken which is relevant to change promotion and that managers feel competent to use that research, each has specific responsibilities. The process of change already outlined is the framework for the responsibilities of researchers and managers (who may all also be clinicians) set out in Box 6.2. Many will (we hope) be recognizable and familiar. We now enlarge on this final component of how we can understand ways of *using* health services research.

Box 6.2 Responsibilities of managers and researchers to change management

Aspects of change management	Responsibilities	
	Researchers	Managers
1 Establishing a sense of urgency. *Bad business creates its own sense of urgency: there is a danger of a good business becoming complacent – managers may have to manufacture crises.*	Essential to communicate important research results, and not expect those simply to be picked up through learned journals and the like.	Develop methods of encouraging communication from research, making the organization more permeable to research results, rather than resistant.
2 Forming a powerful guiding coalition. *This means engaging powerful people in the organization, establishing teamwork, with good team selection and strong leadership.*	Be prepared to get your hands dirty with this sort of operational work.	Researchers can be a continual reminder of the importance of their results for the organization and therefore included in the team.
3 Creating a vision. *'A clear and compelling statement of where all this [is] leading.'*	Can contribute by indicating why they did the research, and why the results matter.	Develop methods of encouraging communication from research, making the organization more permeable to research results, rather than resistant.

4 Communicating the vision. *Means that everyone is convinced by words and deeds.*	With the managers seek out opportunities to communicate the research results.	This is high-level leadership and managers should take advantage of any 'fuel' they can get from researchers.
5 Empowering others to act on the vision. *Removing people who may well block progress, but doing so fairly.*	Engagement of a wide range of participants will have helped to remove some blocks. Mainly take careful political advice from managers regarding transmission of the message.	This is high-level leadership and managers should take advantage of any 'fuel' they can get from researchers.
6 Planning for and creating short-term wins. *May need to find the data to 'prove' wins, but keep the urgency level up.*	Advice on appropriate data and what could be perceived as wins may be very helpful.	This is high-level leadership and managers should take advantage of any 'fuel' they can get from researchers.
7 Consolidating improvements and producing still more change. *Do not declare victory. Go for even bigger change.*	Alert researchers will always be able to identify other areas to investigate.	Develop methods of encouraging communication from researchers, making the organization more permeable to research results, rather than resistant.
8 Institutionalizing new approaches. *'Change sticks . . . when it seeps into the bloodstream of the corporate body' in terms of social norms and shared values.*	Regular communication from researchers will enhance this.	Develop methods of encouraging communication from researchers, making the organization more permeable to research results, rather than resistant.

6.7 Change management: the responsibilities of researchers and managers

Box 6.2 lists the eight aspects of change management[25] and the consequent responsibilities, as we see them, of researchers and managers. Each aspect is discussed in more detail below, emphasizing the roles played by all the different participants.

The sense of urgency

Managers are often expert at this: for example, using the potential judgement of an outside organization to energize an otherwise flagging commitment from their staff. But how often have researchers, in meticulously analysing and picking through their data, come across something which they thought was immensely significant, but with no one to tell? In our new paradigm researchers should be linked to senior managers so that they can inform them about significant findings. Nowadays it is not enough to expect a passive diffusion of knowledge to occur. If something really matters it should be broadcast. It may not be the researcher's responsibility to take action. It is the researcher's responsibility to ensure that those who could take action are aware of what has been uncovered. It can be as important to broadcast the findings that, for example, a certain treatment is not any better than anything else as it is to publish positive findings. This is as true nationally as locally, and the national R&D agenda can instil even greater momentum by ensuring that national programmes are visibly contributing to national policy, or answering national policy issues.

The powerful coalition

Managers are often intuitively experts at this, which, because of its 'political' overtones, may be felt as immensely worrying for researchers, who excuse themselves on the grounds that participation in such groups may be seen as prejudicial to their 'pure' detachment and ability to undertake unbiased research. However, without making these links, researchers will never really understand the full implications of their work, or how the findings can be translated into the language of those who can and will take action when something important is uncovered. Nor will they know the people who should be told. Labels on an organization chart are not necessarily an indication of where power rests, especially the power to make change. One does not need to be an activist to feed the activists who can manage change. But one does need to know who those activists are, and to have trusting and long-term relationships with them.

Creating a vision

This hallmark of good leadership may be one of the most difficult areas for common agreement between researchers and managers, especially if managers are as interested in day-to-day survival as in any long-term change, while researchers may place more value on another slower moving agenda and reference group. There will, however, be common ground; of this there is no doubt. It is the responsibility of all players to seek this common ground. One of the best ways of doing so is of course in the debate about what the real research question is. To ask a good question one needs to have some sense of vision of what to do with the answer, and this is where the excellence of good managers and good researchers can be brought together powerfully. We are also firmly of the opinion that national funders of R&D can create the right ambience, a climate of expectation, within which organizational visions that are valued are those visibly fed by contributions from a wide range of interests. This is a prime responsibility for national R&D in health services: by setting the right example for others to follow, by expecting good research to be multi-interest and by funding only that which directly addresses management issues, their model can inspire others and ensure that this visionary work is legitimately conceived as the product of many collaborators.

Communicating the vision

The challenge here is rather different for researchers and managers. For managers the essence is good communication skills. For researchers the issue is not just communication, but communication that is managed in a way that does not destroy the research approach that has been developed. This can be done, but is best done in the context of an understanding between researchers and managers, on the one hand, of how a shared vision can maintain morale and motivation throughout a service, while, on the other hand, keeping everyone on board with the importance of the research, and a willingness to learn from it.

Empowering others

The very thoroughness that good research requires is an essential foundation here. Meticulous enquiry, addressing the main management questions, will no doubt have already encouraged some change to be considered. The problem of blocking by people who feel they have much to lose is never easily solved, but may precipitate a crisis (as in the first point) if there is not a satisfactory conclusion. Researchers and managers will have to decide if this is likely to be the best way forward. Within this, of course, researchers and managers themselves have to feel empowered, and one sure means of gaining strength is by having commitment to an organization, the sense that it is in one's interest to stay around and participate in much of the day-to-day, rather messy business that is life in complex organizations. Commitment and motivation are not for us to discuss – far more expert writers have contributed vast reams on the topic. However, at a very basic level we all recognize that most of us need some sort of security, and for many health service managers, even on relatively short-term contracts, there is generally a sense that they can develop themselves and their careers as opportunities arise. Not so researchers. Again we make a plea for a national responsibility here: the value of health service researchers must be recognized as integral to any successful organization, not just in terms of intellectual property rights but also in terms of opportunities for career progression and advancement within a field hitherto solely influenced by academe.

Short-term wins

Because the collaboration between researchers and managers means there have to be data, it should be eminently feasible, within this paradigm, for this important aspect of successful change management to bear fruit. The very process of the research will suggest interim milestones that can be used to look at change, as well as ways in which those milestones can be measured and used to praise and reflect back to the organization the achievements that are possible.

Consolidation and further change

Any experienced researcher will be well aware that one of the main conclusions of most research projects is a recommendation for yet more research. This may appear a well worn cliché, but undoubtedly is very much related to enquiring intellects and the ability to recognize the subtle ramifications of various issues as they emerge. In fact, researchers will often be very comfortable with the idea that one research project leads to another. It is managers who might find it hard to bear – they might feel that this means a perpetual no conclusion. In fact, it is an opportunity to be used by both for continuing the ethos of the learning organization, and ensuring that the further research questions are addressed in a properly managed way rather than left floating as the unsatisfactory sole recommendations, which is so often the case when research is conducted in isolation from management decision-making.

Institutionalizing new approaches

This should be the inevitable result of all the previous work, if successfully implemented. In fact, things may not feel 'new' but more part of the culture of the organization (as previously discussed) in terms of how we do things here – learning, improving, valuing each other – because what we are about is really useful health services research.

6.8 Conclusions

We began this chapter with our analogy of a safety net, arguing that multidisciplinary collaborative work gives strength and elasticity. However, we all know that nets are as capable of entrapment as they are of support. Hence arises our lengthy exposition of the ways in which the threads can and should intertwine, whether in terms of decision processes, the cultural context, resolving change management dilemmas, developing a learning organization or acknowledging responsibilities for making change management happen. This coming together with mutual respect in increasingly close and collaborative working should, we hope, convert our open-meshed net almost into a trampoline, and from that, with skilful use, who knows what heights may be reached.

Hence come our recommendations, which we suggest would be of interest to four main groups: managers, researchers, universities and others. The recommendations cover both the short term and the long term, and are summarized in Box 6.3. It will be noted that in the short term we suggest not only reading this book, but reading it with specific purposes in mind, as well as beginning the process of collaborative research and development. There needs to be some sort of locally convenient mechanism by which people can come together, as well as ways in which different groups can learn from each other and work together, possibly on a small scale initially, as a way of learning and understanding. In the long term the whole approach has to be sustainable, and we envisage this partly in terms of acceptable career paths, partly because it will have become a widely diffused technology, partly because key stakeholders will have acquired a range of skills required and partly because they will all have become players in the continuing change that is now almost a given for all health services.

Finally, we suggest that in a few years' time the best way of taking this forward would be for there to be another book, based on these ideas, but showing how well they can be implemented in the practice of promoting change.

Box 6.3 Recommendations for implementing change-promoting R&D

Recommendations	Managers	Researchers	Universities	Others
Short-term				
1 Read the book	Think what existing good practice it calls to mind. Consider what missed or existing opportunities there may be for this collaborative approach. Identify the more technical aspects of research methodology which you would like researchers to clarify for you. Develop your own ideas for taking this forward.	Think what existing good practice it calls to mind. Consider what missed or existing opportunities there may be for this collaborative approach. Which aspects of change management seem problematic or require clarification? How much history of your own local health service do you not understand? Develop your own ideas for taking this forward.	Consider what local examples of good practice might already exist. Identify reasons why the new paradigm may be difficult for you – and possible methods of changing those blocks. Begin to create collaborative research and teaching opportunities using the new paradigm. Develop your own ideas for taking this forward.	Funders of research and development and policy-makers for healthcare should consider how this approach could be integrated with the way they manage their work. Much has already been done in terms of research funding being conditional on multiagency and multi-disciplinary approaches, but considerably more could be achieved.
2 Establish a mechanism for	Local health managers could take	Researchers could also make the first	Forward looking universities might	Funders can encourage

considering collaborative research	a useful lead in inviting colleagues from other organizations.	approach, especially if they have some research ideas which they feel would benefit from managerial input.	well initiate some sort of collaborative research forum, which is at sufficiently senior level to engage the commitment of managers and researchers. In the short term this may simply be in order to fulfil objectives of being perceived as being of value to the local community.	collaborative forums by ensuring that both training and research budgets are conditional on projects demonstrating managerial commitment in addition to research expertise. By liaison with appropriate policy makers they should also be able to identify priority areas which are appropriate for this form of approach.
3 Set up methods of learning from each other	Having made links with a local university or some other group of researchers, share with them a current problem and use it as a means of learning from the researchers how much they can contribute.	There may well be research findings which appear to have gone nowhere. Inviting a senior manager into a research group in order to talk through the complexities of managing any required change within a healthcare organization should	Have change management as an integral, mandatory module of any courses on health services research. Include research understanding as an integral, mandatory module on management courses. Set up modules of	Those who have experience of commissioning research, be it at national or more local level, should set up ways of sharing this expertise with others, ideally to cascade their skills and knowledge throughout the R&D communities.

Recommendations	Managers	Researchers	Universities	Others
		help to elucidate the skills and actions required.	interdisciplinary training.	
4 Identify a pilot project	What apparently small issue could you use as an exemplar where decisions have to be made, but where information may be lacking? Identify an individual of sufficient seniority to be a commissioning manager, and thus to acquire experience of this difficult process through this first-hand experience	Avoid making the perfect the enemy of the good if offered collaborative opportunities. A pilot project which is quick, only moderately clean (not dirty!) and relatively inexpensive may be an immensely helpful learning opportunity for all concerned.	University staff, with their intelligent questioning, could help to facilitate the working up of a collaborative project by managers and researchers. Supporting such a project could well be a very useful 'loss leader' in the first place.	Secondments to and from funding and policy-making organizations, especially in relation to apparently small but specific projects, can prove immensely informative for all concerned.
Longer-term				
5 Making this sustainable	Research experience should be recognized	Researchers may have to trade off being	Again, career structures could	Criteria for judging universities'

as an essential part of a good curriculum vitae for any future healthcare manager. In addition, very senior managers may well be able to be creative about employing researchers within larger organizations on grades which are sufficiently remunerative and offer sufficient opportunities for advancement to retain those individuals as committed contributors to the development of R&D in the organization.

managed, and being commissioned to do specific tasks, against 'freedom'. They should also be able to construct curricula vitae demonstrating how their research has been _used_ rather than just published.

include demonstrable ability to engage, successfully, external healthcare organizations, as well as successful completion of internal requirements.

Discard the arrogant and foolish notion that somehow research council money (e.g. MRC) is superior to that from other sources.

Discard the unwarranted assumption that applied research is inferior to pure research.

Improve the quality of the management of the institutions so that these too use change management in the context of stated goals.

performance (in the UK the Research Assessment Exercise) should include evidence of change promotion, partially, if not completely, replacing any crude measure of a number of publications as an impact factor.

Funders of research will need to continue to be supportive of career development among health service researchers. There is a tension here between long-term funding for research, and managing those limited funds in a flexible way to ensure they are spent only in units with high-quality output. However, competition between research units is not necessarily productive; collaboration, and possible career

Recommendations	Managers	Researchers	Universities	Others
			In relation to the above, discard the notion that so-called academic distinction makes a person a competent manager within the institution.	progression from one unit to another, may be more beneficial. A new journal of change-promoting research could make a useful contribution.
6 Diffusing this 'technology'	Be proud of engaging in collaborative research and share the learning that results – the difficulties as well as the good news.	Publish research focused on change. Develop and share materials which have been successfully used in making some of the more complex methodological issues more transparent to busy managers.	Faculties and departments within a university could be assessed on the basis of the collaborative work they are currently undertaking.	Overall assessment of universities should incorporate some measure of engagement in collaborative R&D. Journal editors should develop a bias towards papers which answer 'so what?', and do not simply present the results of some research in splendid isolation from the healthcare context.
7 Skills development: life-long learning	Become even better at explicitly identifying the	Use acquired experience to construct a model of	Set up multidisciplinary and multi-agency courses.	Those responsible for identifying types of job, be it

	managerial skills which contribute to successful change management, and use management theories from elsewhere, as well as encouraging continuing professional development for all managers in terms of understanding research methodologies.	those research skills which require to be particularly well focused for change-promoting research.	in an academic or healthcare setting, will need to develop flexible ways of valuing what might be termed 'cross-cultural' experiences and learning.	
8 'Change is normal'	All healthcare organizations should become learning organizations.	All research groupings should become learning organizations.	All universities should become learning organizations – not just teaching and researching organizations, but genuinely flexible and adaptive.	Funders and policy makers similarly need to learn and develop.

9 Finally, someone should write a new book showing how well the ideas can work, providing more specific knowledge on the techniques and technologies required and illustrating the career developments and the healthcare organizational developments that result.

NOTES

Chapter 1

1 J. Appleby (1996) Financing the NHS, in P. Merry and C. Ham (eds) *1996/97 NHS Handbook*, 11th edn. Tunbridge Wells: JMH Publishing.
2 A. May (1996) Europe: the emerging issues, in Merry and Ham, *ibid*.
3 D. Hunter (1995) Viewpoint: rationing and priority setting, in C. Ham and P. Merry (eds) *1995/96 NHS Handbook*, 10th edn. Tunbridge Wells: JMH Publishing.
4 House of Lords Select Committee on Science and Technology (1988) *Session 1987, Third Report. Priorities in Medical Research*. London: HMSO.
5 Department of Health (1989) *Priorities in Medical Research. The Government Response to the Third Report of the House of Lords Select Committee on Science and Technology 1987–8 Session*. London: HMSO, Cm 902.
6 M. Peckham (1991) *Research for Health. A Research and Development Strategy for the NHS*. London: Department of Health.
7 B. Stocking (1996) NHS research and development strategy, in Merry and Ham, *op. cit.*, n. 1.
8 A. Culyer (Chairman) (1994) *Supporting Research and Development in the NHS. A Report to the Minister for Health by a Research and Development Task Force*. London: Department of Health.
9 F. Honigsbaum (1995) How the health service evolved, in Ham and Merry, *op. cit.*, n. 3.
10 I. Holliday (1992) *The NHS Transformed*. Manchester: Baseline Books.
11 R. Griffiths (1983) *NHS Management Inquiry*. Letter to the Secretary of State for Social Services, 6 October.
12 Holliday, *op. cit.*, n. 10.
13 C. Ham (1994) *Management and Competition in the New NHS*. Oxford: Radcliffe Medical Press.
14 *Ibid*.
15 National Audit Office (1995) *Clinical Audit in England*. London: HMSO.
16 Department of Health (1997) *The New NHS*. London: Stationery Office.
17 E. Ferlie (1997) Large scale organisational and managerial change in health care: a review of the literature. *Journal of Health Services Research and Policy*, 2(3), 180–8.
18 National Audit Office, *op. cit.*, n. 15.

19 Department of Health (1992) *The Health of the Nation. A Strategy for Health in England.* London: HMSO.
20 M. Deighan and S. Hitch (1995) *Clinical Effectiveness from Guidelines to Cost Effective Practice.* Department of Health and Health Services Management Unit, Manchester. Brentwood: Earlybrave Publications. F. Cluzeau, P. Littlejohns, J. Grimshaw and G. Feder (1997) *Appraisal Instrument for Clinical Guidelines.* London: St George's Hospital Health Care Evaluation Unit.
21 A. Foster, D. Ratchford and D. Taylor (1994) Auditing for patients. *Quality in Health Care,* 3, Supplement, S16–S19.
22 National Audit Office, *op. cit.,* n. 15.
23 K. Walshe and C. Ham (1997) *Acting on the Evidence. Progress in the NHS.* London: The NHS Confederation/ABPI.
24 C. Shaw (1996) Quality in healthcare, in Merry and Ham, *op. cit.,* n. 1.
25 E. A. Balas, S. A. Boren, G. D. Brown *et al.* (1996) Effect of physician profiling on utilisation. Meta analysis of randomised clinical trials. *Journal of General and Internal Medicine,* 11, 584–90. N. Freemantle, E. L. Harvey, J. M. Grimshaw *et al.,* The effectiveness of printed educational materials in changing the behaviour of health care professionals. In the Cochrane Database of Systematic Reviews (quoted in *Evidence-based Medicine,* May/June 1997, 95).
26 H. R. Palmer and L. J. Hargreaves (1996) Quality measurement and improvement among primary care practitioners: results from a multisite randomised controlled test. *Medical Care,* 34(9), Supplement, SS1–SS113 (summarized in *Evidence Based Health Policy and Management,* December 1997, 101, with commentary by D. Somekh). Shaw, *op. cit.,* n. 24. M. Dunning, M. Lugon and J. MacDonald (1998) Is clinical effectiveness a management issue? *British Medical Journal,* 316, 243–4.
27 J. T. Hart (1997) What evidence do we need for evidence based medicine? *Journal of Epidemiology and Community Health,* 51, 623–9.
28 N. Black (1997) Developing high quality clinical databases. *British Medical Journal,* 315, 381–2.
29 E. Scrivens (1997) Putting continuous quality improvement into accreditation: improving approaches to quality assessment. *Quality in Health Care,* 6, 212–18.
30 J. Firth-Cozens (1997) Healthy promotion: changing behaviour towards evidence-based health care. *Quality in Health Care,* 6, 205–11.

Chapter 2

1 Lord Rothschild (1971) The organization and management of government R and D, in *The Lord Privy Seal. A Framework for Government Research and Development.* London: HMSO, pp. 1–25. (Cmnd 4814).
2 M. Peckham (1991) Research and development for the National Health Service. *Lancet,* 338, 367–71.
3 The Cochrane Collaboration. Oxford: Update Software Ltd, published annually. (Includes systematic reviews, abstracts of reviews of effectiveness, a register of controlled trials and a review methodology database.)
4 T. S. Kuhn (1970) *The Structure of Scientific Revolutions.* Chicago: University of Chicago Press.
5 M. Boden (Chairman) (1990) Report to the Advisory Board for the Research Councils from the Working Group on Peer Review, UK, November.

6 K. R. Popper (1974) *The Logic of Scientific Discovery*. London: Hutchinson.
7 Department of Health (1995) *Report of the NHS Health Technology Assessment Programme 1995*. London: Department of Health.
8 D. Berrow, C. Humphrey and J. Hayward (1997) Understanding the relation between research and clinical policy: a study of clinicians' views. *Quality in Health Care*, 6. 181–6.
9 Royal College of Obstetricians and Gynaecologists (1993) *Effective Procedures in Obstetrics Suitable for Audit*. London: RCOG. J. P. Neilson, C. A. Crowther, E. D. Hodnett, G. J. Hofmeyer, M. J. Keirse, L. Daley *et al.* (eds), *Pregnancy and Childbirth Module*, Cochrane Database of Systematic Reviews, Cochrane Collaboration, *op. cit.*, n. 3.
10 S. I. Dawson (1997) Inhabiting different worlds: how can research relate to practice? *Quality in Health Care*, 6, 177–8.
11 D. L. Sackett (1997) Evidence based medicine and treatment choices (letter). *Lancet*, 349, 570.
12 A. Maynard (1997) Evidence based medicine: an incomplete method for informing treatment choices. *Lancet*, 349, 126–8.
13 D. P. Kernick (1997) Letter. *Lancet*, 349, 570. J. Cassell (1997) Letter. *Lancet*, 349, 570–1.
14 K. G. Sweeney, D. MacAutey and D. Pereira Gray (1998) Personal significant: the third dimension. *Lancet*, 351, 134–6.
15 B. Russell (1961) *The History of Western Philosophy*. London: Unwin Paperbacks.
16 J. McCormick (1996) Death of the personal doctor. *Lancet*, 348, 667–8.
17 P. B. Haynes, D. L. Backett, G. H. Guyatt, D. J. Cook and J. A. Muir Gray (1997) Transferring evidence from research into practice: 4. Overcoming barriers to application, *Evidence Based Medicine*, 2(3), 68–9.
18 A. Coulter, Health care outcomes, in C. Ham and P. Merry (eds) (1995) *NHS Handbook 1995/6*. Tunbridge Wells: JMH Publishing.
19 J. C. Hall and C. Platell (1997) Half life of truth in surgical literature. *Lancet*, 350, 1752.
20 Popper, *op. cit.*, n. 6.
21 D. L. Sackett and J. E. Wennberg (1997) Choosing the best research design for each question. *British Medical Journal*, 315, 1636.
22 M. Hotopf, G. Lewis and C. Normand (1997) Putting trials on trial – the costs and consequences of small trials in depression: a systematic review of methodology. *Journal of Epidemiology and Community Health*, 51, 354–8.
23 Editorial (1997) Overmanaged medical research. *Lancet*, 349, 145.
24 D. Horrobin (1996) Peer review of grant applications: a harbinger of mediocrity in clinical research? *Lancet*, 348, 1293–5.
25 M. Isohanni and K. Nevala (1997) Psychological and managerial aspects of the scientists and the research team. *Journal of Health Services Research and Policy*, 2(3), 135–6.
26 I. Lau, J. P. A. Ioannidis and C. H. Schmid (1998) Summing up evidence: one answer is not always enough. *Lancet*, 351, 123–7.
27 J. Popay and G. Williams (1996) Public health research and lay knowledge. *Social Sciences and Medicine*, 42(5), 759–68.
28 B. N. Ong, K. Jordan, J. Richardson and P. Croft, Experiencing long term limiting illness. *Health and Social Care in the Community*, in press.
29 S. Harrison, NHS management, in Ham and Merry, *op. cit.*, n. 18.
30 HSC (1998) *Sildanefil (Viagra)*. Leeds: Department of Health.

31 DoH (1998) *Our Healthier Nation. A Contract for Health.* London: HMSO.
32 The National Cancer Alliance (1996) *'Patient-centred Cancer Services?' What Patients Say.* London: The National Cancer Alliance.
33 Harrison, *op. cit.*, n. 29.
34 E. Scrivens (1997) Putting continuous quality improvement into accreditation in improving approaches to quality assessment. *Quality in Health Care*, 6, 212–18.
35 N. Black (1997) A national strategy for research and development: lessons from England. *Annual Review of Public Health*, 18, 485–505.
36 T. Turrill (1986) *Change and Innovation. A Challenge for the NHS.* London: Institute of Health Service Managers.
37 J. Firth-Cozens (1997) Healthy promotion: changing behaviour towards evidence-based health care. *Quality in Health Care*, 6, 205–11.
38 Popay and Williams, *op. cit.*, n. 27.
39 A. Cornwall and R. Jewkes (1995) What is participatory research? *Social Sciences and Medicine*, 41(12), 1667–76.
40 S. B. Rilkin (1996) Paradigm lost: towards a new understanding of community participation in health programmes. *Acta Tropica*, 61, 79–92.
41 S. C. White (1996) Depoliticising development: the uses and abuses of participation. *Development in Practice*, 6(1), 6–15.
42 Harrison, *op. cit.*, n. 29.
43 K. Manning, Viewpoint: trusting in management, in Ham and Merry, *op. cit.*, n. 18.
44 R. Smith (1995) The scientific basis of health services (editorial). *British Medical Journal*, 311, 961–2.
45 A. S. St Leger, H. Schnieden and J. P. Walsworth-Bell (1992) *Evaluating Health Services' Effectiveness.* Buckingham: Open University Press.
46 A. S. St Leger (1992) Making 'Peckham' work for managers. *Journal of Management in Medicine*, 6, 6–12.
47 Development Task Force (Chair Professor Anthony Culyer) (1994) *Supporting R&D in the NHS: a Report to the Minister for Health.* London: Department of Health, September.
48 Department of Health (1996) *Report of the NHS Health Technology Assessment Programme 1996.* London: Department of Health.

Chapter 3

1 A. S. St Leger, D. Allen and K. V. Rowsell (1989) Procedures for the evaluation of innovatory proposals. *British Medical Journal*, 299, 1017–18.
2 J. M. Hantman (1994) An evaluation of the medical innovation fund. Master of science thesis, University of Manchester.
3 A. S. St Leger (1992) Making 'Peckham' work for managers. *Journal of Management in Medicine*, 6, 6–12. Michael Peckham was the first National Director of R&D in the NHS.

Chapter 5

1 A. S. St Leger, H. Schnieden and J. P. Walsworth-Bell (1992) *Evaluating Health Services' Effectiveness.* Buckingham: Open University Press.

2 A. Donabedian (1980) *Explorations in Quality Assessment and Monitoring. Volume 1. The Definition of Quality and Approaches to Its Assessment.* Ann Arbor, MI: Health Administration Press.

3 R. Dingwall, E. Murphy, P. Watson *et al.* (1998) Catching goldfish: quality in qualitative research. *Journal of Health Services Research and Policy*, 3, 167–72.

4 A. L. Cochrane (1972) *Effectiveness and Efficiency: Random Reflections on Health Services.* London: Nuffield Provincial Hospitals Trust.

5 We use the word meticulous as meaning vice rather than virtue, i.e. 'giving . . . excessive attention to details' (*The Concise Oxford Dictionary*, 1990).

6 M. Peckham (1991) Research and development for the National Health Service. *Lancet*, 338, 367–71.

7 J. Rush, R. Fiorino-Chiovitti, K. Kaufman *et al.* (1990) A randomized controlled trial of a nursery ritual: Wearing cover gowns to care for healthy newborns. *Birth*, 17, 25–30.

8 T. A. Conine, D. Daechsel, A. K. Choi *et al.* (1990) Costs and acceptability of two special overlays for the prevention of pressure sores. *Rehabilitative Nursing*, 15, 133–7.

9 A. S. St Leger, A. L. Cochrane and F. Moore (1979) Factors associated with cardiac mortality in 18 developed countries with particular reference to the consumption of wine. *Lancet*, i, 1017–20.

10 Department of Health and Social Security (1986). *Breast Cancer Screening* (the Forrest Report). London: HMSO.

11 The pitch has been queered by so much (moderately strong but not wholly consistent) circumstantial evidence of the effectiveness of cervical screening that most commentators would now regard it as unethical to embark on an RCT. This would also be impracticable in developed countries because many women regard screening to be self-evidently good and a right. Perhaps the developing world should not repeat the mistakes of the developed nations and begin with no prior assumptions of the cost-effectiveness of cervical screening in their societies.

12 Conditional and unconditional logistic regression respectively for analysis of stratified data or unstratified data.

13 It would have been natural and in keeping with our approach to evaluation to term this cost-effectiveness and the relating of cost to efficacy, in the item above, cost-efficacy. However, that would have conflicted with the current usage of cost-effectiveness in health economics.

14 The statistical inference procedures that assume simple random sampling usually also assume that the sampling was with replacement (thus a study unit could figure more than once in the sample). In practice, sampling without replacement has the same statistical properties as sampling with replacement if the sample size is small relative to the size of the sampling frame. This is a pedantic point and may be ignored by most people doing R&D.

15 There is a loose analogy to sequential clinical trials.

16 Those who give no heed to maintaining precision in the use of language insist on calling it a rate. It would be a rate only if response per unit of time were being measured.

17 In the sense of being followers of William James, the American philosopher, rather than, as in an everyday connotation of the word pragmatism, being opportunistic and unconcerned by values.

18 Some commentators define proportions as an additional scale. Proportions are derived from nominal measures. It is a matter of personal taste whether one defines scales according to the initial measurements or by the indices that may be derived from those measurements. Proportions have special properties that have to be taken into account during statistical analysis.

19 For the sake of simplicity in the following illustrations it is being assumed that the measures are on an interval or ratio scale, or are counts represented as proportions.

20 A null hypothesis is merely a construct for significance tests. It need have no, and usually does not, connection to the study hypothesis. The study hypothesis is usually closer to the alternative hypothesis of a significance test (e.g. that a real difference exists). Thus, when researchers start a presentation by saying 'my null hypothesis is . . .' they are conveying nothing of much interest to the audience.

21 There are formulae to help in the selection of an appropriate nominal significance level for a given number of comparisons.

22 In this book we refer only to the frequentist school of statistics. Bayesian methods are less often used in practice, are generally computationally more difficult and are not to our taste because the analysts weave their preconceptions into the fabric of the analysis in such a way that a critic of their findings cannot unpick them. However, the Bayesian approach does lead to a more appealing definition of confidence intervals. Bayes' theorem itself is inoffensive and used within frequentist statistics.

23 N. C. Curran, V. Klimach, W. Rankin, I. McKinlay and A. S. St Leger (1997) Lessons for school health: a survey of facilities for screening tests and medical examinations in schools. *Ambulatory Child Health*, 2, 211–19.

24 This is unlikely to arise as an R&D issue but it makes for easy illustration.

25 R. Lilford and G. Royston (1998) Decision analysis in the selection, design and application of clinical and health services research. *Journal of Health Services Research and Policy*, 3, 159–66.

26 We are not distinguishing between perturbations due to ignorance of fine details and perturbations consequent upon measurement error. The former are amenable to improvement through creative development of theory, the latter through attention to study design and experimental technique.

27 This is not universally true. However, it is sometimes found that a transformation of the original scale (e.g. taking logarithms) results in a more nearly normal distribution.

28 It can be shown that the sum of a large number of random variables, each of which has a small effect, tends towards following a normal distribution. This is so (almost) regardless of the nature of the probability distributions followed by each of the random variables.

29 The term *statistical model* is being used to mean a general purpose tool or approach such as multiple linear regression. Models may also be wholly theoretical in the sense that they explicitly state the relationships between the entities which a theory determines to be measurable, i.e. the model embodies the theory. Models of this kind may nevertheless have a probabilistic element to allow for the effects of small influences which as yet do not fall within the domain of the theory; these are called *stochastic* models, e.g. models used to describe the behaviour of epidemics. As is shown in the subsequent discussion, statistical models may include structures and

relationships determined by theory. However, these models are descriptive rather than predictive.

30 In this instance adherence to the *blending theory* of inheritance would have altered nothing.

31 The best fitting models do not necessarily reflect the geometric relations as expected. For example, FEV_1 in adults is proportional to body height squared rather than height cubed.

32 Gathering data on the off-chance that something interesting will emerge.

33 The standard statistical term.

34 Translation from the pseudo-equation to a formal model may entail some mathematical function of the structural components, e.g. dependent variable = f(linear combination of coefficients and their associated independent variables) + random error, where $f(\ )$ is a mathematical function.

35 In principle, interaction terms can extend up to various combinations of powers of the variables. This is akin to the first terms of a Taylor series and thus allows for the possibility of quite non-linear relationships (though still linear in the coefficients). Higher-order interactions are usually meaningless in the absence of all the lower-order ones and the corresponding non-interaction terms. Generally, it is not necessary to go beyond first-order interactions and to do so can be confusing.

36 Sometimes it is not obvious whether a variable should be represented on a nominal scale or some other. For example, social class can be represented by categories of occupations ranging from professional and managerial groups, through semi-skilled workers down to the unskilled. There is an implied ordering in these categories because they correlate highly with, for example, educational achievement and income. Although an ordinal scale is credible a ratio scale is difficult to justify: it would imply that social class I (learned professions etc.) is one-fifth in some attribute of social class V (unskilled). There is a temptation to enter social class into a regression model as a variable coded from, say, 1 to 5. Unfortunately, standard regression models cannot distinguish between ordinal scale variables and ratio scale variables (or interval) – all are treated as being on the ratio scale. Thus, in such cases, if ratio scale properties are unpalatable the nominal scale should be retained. Dichotomous variables (e.g. sex) can safely be coded 0 and 1, or whatever, since this gives exactly the same result as treating them formally (as factors) as being on a nominal scale.

37 Generally, if there are N categories there will be $N-1$ component coefficients. The remaining coefficient is in fact amalgamated with the overall mean (A). It is largely arbitrary what contrasts among the N hypothetical coefficients are used to generate $N-1$ actual coefficients.

38 'Entities are not to be multiplied beyond necessity.' Attributed to William of Occam, who lived during the first half of the fourteenth century.

39 Those which have sufficiently common aims and methods, and are methodologically sound according to strictly defined criteria.

40 Material, such as in-house reports, not formally published in journals or books, and not deposited in copyright libraries.

41 H. J. Eysenck (1994) Systematic reviews: meta-analysis and its problems. *British Medical Journal*, 309, 789–92. (This was part of an interesting set of articles on systematic review published in the *British Medical Journal* from 3 September to 19 November 1994.)

42 It is not sufficient for meta-analysts to try to get around this objection by using within-group random effects models rather than fixed effects ones. The issue remains that, almost certainly, unlike studies are being combined and it is hard to quantify whether the differences are in practical terms acceptable. Moreover, the apparent precision of the statistical procedure cannot undo fundamental flaws in the data. However, it can fool the unwary.

43 Adapted from the US Task Force on Preventive Health Care and published in A. Stevens and J. Raftery (eds) (1997) *Health Care Needs Assessment: the Epidemiologically Based Needs Assessment Reviews*, second series. Oxford: Radcliffe Medical Press.

Chapter 6

1 B. Heirs and P. Farrell (1986) *The Professional Decision Thinker*. London: Grafton/ HarperCollins.

2 R. Lilford and G. Royston (1998) Decision analysis in the selection, design and application of clinical and health services research. *Journal of Health Services Research and Policy*, 3(3): 159–66.

3 B. G. Charlton (1993) Medicine and postmodernity. *Journal of the Royal Society of Medicine*, 86, 497–9.

4 The relationship between facts and the constructs that legitimize them (theories) is more complicated than we indicate here (see Box 2.2); as is the notion of truth. However, our point is that R&D concerns the world experienced by people and is based on the premise that the world really can be changed.

5 D. Plamping (1998) Change and resistance to change in the NHS. *British Medical Journal*, 317, 69–71.

6 R. Griffiths (1983) NHS Management Inquiry. Letter to the Secretary of State for Social Services, 6 October.

7 L. R. Beach (1993) *Making the Right Decision*. Englewood Cliffs, NJ: Prentice Hall.

8 I. Smith and T. Knight (1998) *Towards a Partnership of Equals*. Report for South Staffordshire Health Authority, University of Birmingham HSMC.

9 T. Turrill (1986) *Change and Innovation. A Challenge for the NHS*. London: Institute of Health Service Management.

10 N. Freemantle, J. Wood and F. Crawford (1985) Evidence into practice, experimentation and quasi-experimentation: are the methods up to the task? *Journal of Epidemiology and Community Health*, 52, 75–81.

11 A. S. St Leger, H. Schneiden and J. P. Walsworth-Bell (1992) *Evaluating Health Services' Effectiveness*. Buckingham: Open University Press.

12 COHRED (1997) The Chagas disease saga. Research into action. *Newsletter of the Council on Health Research for Development*, 11, 1–3.

13 T. J. Peters and N. Austin (1985) *A Passion for Excellence*. New York: Collins.

14 C. B. Handy (1985) *Understanding Organisations*. London: Penguin.

15 A. McColl, H. Smith, P. White and J. Field (1998) General practitioners' perceptions of the route to evidence based medicine: a questionnaire survey. *British Medical Journal*, 316, 361–5.

16 NHS R&D National Co-ordinating Centre for Health Technology Assessment, Southampton. Regular reports.

17 NHS Executive (1996) *Good Practice. Clinical Guidelines*. Leeds: NHSE, May.

18 R. D. Fox and N. L. Bennett (1998) Learning and change: implications for continuing medical education. *British Medical Journal*, 316, 166–8.

19 NHS Executive (1998) *The New NHS: Modern and Dependable. Establishing Primary Care Groups*. Leeds: NHSE, April.

20 I. B. Quinn, P. Anderson and S. Finkelstein (1996) Managing professional intellect: making the most of the best. *Harvard Business Review*, March/April, 71–83.

21 Turrill, *op. cit.*, n. 9.

22 J. Gosbee (1998) Communication among health professionals. *British Medical Journal*, 316, 642–3.

23 Turrill, *op. cit.*, n. 9.

24 K. E. Watkins and V. J. Marsick (1993) *Sculpting the Learning Organization. Lessons in the Art and Science of Systemic Change*. San Francisco: Jossey-Bass.

25 J. P. Kotter (1995) Leading change: why transformation efforts fail. *Harvard Business Review*, March/April, 59–67.

FURTHER READING

Project management

Aquilano, N. J. and Chase, R. B. (1991) *Fundamentals of Operations Management.* Homewood, IL: Irwin Publishers.

Krajewski, U. and Ritzman, L. P. (1998) *Operations Management: Strategy and Analysis,* 5th edn. London: Addison Wesley Longman Higher Education.

Slack, N., Chambers, S., Harland, C., Harrison, A. and Johnston, R. (1997) *Operations Management,* 2nd edn. London: Financial Times and Pitman Publishing.

Vonderembse, M. A. and White, G. P. (1995) *Operations Management: Concepts, Methods and Strategies,* 3rd edn. Minneapolis/St Paul: West Pub. Co.

Research methods

Abrahmson, J. H. (1986) *Survey Methods in Community Medicine: an Introduction to Epidemiological and Evaluative Studies,* 3rd edn. London: Churchill Livingstone.

Bowling, A. (1997) *Research Methods in Health.* Buckingham: Open University Press. (A comprehensive guide to qualitative and quantitative research methods.)

Frankfort-Nachmias, C. and Nachmias, D. (1992) *Research Methods in the Social Sciences,* 4th edn. London: Edward Arnold.

Pocock, S. J. (1983) *Clinical Trials: a Practical Approach.* Chichester: John Wiley and Sons.

St Leger, A. S., Schnieden, H. and Walsworth-Bell, J. P. (1992) *Evaluating Health Services' Effectiveness.* Buckingham: Open University Press.

Silverman, D. (1993) *Interpreting Qualitative Data: Methods for Analysing Talk, Text and Interaction.* London: Sage Publications.

Stake, R. E. (1995) *The Art of Case Study Research.* London: Sage Publications.

Stringer, E. T. (1996) *Action Research: a Handbook for Practitioners.* London: Sage Publications.

Health outcome measures

Bowling, A. (1991) *Measuring Health.* Buckingham: Open University Press. (An excellent review of many measures of functional disability, health status, well-being etc.)

Bowling, A. (1995) *Measuring Disease*. Buckingham: Open University Press. (A valuable extension to *Measuring Health*.)

Economic analysis

Drummond, M. F., Stoddard, G. I. and Torrance, U. W. (1987) *Methods for the Economic Evaluation of Health Care Programmes*. Oxford: Oxford University Press.

Lockett, T. (1996) *Health Economics for the Uninitiated*. Abingdon: Radcliffe.

Mooney, G. (1992) *Economics, Medicine and Health Care*. London: Harvester Wheatsheaf.

Statistics

Armitage, P. and Berry, U. (1987) *Statistical Methods in Medical Research*, 2nd edn. Oxford: Blackwell. (A useful 'bench book' for researchers.)

Bland, M. (1995) *An Introduction to Medical Statistics*. Oxford: Oxford University Press. (Useful for intermediate level courses.)

Gardner, M. J. and Altman, D. G. (eds) (1989) *Statistics with Confidence*. London: British Medical Journal Publishing Group. (Pitched at an elementary level and easily read.)

Organizations and management

Handy, C. B. (1985) *Understanding Organisations*. London: Penguin.

Heirs, B. and Farrell, P. (1986) *The Professional Decision Thinker*. London: Grafton/ Harper Collins.

Watkins, K. E. and Marsick, V. J. (1993) *Sculpting the Learning Organization. Lessons in the Art and Science of Systemic Change*. San Francisco: Jossey-Bass Publishers.

Critical appraisal, systematic review and dissemination

Chalmers, I. and Altman, D. (eds) (1995) *Systematic Reviews*. London: British Medical Journal Publishing Group.

Crombie, I. K. (1996) *The Pocket Guide to Critical Appraisal*. London: British Medical Journal Publishing Group.

Greenhalgh, T. (1997) *How to Read a Paper, the Basics of Evidence Based Medicine*. London: British Medical Journal Publishing Group.

Hawkins, C. and Sorgi, M. (1985) *Research. How to Plan, Speak and Write About It*. Berlin: Springer-Verlag.

Cochrane, A. L. (1972) *Effectiveness and Efficiency: Random Reflections on Health Services*. London: Nuffield Provincial Hospitals. (A seminal work).

Philosophy

Feyerabend, P. (1975) *Against Method*. Thetford: The Thetford Press.
James, W. (1907) *Pragmatism: a New Name for Some Old Ways of Thinking*. London: Longmans, Green and Co. (The patron philosopher of the new paradigm.)
Kuhn, T. S. (1970) *The Structure of Scientific Revolutions*, 2nd edn. Chicago: University of Chicago Press.
Popper, K. R. (1959) *The Logic of Scientific Discovery*. London: Hutchinson. (The discarded philosopher in the new paradigm.)

INDEX

EVALUATING HEALTH SERVICES' EFFECTIVENESS
A GUIDE FOR HEALTH PROFESSIONALS, SERVICE MANAGERS AND
POLICY MAKERS

A. S. St Leger, H. Schnieden and J. P. Walsworth-Bell

Resources can never keep pace with the demand for more and better health services. Health service clinicians, managers and policy makers must make increasingly difficult choices among many options, seeking not only economy and efficiency but benefit to individual patients and to the community.

This book is aimed at all those involved in planning, carrying out and acting upon evaluations of health services' effectiveness. It provides an essential and comprehensive guide to the theory, practice and interpretation of evaluation. Throughout this book, the reader is provided with practical tips, case studies and discussions of advantages and disadvantages of particular techniques or procedures. Whilst the authors have based the book on their experiences as practising public health physicians in the British National Health Service, it is applicable to any kind of health service – nationalized or private.

Contents
An overview of evaluation – Key concepts and the setting of objectives – Planning and executing health service evaluation – Using routinely gathered data to assist in evaluation – Some basic economic concepts and their uses – Descriptive, testimony, case studies and case-control studies – Intervention studies – Assessing patient satisfaction – The evaluation of disease prevention services – Technology assessment – Important methodological issues – Making evaluation work – Obtaining data – Appendix B: Template of a checklist for the evaluation of innovatory proposals – References – Further reading.

224pp   0 335 15742 4 (Paperback)   0 335 15743 2 (Hardback)

RESEARCH METHODS IN HEALTH
INVESTIGATING HEALTH AND HEALTH SERVICES

Ann Bowling

- What research methods are used in the investigation of health and health services?
- What are the principles of the research method that should be followed?
- How do I design a research project to describe the topic of interest and to answer cause and effect questions?

This is the first comprehensive guide to research methods in health. It describes the range of methods that can be used to study and evaluate health and health care. Ann Bowling's impressive range and grasp of research methodology are manifest in the simplicity of her style and in the organization of the book. The text is aimed at students and researchers of health and health services, including those in: demography, economics, epidemiology, health management, health policy, health psychology, health sciences, history, medical sociology, medicine, nursing, pharmaceutics and other health care disciplines. It has also been designed for health professionals and policy makers who have responsibility for applying research findings in practice, and who need to know how to judge the value of that research.

Contents

Preface – Section 1: Investigating health services and health: the scope of research – Evaluating health services: multidisciplinary collaboration – Social research on health: sociological and psychological concepts and approaches – Health needs and their assessment: demography and epidemiology – Costing health services: health economics – Section 2: The philosophy, theory and practice of research – The philosophical framework of measurement – The principles of research – Section 3: Quantitative research: sampling and research methods – Sample size for quantitative research – Quantitative research: surveys – Quantitative research: experiments and other analytic methods of investigation – Sample selection and group assignment methods in experiments and other analytic methods – Section 4: The tools of quantitative research – Data collection methods in quantitative research: questionnaires, interviews and their response rates – Questionnaire design – Techniques of survey interviewing – Preparation of quantitative data for coding and analysis – Section 5: Qualitative and combined research methods, and their analysis – Unstructured and structured observational studies – Unstructured interviewing and focus groups – Other methods using both qualitative and quantitative approaches: case studies, consensus methods, action research and document research – Glossary – References – Index.

448pp   0 335 19885 6 (Paperback)   0 335 19886 4 (Hardback)

ASSESSING HEALTH NEED USING THE LIFE CYCLE FRAMEWORK

Chrissie Pickin and Selwyn St Leger

Assessing the health needs of populations is a prerequisite for the planning and delivery of effective health services. This book presents the life cycle framework as a means of organizing thought about this task from health district down to neighbourhood levels. The framework brings together in a coherent manner the diverse influences (e.g. biological, social, environmental, ethnic and geographical) on people's propensity for good health and their ability to avail themselves of services. It also identifies routinely available sources of information. The book is self-contained in that no prior knowledge of epidemiology is demanded of the reader. The intended readership includes a wide range of health professionals, managers and policy makers and those in other public sectors (e.g. local government) whose actions influence health. The life cycle framework can also be used to assist in teaching social medicine to medical and nursing undergraduates and will be a valuable aid to trainees in public health medicine.

Contents

The new NHS: opportunities and challenges – What is health needs assessment? – An introduction to essential demographic and epidemiological concepts – Sociological approaches to collecting information on health needs – The life cycle framework: its rationale, structure and use – Life stage: from late pregnancy to one week after birth – Life stage: from one week to one year – Life stage: from one to four years – Life stage: from five to 14 years – Life stage: from 15 to 24 years – Life stage: from 25 to 44 years – Life stage: from 45 to 64 years – Life stage: from 65 to 74 years – Life stage: 75 years and over – The challenge of purchasing for health gain – Appendix one – Appendix two – Appendix three – Appendix four – Glossary – Further Reading – Index.

224pp   0 335 15742 4 (Paperback)   0 335 15743 2 (Hardback)